Lifestyle and Social Structure

Concepts, Definitions, Analyses

This is a volume of
Quantitative Studies in Social Relations
Consulting Editor: Peter H. Rossi, University of Massachusetts,
Amherst, Massachusetts
A complete list of titles in this series appears at the end of this volume.

Lifestyle and Social Structure

Concepts, Definitions, Analyses

Michael E. Sobel

Office of Research Methods and Standards
Bureau of Labor Statistics
Washington, D.C.

ACADEMIC PRESS
A Subsidiary of Harcourt Brace Jovanovich, Publishers
New York   London   Toronto   Sydney   San Francisco

To my parents, Irvin and Peggy Sobel

ACADEMIC PRESS, INC.
111 Fifth Avenue, New York, New York 10003

United Kingdom Edition published by
ACADEMIC PRESS, INC. (LONDON) LTD.
24/28 Oval Road, London NW1 7DX

Library of Congress Cataloging in Publication Data

Sobel, Michael E.
    Life style and social structure.

    (Quantitative studies in social relations)
    Bibliography: p.
    Includes index.
    1. Life style. 2. Social structure. I. Title.
II. Series.
HM73.S625   305   81-19055
ISBN 0-12-654280-5   AACR2

PRINTED IN THE UNITED STATES OF AMERICA

82 83 84 85   9 8 7 6 5 4 3 2 1

Contents

8

Social Structure and Stylistic Unity 117

9

Lifestyle, Stratification, and Alienation: Conclusions and Speculations 165

APPENDIX A

Creation of the Education Codes 175

APPENDIX B

Creation of the SEI Scores 177

APPENDIX C

Creation of the Dependent Variable 181

Preface

The primary focus of this book is the relationship between lifestyle and social structure. In order to understand and model this relationship, it is first necessary to construct a meaningful concept of lifestyle. Unlike prior treatments of lifestyle, I do not derive the concept within the framework of some other primary substantive interest, because this conventional treatment inherently limits the scope of the phenomenon itself, directing attention only to those features which appear to be germane within an already restricted framework. The general formulation of the concept hinges on the descriptive word *style*, defined as "any distinctive, and therefore recognizable way in which an act is performed or an artifact made or ought to be performed and made" (Gombrich, 1968, p. 352). After developing the implications of the definition, lifestyle is defined, by analogy, as "any distinctive, and therefore recognizable mode of living." Since this definition parallels the definition of style, the implications are similar. Thus, it is argued that a lifestyle consists of expressive behaviors that are directly observable or deducible from observation.

Having derived the concept in this fashion, I then argue that consumption is the one behavior that best indexes lifestyle in post-World War II America. Next, the notion of social structure is introduced; briefly, the

argument is that structural differentiation engenders lifestyle differentiation.

The remainder of the work is concerned primarily with the modeling
of this relationship using data from the 1972–1973 Survey of Consumer
Expenditures, and with the concept of stylistic unity. This is a matter of
emphasis; it neither means that the value of the concept itself is limited to
this framework, nor that the concept itself is only of sociological interest.
In fact, other meaningful relations are hinted at or discussed in the text.
For example, the relationship between the theory of lifestyle differentiation and modern economic utility theory is taken up in Chapter 5, and
psychographic notions of lifestyle are discussed in Chapter 2. Finally, in
Chapter 9, the relationships between lifestyle and other key sociological
concepts (stratification, alienation) are discussed, and it is argued that the
concept of lifestyle should be of interest to a broad range of applied and
theoretical researchers.

Acknowledgments

This book is an outgrowth of my dissertation, which was completed at the University of Wisconsin—Madison in January 1980. In particular, I wish to acknowledge Halliman H. Winsborough for his role in this project. In large part, he is responsible for teaching me the perspective on research which is reflected in this work.

No one could have asked for a better or more conscientious advisor. Despite a busy schedule, Winsborough spent many hours discussing all aspects of this work with me, and his insights are responsible for some of the most important points in this piece. While I am especially grateful for his contributions in the area of substantive interpretation, in particular those which pertain to the descriptive form of lifestyle, I have also benefited substantially from his editorial advice.

I also wish to thank the other members of that committee, David Featherman, William Sewell, Maurice MacDonald, and Charles Halaby. Featherman argued with me about the early chapters, and forced me to develop the argument more cogently. MacDonald helped me with the economic aspects of this work. Sewell encouraged this work and discovered several sins of omission. Finally, Halaby encouraged me to develop the argument more articulately.

In addition, I have benefited from my conservations with many other persons. Neil Fligstein discussed many facets of this work with me, read selected portions of the manuscript, and more than once helped me formulate arguments cogently. Donald Treiman encouraged me to speculate on the results and to examine the potential value of the lifestyle concept in general sociological work. Albert Simkus first realized the potential of the data source. James Dennis discussed the art historical material with me and suggested specific readings. Paul Gertler and Chris Alaouze discussed consumer theory with me on several occasions and read selected portions of the manuscript. My conversations with Peter Piett on selected aspects on the statistical analysis were both enlightening and instrumental. Robert Dalrymple, Gordon Caldwell, Mike Watts, and Robert Mislevy assisted with various aspects of the computer work. Lori Hayward was responsible for the production of the manuscript, which benefits from her considerable editorial and clerical skills. Finally, it has been both valuable and enjoyable to work with the staff of Academic Press.

For financial and material support I am grateful to the Center for Demography and Ecology at the University of Wisconsin—Madison, under the auspices of the National Institute of Child Health and Human Development grants HD05876 and HD07014.

Finally, I wish to thank my parents Irvin and Peggy Sobel, and my friends Eileen Mortensen-Fligstein, Handy Gelbard, Laureen Du Pree, and Neil Fligstein, for their support and encouragement.

CHAPTER 1

Introduction

Lifestyle is currently one of the abused words of the English language. Social scientists, journalists, and laymen use it to refer to almost anything of interest, be it fashion, Zen Buddhism, or French cooking. The more this word is bantered about, the less it seems to mean. If the 1970s are an indication of things to come, the word *lifestyle* will soon include everything and mean nothing, all at the same time.

Imprecise popular usage is forgivable. However, that sociologists, who presumably are scientists, use the term in a nebulous manner is not. In this study, I attempt to give some systematic meaning to the word *lifestyle* and empirically examine the structural sources of lifestyle differentiation in contemporary American society.

The study is by no means descriptive, but is, rather, analytical, the objective being to answer the question "why" rather than to describe and classify. Reasons for this choice are elaborated in the text; the basic rationale is that the sources of lifestyle differentiation are of primary sociological interest, the concrete form constituting a somewhat arbitrary manifestation of these underlying sources.

The study is divided into three parts. In the first, I discuss the concept of lifestyle both abstractly and as applied to the American experience. In the second part, I focus on the sociological sources of lifestyle differentiation, and in the third I estimate statistical models to test hypotheses generated in the second part. The second and third parts are most closely intertwined. The first part builds the abstract, conceptual framework, a task that must be completed prior to a more concrete theoretical and empirical examination.

Since this study is somewhat lengthy, in this introduction I shall sketch the logical structure of the argument with enough detail to provide a prelude to the specific arguments used later. Each subsequent chapter constitutes an argument or a set of evidence that examines the validity of an argument. Since there is a sequential logic to the chapter arrangement, it suffices to take up each in turn.

In Chapter 2, I review literature from several disciplines that touches upon or is directly concerned with notions of lifestyle. The review is written to emphasize that there is almost no agreement either empirically or conceptually as to what constitutes a lifestyle. There is not much explicit disagreement either. Rather, the literature is idiosyncratic. As a result, it is not clear whether a lifestyle belongs to an individual or to some aggregate. The causes and consequences of lifestyles are not separated analytically from the phenomenon itself. Furthermore, virtually no discussions of lifestyle as a phenomenon in its own right are to be found. In short, social scientists use this term to refer to whatever they wish, failing to realize that it has little intersubjective meaning, and that without more formal definition, their use is no more informative than the layman's. This state of affairs implies either the need for exorcism of the word *lifestyle* from that literature which purports to be scientific, or it implies the need for meaningful conceptualization of the word itself.

Since little of value can be culled from the previous literature, the conceptual task must be initiated at the most elemental level. This process is begun in Chapter 3 in which the word *style* is discussed at some length. The word *style,* it is found, is profitably used in several ways. Although three modes of usage are identified, it is safe to say that the word is used either in a fashion that is primarily laudatory or derogatory or in a manner that is primarily descriptive. This is the case in both ordinary language and the more formal discussions of style found in the literature of art history.

Since the concept of style has proved extremely useful as a framework for art history, there is a priori reason to believe that application of the concept in the present context may prove fruitful. Drawing heavily upon descriptive notions of style as developed by art historians, *style* is defined as "any distinctive, and therefore recognizable, way in which an act is performed or an artifact made or ought to be performed and made

[Gombrich, 1968, p. 352]." Implications of this definition are drawn out and used to make further distinctions, still in the context of art history. Then, by analogy, *lifestyle* is defined as "any distinctive, and therefore recognizable, mode of living." This definition, I believe, constitutes a baseline meaning to which all social scientists can agree. Implications developed from the previous argument are then used to argue that a lifestyle consists of "expressive" behaviors that are directly observable or deducible from observation. While this argument does not allow us to choose among behaviors, it at least restricts the domain of content to this class of phenomena.

From the restricted domain of content, appropriate behaviors must be chosen. In Chapter 4, I argue that a reasonable way to choose appropriate behaviors is to select those that are most salient within a given time and space. By implication, the appropriate behaviors may then vary across either or both of these dimensions. As discussed in Chapter 4, this circumstance has both advantages and disadvantages.

Following this secondary criterion of spatio-temporal salience, consumption is selected as the one expressive behavior that best indicates lifestyle in post–World War II America. Reasons for excluding leisure and work are given there; the basic argument is that leisure falls under the consumption umbrella, and work is not typically an expressive activity. The chapter is written historically, to indicate the importance of consumption to American society and to establish the connection between consumption and the individual psyche. European experience is not considered, so it has not been argued that consumption best indicates lifestyle in contemporary Western Europe. Nonetheless, there is every reason to believe that this is the case (Lefebvre, 1971).

Having defined lifestyle and indicated how one might characterize the American experience, the focus of the argument changes. In Chapter 5, individual lifestyle variation is addressed. The argument is made that the sources of lifestyle differentiation are rooted in the different *reference sets* that individuals maintain. These reference sets are engendered by the positions that individuals occupy and the different demands placed upon incumbents of various positions. Thus, lifestyle variation stems from differentiation within social structure. Of particular interest in the ensuing portion of the study are socioeconomic differences among individuals. Here we follow a lead suggested by Weber, who stated that status differences are the conditional source of the stylization of life (see Chapter 2). Next, sociological theories about alternative lifestyles are considered in relation to the theory just posited, and it is demonstrated that these are subsumed by the more general theory I have proposed.

Following this, the relationship of the general sociological theory of lifestyle differentiation to the economic theory of utility maximization is considered. It should be pointed out that in economic parlance, our explanation of lifestyle differentiation is equivalent to the argument that role differences are the source of tastes and preferences, which are manifested in different commodity bundles. This translation is important for two reasons. First, microeconomists have long considered tastes and preferences exogenous. The economist's justification for this choice usually consists of an attack on other disciplines, namely, psychology and sociology, for not considering the problem of tastes and preferences, and hence not providing a coherent explanation of these phenomena. To put the matter somewhat differently, microeconomists think that it is not their job to provide an explanation of tastes and preferences, and that in the absence of such an explanation, it is legitimate to consider these exogenous.

Translation into economic terminology is also important because it indirectly forces the consideration of theoretical alternatives that may yield empirical results consistent with the explanation that hinges on tastes and preferences. Specifically, we refer to Michael's (1972) theory that education is an "efficiency" variable.

The remainder of this work is primarily empirical. Chapter 6 is the data and methods chapter. It is unconventional in that specific techniques are not discussed. Rather, the purpose of the chapter is to bridge the gap between the theoretical and empirical, to discuss dimensions of consumption, to make clear the advantages and disadvantages of operationalizing consumption as a vector of expenditures, and to propose plausible models that stem from the economic and econometric literature.

In the next chapter, using data from the 1972–1973 Survey of Consumer Expenditures, the regression of 17 lifestyle items on sets of the social structural variables is considered. Our concern is not so much with the individual items, which are viewed as somewhat arbitrary forms, but rather with the pattern of significance of the coefficients of the independent variables. Of particular interest are the education, occupational status, and income coefficients. First, Michael's (1972) theory receives little empirical support from these data. Education does not appear salient to lifestyle differentiation, but occupational status and income are clearly salient. Furthermore, the effects of all three variables vary across levels of the stratification system, that is, the parameters of interest tend to take on different values at different levels of the socioeconomic hierarchy in a substantial number of the equations. This is somewhat less true of the education parameters. Finally, the effects of occupational status and the effects of income are weakly substitutable with respect to lifestyle.

Chapter 8 takes up a related question. In Chapter 3, a distinction between style and stylistic unity was made and it was argued that style always exists regardless of whether stylistic unity exists. Chapter 8 is concerned with the meaning of the term *stylistic unity* as applied to the concept of lifestyle. This is an important issue because stylistic unity is the basis for perception and evaluation of an observed lifestyle. Furthermore, by intervening between social structure and lifestyle, stylistic unity becomes the proximate cause of a lifestyle. Therefore, the effects of social structure on stylistic unity are of concern. In order to model the theory, MIMIC models that simultaneously consider the form of stylistic unity and its structural sources in role differentiation are estimated, after an extensive exploratory analysis. Descriptively, stylistic unity emerges as a four-factor form that is organized around prestige, maintenance, and two entertainment patterns. It is argued that at the abstract level, this organization is common to advanced Western countries. Furthermore, all three socioeconomic variables differentiate stylistic unity. The conclusion that education is unimportant with respect to lifestyle differentiation was therefore premature. As before, the effects of the socioeconomic variables vary across levels of the stratification system. There is evidence of status-related conspicuous consumption in these data. Occupational status and income appear to be weakly substitutable, but the effects of education are sometimes inverse to the effects of status.

Finally, in Chapter 9, the empirical results are summarized. Following this, I speculate on the role of the lifestyle concept in sociological thought, arguing that lifestyle, in its modern form, is both a deference entitlement and possibly a solution to the existential problem of alienation. Next, some limitations of this work are discussed, and suggestions for further research are offered. These include cross-cultural and intertemporal comparisons and longitudinal analyses.

CHAPTER 2

Lifestyle and Sociological Thought

In this chapter, I discuss prior research on lifestyles, concluding that the term *lifestyle* has been used too loosely to permit good research on either the phenomenon itself or on the relationship between it and other aspects of social life. Unless present utilization of the word is dramatically improved, sociologists would be well advised not to use it in a serious fashion.

Early Theoretical Approaches

Sociological interest in lifestyles can be traced to the fathers of the discipline. However, they treated lifestyles as a derived, rather than as a primary issue.

For example, Marx discusses "commodity fetishism" and "bourgeois decadence," yet says little or nothing about lifestyle per se. In the Marxian order, lifestyle is a phenomenon determined primarily by an individual's objective position in the production process, that is, in the structure that loosely shapes values and attitudes and determines critical life experiences (Bendix and Lipset, 1966, p. 8).

7

Nevertheless, Marx is presumably concerned with lifestyles in some teleological fashion. Indeed, the aim of Marxian revolution is to bring into existence a society in which individuals are free to develop their lives without subjecting themselves to the brutalizing and alienating forces of capitalism. In other words, post-revolutionary society is characterized by the equivalence of lifestyle and life substance.

Marx's successor and critic, Max Weber, is more explicitly interested in lifestyle. In the seminal essay "Class, Status, and Power," Weber discusses the sociological meaning of these three terms. Having defined them, he proceeds to develop their sociological importance and in so doing, he introduces the term *lifestyle*.

Briefly, Weber argues that *class situation*—"the typical chance for a supply of goods, external living conditions, and personal life experiences, in so far as this chance is determined by the amount and kind of power, or lack of such, to dispose of goods or skills for the sake of income in a given economic order [Weber. 1966, p. 21]"—structures lifestyle in so far as it "in itself creates specific life chances [Weber, 1966, p. 22]."

But class status is only an initial condition for a style of life. Alone it does not warrant membership in the status group from which both status honor and lifestyle form are derived. Once the initial conditions are satisfied, status situations—"every typical component of the life fate of men that is determined by a specific, positive or negative social estimation of honor [Weber, 1966, p. 24]"—appear in the foreground of analysis. Indeed, Weber goes so far as to make the following argument: "The decisive role of a 'style of life' in status 'honor' means that status groups are the specific bearers of all 'conventions.' In whatever way it be manifest, all 'stylization' of life either originates in status groups or is at least conserved by them [1966, p. 26]."

Because honor derives from group affiliation, and because the status group demands that its members share a specific style of life, lifestyle becomes the descriptive manifestion through which affiliation, hence status, can be perceived. Given the critical role of lifestyle in this signification process, it is not surprising that influential status groups exercise both informal and formal monopolies on a variety of conspicuous lifestyle elements.

Having made these points, Weber returns to the central theme, and concludes:

> With some over-simplification, one might thus say that "classes" are stratified according to their relations to the production and acquisition of goods; whereas "status groups" are stratified according to the principles of their consumption of goods as represented by special "styles of life"[p. 27].

Thus, in the Weberian framework, lifestyle is of interest primarily because it is the descriptive means by which status can be differentiated from class. In other words, it is a secondary concept, unworthy (at least in this context) of independent explication.

Motivated by his interest in the structure of production in industrial society, Veblen (1966) is led to consider the form and meaning of lifestyle at some length. Nevertheless, his interest in lifestyle is also derivative, and the concept itself does not receive close examination.

Veblen's argument is grounded in the assumption that esteem is derived primarily from prowess. In predatory societies, prowess was best evidenced by physically aggressive activity, for example, war. However, in industrial societies, the limited opportunity for such displays necessitates the development of alternative measures of prowess. In such a fashion, ownership (the possession of wealth) becomes the primary evidence of successful activity in industrial society and hence the dominant basis of esteem.[1]

But like prowess, the possession of wealth cannot accrue esteem to its owner in the absence of visible activity. Thus the translation of wealth into appropriate observable symbols is imperative. Traditionally, this is accomplished through the display of conspicuous leisure, as manifested by

> quasi-scholarly and quasi-artistic accomplishments and a knowledge of processes and incidents which do not conduce directly to the furtherance of human life [Veblen, 1966, p. 40].

With the rise of urbanization, conspicuous leisure is no longer an effective indicator of status. Since the generation of esteem requires recognition of "merit," the wealthy now tend to translate their money into symbols that are visible to the more casual observer. Like conspicuous leisure, these signs must be exclusive. They are made so by matching the hierarchy of exchange value with the hierarchy of taste. In this fashion conspicuous consumption becomes more important than conspicuous leisure. This is not to say that conspicuous leisure loses all significance. It does not: Conspicuous consumption and conspicuous leisure are closely related. For example, consider the matter of dress—white suits indicate abstention from menial activity.

---

[1] While Weber argued that class status is an initial condition for membership within the status group, he also argued that in the long run, class tends to be a sufficient condition:

> Property as such is not always recognized as a status qualification, but in the long run it is, and with extraordinary regularity [1966, p. 24].

Whereas Weber and Veblen do not entirely agree upon the structural source of prestige, both view lifestyle as its observable manifestation. The extent to which this viewpoint has structured subsequent thinking about lifestyles is remarkable and accounts for the advent of several research traditions. Among the most prominent of these is the symbolic approach to the measurement of social status, that is, the measurement of place in the stratification system by lifestyle.

The Symbolic Approach

The symbolic approach is widespread, both in the sociological and lay worlds. In the former, the approach owes its formal existence to Chapin, whose primary interest is in the measurement of socioeconomic status. This he defines as

> the position that an individual or a family occupies with reference to the prevailing average standards of cultural possessions, effective income, material possessions, and participation in the group activities of the community [Chapin, 1935, p. 374].

In empirical research, he finds that a scale constructed from items within the familial living room correlates highly with an index of socioeconomic status based on measures of these phenomena. In fact, the correlation is strong enough to warrant the use of the scale as an alternative measure of status.

Drawing on Chapin's work, Sewell (1940) argues that more traditional measures of socioeconomic status differentiate very poorly within farm populations. Therefore, he devises a "Farm Family Socio-economic Status Scale," consisting of a linear combination of social participation measures, material and cultural possessions.

Since the 1940s, very little research has been done that measures socioeconomic position in this manner. But the idea that lifestyle can be construed as an indicator of social position is far from dead. As Bernard Barber (1957) puts the matter:

> Symbolic activities and possessions are also a useful indicator of social class position for the social scientist. For him, and for the applied researcher who wants to identify easily, if somewhat roughly, people's social class positions, symbolic indicators are often easier to ascertain than are verbal evaluations or actual patterns of intimate association. For example, it is very easy to ascertain the relative size of a man's house, the cost of his car, or the character of his residential neighborhood and to use any or all of these as rough indicators of his social class position [135–136].

The symbolic approach, while interesting in its own right, is relevant primarily because it further channeled subsequent research. The next wave of research takes the nexus between lifestyle and social position (that which symbolic researchers either assume or attempt to demonstrate) as the issue itself. This is not to say that the logical existence of the connection is questioned; it generally is not. In fact, the connection is usually assumed, and the empirical work in this tradition focuses on either status (class) correlates or temporal trends in lifestyle among the occupants of distinct hierarchical positions.

At the same time (indeed, before), it was increasingly recognized that lifestyle variation was associated with other dimensions of social life. Researchers interested in subcultural affiliation, rural–urban or city–suburban differences, ethnicity, race, and social psychology found the concept of lifestyle descriptively (and occasionally, analytically) useful in their work. The advent of this tradition was clearly responsible for broadening sociological interest in lifestyles. However, the tradition shared and still does share at least one important communality with lifestyle research in the stratification literature. That is the previously noted tendency to treat lifestyle as a secondary phenomenon that merits inspection only within some other context of primary concern.

In conjunction with the expansion of interest itself, the treatment of lifestyle as a derived issue has engendered such a diversity of usage that it is now difficult to understand what a lifestyle is, because it is even more difficult to understand what it is not.

In the next section, I examine representative empirical literature from the preceding two traditions. The point of this exercise is not to review the literature per se (for a more extensive review, see Zablocki and Kanter, 1976), but to pinpoint the critical differences that have generated the ambiguity underlying the current use of the word *lifestyle*. This illustrates the need for an independent examination of the term *lifestyle* and indicates the types of issues with which a successful definition of lifestyle must be able to contend.

Some Empirical Inquiries

Within the framework of the first tradition, researchers have demonstrated that social position is related to a variety of attitudes and values, behavioral orientations, and behaviors that are viewed as indicative of lifestyle. For example, social position is related to sexual behavior (Kinsey, Pomeroy, and Martin, 1948) and happiness (Inkeles, 1960), and hence lifestyle.

Also related to social position are attitudes regarding child rearing (Bronfenbrenner, 1958), the way in which the members of different classes view one another (Rodman, 1964), fertility (Ryder and Westoff, 1971), and the different manner in which the members of distinct classes communicate (Schatzman and Strauss, 1955).

In addition, members of the middle class are purported to attend church more often (Demerath, 1965) and to attend churches of higher status than do members of the lower classes. They are also more likely to join and participate in voluntary organizations and to participate in different types of organizations. Furthermore, political participation, both in form and in content, varies with social position.

With respect to leisure, the middle classes read more books and magazines than the lower classes do. Furthermore, type of reading material varies with class (Noe, 1974). The middle classes also watch less television, entertain and dine out more frequently, attend concerts and plays with greater regularity, and are less likely to attend sporting events as spectators, or to use their vacations and weekends for outdoor recreational activities (Burdge, 1969; Clarke, 1956; Havighurst and Feigenbaum, 1959; Meyersohn, 1968; White, 1955; Matras, 1975; Berger, 1960).

All these phenomena, it is claimed (not necessarily by the original authors), fall under the rubric of lifestyle. For example, Tumin (1970) includes the pieces by Inkeles and Bronfenbrenner in his chapters on lifestyle.

A different set of findings has been generated by sociologists interested in the temporal trend of class-related phenomena. Much of this research is specifically addressed to the question of whether the lifestyles of blue- and white-collar workers are converging, and if so, in what manner. The Marxist argument is that lifestyles can be expected to converge, as white-collar workers become proletarianized. The more usual argument (the embourgeoisement hypothesis) is that with the narrowing of income differentials, significant proportions of blue-collar workers are able to maintain middle-class styles of life (Mayer, 1955, pp. 41–42) and do so.

Despite the ease with which the two competing theories could be tested, most sociologists have assumed the Marxist argument away. Furthermore, on the basis of observed differentials at a single point in time, they have argued that the embourgeoisement hypothesis itself seems to be incorrect. While the use of cross-sectional data will not admit these conclusions about temporal change, the findings that have emerged from this body of research are nonetheless of some value.

In this vein, Hamilton (1964) studied, among other things, political orientation, attitudes toward foreign and domestic affairs, and attitudes toward education. He finds substantively significant differences between clerical and sales workers, as opposed to craftsmen and foremen (these two groups are close to each other in the occupational ladder; see Blau and Duncan, 1967). On a fair number of questions, the latter group more nearly resemble operatives in their answers. A similar type of argument (without any data) is made by Goldthorpe and Lockwood (1962) with respect to the British case.

Handel and Rainwater (1964), in an article entitled "Persistence and Change in Working-Class Life Style" argue that

> Certain behaviors and attitudes increasingly found in the working class have a surface similarity to those in the middle class, but they have a different meaning for the working class than they do for the middle class . . . In the areas of family life and social participation, the working class seems to be dividing into two main groups, which might be characterized as traditional and modern. In these life areas, the modern working-class group begins to approximate lower-middle-class values and behaviors [p. 37].

But the authors also argue that

> In the area of consumer behavior, working-class behavior resembles middle-class behavior in spending for hard goods, but not in other types of expenditure. This difference in expenditure pattern reflects persisting differences in working-class and middle-class life styles [p. 37].

And, in their summary (p. 41) the authors point out that (a) the proportion of income spent on education is smaller in working-class than in middle-class families, (b) working-class men are more likely than middle-class men to work on their homes and to repair their cars, and (c) working-class men are less likely than middle-class men to purchase suits. It is now also known that members of the different classes shop at different types of stores (Rich and Jain, 1970; Martineau, 1958), that the form of saving differs by social class (Martineau, 1958), that automobile and home ownership vary by income levels (Katona, 1964, 1971), that the middle classes typically spend a larger proportion of their income on clothing than the working class, and that the middle classes own more appliances.

Lifestyle variation also occurs within groups similarly placed in the hierarchical order. Commonly specified axes of further differentiation include ethnicity (Gans, 1962; Gans, 1951; Gordon, 1964), race (McCord, Friedberg, and Harwood, 1969; Liebow, 1967), age (Lofland, 1970; Coleman, 1974), urban versus suburban residence (Bell, 1958; Tallman and

Morgner, 1970; Tomeh, 1964; Willmott and Young, 1960; Wirth, 1938), subcultural affiliation (Matza, 1967; Merton, 1969; Reed, 1972; Zablocki, 1971), and even sexuality (Hoffman, 1972).

The existence of overlap among these variables (as well as with respect to social position) is recognized and occasionally taken into account. Much of this research, like that cited previously, covers a broad range of phenomena that are viewed as indicative of lifestyle. However, some of the criteria, for example, urban versus suburban residence and subcultural affiliation, are viewed by some as part and parcel of lifestyle, by others as factors influencing lifestyle.

A good example concerns the role of family status. Implicitly adopting the view that family status is part of lifestyle, Matras (1975) states in his section entitled "Styles of Life and Leisure":

> The dimensions of family life which have been found to vary among the different strata include: (1) the range and importance of kinship relations, (2) the pattern of authority, role differentiation, and role segregation, (3) sexual relations, (4) fertility control and family size, and (5) family economic cooperation and characteristics, e.g., the extent to which wives and children are involved in earning the family income, and occupational "inheritance" (entrance into occupations and industries through family connections) [p. 187].

Implicitly adopting the other point of view, Zablocki and Kanter (1976) discuss the special lifestyle of the two-career family, its problems, particularly with respect to the utilization of time, and the future implications of the increase of two-career families. Similarly, Vanek (1974) demonstrates the existence of differentials in time spent keeping house between working and nonworking wives, though she does not mention lifestyle per se.

It should now be clear that consideration of the empirical literature does little to clarify the nature of lifestyle. However, it does generate several questions. What best indexes lifestyle? What is to be done with the fact that one author's determinants are another's criteria? What about the conjunction of lifestyle variables? Is it appropriate to study variables one at a time, as all this research does? That is, is it sufficient to study the separate marginal distributions of the variables rather than the joint distribution and string the findings together with commas?

These are the types of questions a successful definition of lifestyle must be able to resolve. Before an attempt at resolution is made, several previous attempts to conceptualize the notion of lifestyle are examined. This is helpful in further pinpointing and illustrating the types of issues that must be considered in any attempt at resolution.

Defining Lifestyle

Given the interplay between findings and theory, it is not surprising that the problem of separating determinants from criteria also arises in the more conceptual literature. According to Tumin (1970):

> Max Weber used the term "life styles" to refer to those modes of conduct, dress, speech, thought, and attitudes, that defined various "honor" groups and that in turn served as models of behavior for those who aspired to be members of these groups. By extension, the term is often used now to include the range of distinctive behavior patterns, including institutional patterns such as family styles, value orientations to the world in general, and patterns of interpersonal and intergroup conduct [p. 179].

But according to Myers and Gutman (1974), lifestyle is the essence of social class. "The social class construct is in reality only a subset of the indicators of life style [p. 236]." Both these viewpoints differ from the perspective of Zablocki and Kanter (1976):

> Life-style is to be distinguished from culture and subculture. A given life-style may be characteristic of a specific social class, status group, or sub-culture; but since life-style is defined solely in terms of shared preferences, it is possible and indeed is often the case that a life-style may be defined over a collectivity that otherwise lacks social and cultural identity. . . . Life-style is also to be distinguished from social class and social status, though it may stem from both [p. 271].

The preceding quotations illustrate the ambiguity surrounding the role of sociological variables in analyses of lifestyle. Even if this ambiguity is removed, the problem of what or what else constitutes lifestyle remains. For example, Reynolds and Darden (1974, p. 83) adopt a psychological perspective, arguing that a lifestyle is a construction system built from consistent combinations of personal constructs. In other words, lifestyle is some undefined state of mind. While this definition is unsatisfactory for a variety of reasons,[2] it is still instructive to contrast it with others.

Zablocki and Kanter (1976) hint at a definition when they state

> An ultimate goal should be to provide a distinct and analytically useful definition of life-style in terms of shared values or tastes as reflected primarily in consumption patterns but applicable also to the evaluation of intangible and/or public goods. A life-style might be defined over a given collectivity to the extent that the members are

---

[2] Among other things, the definition is devoid of specific content and stands in violation of almost all ordinary notions about the phenomenon itself.

> similar to one another and different from others both in the distribution of their disposable incomes and the motivations that underlie such distributions. A purely statistical definition of life-style, therefore, would have to use as input data motivations as well as consumption frequencies [p. 270].

There are problems with this definition as well. However, it is an attempt to address the content of a lifestyle directly. The more common approach is circumvention. This is explicit in Tallman and Morgner (1970):

> The lack of constituent meaning for a concept such as "life-style" makes any set of indicators vulnerable to the criticism that they are not appropriate measures and do not tap "significant" aspects of the phenomenon. We view life-style as a broad rubric under which a number of behavioral activities and orientations can be included, each of which requires a distinctive investment of the individual's resources of time, energy, and money. The behaviors investigated are not exhaustive of all possibilities but are representative of the concerns of many social scientists interested in the relationship between behavioral modes and community types [p. 337].

In the present context, two aspects of this quotation are interesting. First, the issue of lifestyle is confronted by an argument to the effect that the issue is not confrontable. Nonetheless, the authors believe the phenomenon is behavioral, so their measures consist of behaviors and behavioral orientations. The next issue is which behaviors and orientations are relevant. Since the construct "lacks constituent meaning," it is acceptable to answer by appealing to the specific interest in community types, that is, to phenomena relevant to the specific research concerns.

The use of circumvention, while rarely explicit, is nevertheless the predominant approach to lifestyles in the sociological literature. This explains why researchers typically define lifestyle as a mode of living, a seemingly innocuous tautology, and then proceed directly to an eclectic and/or ad hoc set of measures.

This characterization can also be applied to most psychographic research. Researchers who implicitly accept some type of social-psychological or psychological definition typically use measures intended to capture personality traits and self-conceptions, or value systems, or activities, interests, and opinions. Other researchers focus on the consumption of goods and services. Nor is it uncommon to find researchers who wish to use combinations of these different types of measures.[3]

---

[3] I have good reason for not discussing these particular measures in detail. Since the intent of most of this research is pragmatic, justification of measures will tend to be pragmatic as well. It would be inappropriate here to enter into a discussion of why some attitude measures predict who buys toothpaste, while others are better overall predictors of more general buying behavior.

Given the precarious and shifting meaning attached to the notion of lifestyle, it seems more than reasonable to eschew the use of the term itself in serious future research. This would lead to greater precision in sociological work, as researchers would be forced to indicate what they mean. Of course, lifestyle might still be a very reasonable term to use in ordinary language.

On the other hand, the fact that some overwhelming problems in the use of the concept can be elucidated does not constitute grounds for its abandonment; justification of this sort must be sought elsewhere. The study of lifestyles seems to have some basis in the social and sociological worlds and may therefore be viewed as a legitimate sociological subject. Furthermore, the notion of lifestyle seems to capture and be related to some phenomena that already possess "legitimate sociological interest." Either one of these related reasons implies that the notion itself possesses "legitimate sociological interest." Therefore, abandonment is unacceptable.

It is clear that the concept of lifestyle demands reconceptualization by means of extensive primary analysis. Such an analysis takes place in the next two chapters. To begin with, I first examine the word *style*.

CHAPTER 3

From Style to Lifestyle:
An Analogy to Art History

The intent of this chapter is to construct a meaningful definition of the word *lifestyle* and to examine important properties of the definition itself. The first step in this process involves extensive consideration of the word *style* and its use in both ordinary language and art history. Primary attention is given to the descriptive (as opposed to normative) use of the word. After defining style and considering implications of the definition, lifestyle is defined by analogy as "a distinctive, hence recognizable, mode of living." Next, the implications drawn from the previous discussion are used to explicate the properties of *lifestyle*. This facilitates the utilization of the term in a clear conceptual fashion and makes possible the resolution of those questions raised in the previous chapter.

Style in Ordinary Language

It is important to consider the use of *style* in ordinary language. This paves the way for a more complete understanding of the parallel treatment given by scholars, thereby encouraging the development of a useful and unambiguous formal definition of lifestyle that stems ultimately from ordinary language itself.

There are three broad ways in which style is employed in ordinary language. First, it is used in a normative or judgmental fashion. Second, it may be used to render an idiosyncratic but nonnormative description. Third, the word is often used in a more general descriptive manner.

Since *style* is not an inherently scientific term it is not surprising that the word itself is loosely used. Although sociologists do not typically use the word lifestyle in the normative or idiosyncratic sense, there is much to be learned from consideration of these uses. Furthermore, there is a communality that underlies the use of the word *style* that does not underlie sociological usage of the word lifestyle, even though the latter usage is more restricted. It is the strength of this communality that ultimately permits a definition of lifestyle that stems from ordinary language.

As an example of normative usage consider the sentence, "The lady has style." When *style* is used in this fashion, it is customarily without further elaboration; indeed, elaboration of this summary quality seems superfluous. The context provides the meaning in a very special fashion, that is, by contrast. For, by saying that the woman has style, it is implicitly meant that she possesses certain characteristics that distinguish her from others in the same reference class, that is, from other women. If this were not the case, that is, if all women possessed style, the remark would be vacuous.

It may have been the way the woman was dressed, or the manner in which she carried herself that prompted the comment. No matter. The main point is that the woman possesses characteristics that either separately, or in conjunction with one another, create an impression that is sufficient to cause an observer to make the remark.

Since the characteristics need not be known explicitly, the same observer might make the same remark in a rather "different" situation, and yet it might be equally apropos. Or, in a very similar situation, the observer might not comment at all. Perhaps some quality or combination of qualities present in the first situation is missing, or not quite the same. An observer, then, need not be consistent in his usage of the term. Certainly two observers need not agree, even if it appears that they are using implicitly similar criteria.

To summarize: when the word style is used in this fashion, it is "a laudatory term denoting a desirable consistency and conspicuousness that makes a performance or artifact stand out from a mass of 'undistinguishable' events or objects [Gombrich, 1968, p. 353]."

Another common usage is illustrated by the sentence, "That's not my style." The sentence may refer to an object, such as a sweater, in which case the person making the remark is saying that he or she does not think the particular sweater is befitting. Perhaps the colors are not those he or she wears, or the sweater is cut too baggily. Or perhaps the fabric, the texture of the fabric, or the presence or absence of design is somehow inappropriate. When *style* is used in this fashion, qualities or combinations of qualities characteristic of the object evoke a personal preference. The person making the remark is not necessarily claiming that the object either has or does not have style, as in the preceding example, although he may think that this is the case. Implicitly all objects in the same class possess style. But some styles (there are at least two, namely, "my style" and "not my style") are more suitable than others. That is, for whatever reasons, the person thinks that some sweaters are more suitable for him than others. Perhaps a preferred image is more appropriately symbolized by one type of sweater than another.

The sentence "That's not my style" need not refer to an object, as in the preceding example. It can also refer to a variety of events, either real or contemplated, as when we say: "I don't think I'll do it that way. It's not my style." Here again, the word is used in the second sense; there are at least two styles, as before. But now, the reference class is no longer sweaters but activities. Style refers to the manner in which an individual performs an act. The individual might even choose not to perform at all.

Although it might appear otherwise, both usages are easily reconciled. One judges the sweater with respect to the manner in which one dresses. Therefore, both examples refer to a characteristic mode of performance. Style resides in the characteristic mode itself, in which case both the sweater and the act possess style. Hence the two uses are by and large equivalent.

In these examples a personal preference of a descriptive sort is rendered. No acclaim is attached to the preference itself, as in the normative use of the word. Personal judgments are still made, as in the first example, but the evaluation now takes place on an axis that implicitly grants equality of style to all objects (activities) in the class. (In actuality, the word is often used in a manner that combines both descriptive and normative notions.)

Personal preferences are meaningless if the individual is unable to express them. When alternatives are unavailable, or choice is somehow constrained independently of the alternatives, it does not make a great deal of sense to use the word *style*. When alternative expression is impossible, style is uniform, and there is nothing at all characteristic about the particular style. There is only one style, and without an appropriate contrast, it makes no sense to use the term at all. That is, when choice is severely constrained (forced), style is unobservable, and use of the word is then vacuous.

There is one more way the term *style* is commonly used in ordinary language. When we say: "He dresses in a traditional style," a description is still rendered, as in the second use of the word. However, the description is now more general because there are typically more than two categories, and the basis for classification is no longer idiosyncratic. But because the word is used in conjunction with the adjective preceding it, an effective description depends upon shared perceptions, in contrast with both prior uses. The components of a traditional style must be known, if only implicitly. Again, since alternative styles exist, the traditional style may be defined by contrast, either with other styles or with explicit other styles, such as modern, etc.

In short, when style is used in this manner, that is, in conjunction with a descriptive adjective, it is possible (at least in principle) to construct either a (not necessarily unique) taxonomy or an ideal-typical set of states with formal criteria of exclusion and inclusion. (Unlike taxonomies, ideal types need not be empirically realized, nor need the classification criteria be mutually exclusive and exhaustive. Ideal types are merely "tendencies" of some sort.)

Esthetic Style

The use of the word *style* as a formal esthetic concept parallels normative usage in ordinary language. For example, good and bad literature are often distinguished by the presence or absence of style. The former is said to possess style, whereas the latter does not. Henri Beyle (Stendahl) claims: "Style consists in adding to a given thought all the circumstances calculated to produce the whole effect that the thought ought to produce." That is, style is the literary production of the correct emotion. It is laudable, characteristic, and consistent. To be sure, it is idiosyncratic, but it also transcends mere idiosyncracy. As Murry (1965) says: "Style, in this absolute sense, is a complete fusion of the personal and the universal . . . absolute style is the complete realization of a universal significance in a personal and particular expression [p. 7]." It is "the highest achievement of literature [p. 7]."

These notions of style rely upon ideas about "whole effect," "complete realization," etc. Style depends upon the manner in which the elements of writing combine with one another; that is, they combine so as to produce a totality. Style is, above all else, holistic.

As in ordinary language the presence or absence of style depends upon the observer's perceptions. However, there now exists an explicit, if unwieldy criterion by which to determine the presence of style. One looks for the correct emotion or universal significance. If it exists, analysis of the work itself reveals the manner in which the achievement is attained.

Similar ideas can be found in art. In the widely read work, *Art,* Clive Bell (1958) attempts to distinguish between those objects that are "art" and those that are not. Bell starts with the existence of the "aesthetic emotion" as given. The problem is then to discover those characteristics of the object that provoke the emotion itself.

According to Bell, the quality that discriminates among objects is "significant form" (a synonym for, or description of, style), that is, "lines and colours combined in a particular way, certain forms and relations of forms [p. 17]." Subject matter and the manner in which it is represented are unimportant. The "representation of three-dimensional space is neither irrelevant nor essential to all art . . . every other sort of representation is irrelevant [p. 28]."

There are a variety of reasons why one might wish to quarrel with Bell and with notions of style such as these. This is not at issue. The important point is that *style,* in the esthetic sense, is a fusion of formal elements that engenders emotions of a certain character. The formal elements are amenable to direct observation and, in principle, formal analysis.

Idiosyncratic Style

The idiosyncratic use of *style* ("my style") is more prevalent in ordinary language than in the language of the sciences or the arts. Nonetheless, the application of "idiosyncratic style" has proved fruitful, even without the formal explication of the notion itself.

For example, the authorship of several of the Federalist papers was disputed; both Jefferson and Hamilton claimed to have written the pieces in question. In the early 1960s several Harvard statisticians analyzed the disputed pieces by comparing them to other pieces known to be written by one or another of these authors. Using criteria such as sentence length, frequency of usage of certain definite articles, they concluded that the disputed pieces were written by Jefferson.

In art history, questions like these are generally decided by connoisseurs. The criteria they use are diverse and include medium, technique, quality, size, X rays, and formal elements of the work itself. The connoisseur uses a loose, idiosyncratic notion of style to make fine distinctions. He may use more formal notions of style as well.

Unlike the notion of idiosyncratic style in ordinary language already discussed, personal preferences are not at issue. What the two notions have in common is the potential ability to discriminate on the basis of analysis of formal elements and (or) their conjunction.

Descriptive Style

In the descriptive context, *style* has received its most serious consideration from art historians. There are two broadly related ways in which art historians use the word itself. The first is in conjunction with a descriptive adjective or set of adjectives. The second is as a formal concept in and of its own right. Careful consideration of both usages is essential to the derivation of a useful concept of lifestyle.

As an example of the first use, *Baroque style* is considered. Initially, the adjective Baroque signified elaborate ornamentation, and by analogy, cultural decadence, hence decay.[1] However, Baroque is no longer used normatively by art historians, and its normative use is not at issue here.

In the modern context, Baroque may be used to indicate that a work was made at a certain point of time (period style) or that a work exhibits observable characteristics, either separately or in conjunction with one another, that make this work very similar in character to other works that have been labeled Baroque (theoretical style). In the first case, the referent is clearly temporal, and the addition of the word *style* to the word *Baroque* is, in many respects, gratuitous.[2] In the second, however, the referent is to an underlying set of formal criteria that define style, and the addition of the word *Baroque* to the word *style* is equally gratuitous, at least in a logical sense.

In the "empirical world," it turns out that the association between period style and theoretical style is nearly perfect. Even art historians who disagree about the important elements in a theoretical style usually agree about which style the work exhibits. Baroque works are simply not made in the Early Renaissance. Thus, art historians who disagree about the exact nature of theoretical style nonetheless can agree about the period style that is represented.

This occurs for several reasons. First the works of a period are homogeneous by contrast with those of other periods. Second, the formal

[1] Art historians had adopted an organismic analogy in which the relationship of art to culture was very close. Culture was held to evolve through three stages: The first stage was adolescence, the second, maturity, the third, old age. Corresponding to these stages were primitive, classical, and Baroque art, respectively. The former was characterized by primitive forms, the classical by simple elegance, and the Baroque by elaborate ornamentation.

[2] For period we we could have just as easily used a geographic criterion.

elements that comprise style exhibit stylistic unity; that is, certain characteristics occur only with certain others, etc. This last fact, and it is an empirical fact rather than a fact that follows from necessity, makes matters simple for the art historian. Out of all the potential combinations only a few occur with much frequency. Taken together, these two considerations admit the establishment of a simple one-to-one correspondence between time and any manifestation of theoretical style. In turn, this accounts for the high degree of consensus among art historians.

In addition, the existence of the correspondence allows a sense of descriptive reality to be imparted by means of appropriately chosen labels, for example, Baroque. However, the absence of either condition destroys the utility of labeling. In the absence of temporal homogeneity, labeling is ambiguous, and because the correspondence between period style and theoretical style breaks down, the concept of period style becomes meaningless. In the absence of stylistic unity, the realization of many distinct combinations makes labeling unwieldy. In that case, an analysis of the formal characteristics of a work and the manner in which these are conjoined can still be conducted. That is, the notion of theoretical style remains intact.

Having made these points, to which we shall return, the theoretical use of the word style can be considered, apart from any of the adjectives that usually precede it. Three different notions are discussed and compared.

Ackerman argues that style is "a way of characterizing relationships among works of art that were made at the same time and/or place, or by the same person or group [1963, p. 164]." For the concept to fulfill these functions it must consist of

> characteristics that are more or less stable in the sense that they appear in other products of the same artist(s), era or locale, and flexible, in the sense that they change according to a definable pattern when observed in instances chosen from sufficiently extensive spans of time or of geographic distance. A distinguishable ensemble of such characteristics we call a style [p. 164].

Of course Ackerman is merely arguing that since the concept is used empirically, it should consist of phenomena that discriminate well. That is, a useful notion of style is one that does its job well; the argument is for predictive validity. In fact, Ackerman goes so far as to claim that it is silly to ask what style is apart from its empirical context.

It is true, if one begins with recognizably different period styles, that contrasts between the styles should be made in terms of cogent criteria. But Ackerman's argument encourages operationalization without conceptualization. Style becomes the set of empirical indicators, but there is no real theoretical concept to which these correspond. In this instance, it would be just as well to speak of X (X consists of the set of empirical indicators) as to speak of style.

A different approach is taken by Schapiro, who states:

> By style is meant the constant form and sometimes the constant elements, qualities, and expression in the art of an individual or a group . . . style is above all, a system of forms with a quality and a meaningful expression through which the personality of the artist and the broad outlook of a group are visible. It is also a vehicle of expression within the group, communicating and fixing certain values of religious, social, and moral life through the emotional suggestiveness of forms [1961, p. 81].

By qualities Schapiro means that lines and colors, as well as relationships between lines and between colors, are better expressed in qualitative terms (i.e., a line is hard or soft, a color light or dark) than in quantitative terms. Furthermore, these qualities, which are "not comprised in a compositional schema of the whole [p. 84]" are important to the structure of the work itself. By expressiveness he means a holistic, summary quality, suggested by the configuration of forms and qualities.

But Schapiro goes too far. He seems to argue that style is a manifestation of personality and/or broad outlook, in the aggregate. Because he is not careful, this can be read to mean that style blatantly mirrors personality. If this is in fact what he means, then the argument bears little resemblance to the evidence. If, on the other hand, he means that in a non-deterministic fashion one can sometimes make reasonable speculations concerning some aspects of personality (e.g., Van Gogh was probably schizophrenic), or, that in the aggregate, broad outlooks (e.g., Western Renaissance people tended to view physical reality as they perceived it, witness the use of perspective projection; but Eastern people tended to view physical reality as it is, witness the use of geometric projection) may be discernable, there is little room for disagreement. Personality and outlook are causally associated with style, but are not part of style itself.

The broadest definition is due to Gombrich (1968): "Style is any distinctive, and therefore recognizable, way in which an act is performed or an artifact made or ought to be performed and made [p. 352]."

But it is only meaningful to speak of style when certain initial conditions are satisfied: "Only against the background of alternative choices can the distinctive way also be seen as expressive. . . . There can be no question of style unless the speaker or writer has the possibility of choosing between alternative forms of expression [p. 353]."

Despite the differences in the three definitions all share one common feature: either explicitly or implicitly, style resides within the completed product or is formally deducible from the product itself. This is most clear in Ackerman's and Schapiro's definitions, which are not far from an operational definition. This is less clear in Gombrich's definition, which is the most abstract and general; nonetheless, it is implicit. The manner in which a performance is rendered or an object made refers to a behavioral activity, i.e., to artistic activity. The evidence of the manner, however, resides in the product itself.

While this communality in the definitions is by far the most important point, there are three differences between the definitions that merit discussion. First, in all but Gombrich's definition, some notion of stylistic unity (patterned elements) is hinted at: Ackerman uses the words "distinguishable ensemble," while Schapiro refers to a "system of forms." Gombrich, however, does not introduce such a notion. His definition is technically compatible with a lack of stylistic unity. That is, a work may exhibit distinctiveness, hence style, without necessarily exhibiting stylistic unity. This is an important point, one which is often overlooked because great art does tend to possess unity. But, as Hauser (1958) points out, a formal analysis of the style(s) in folk art could certainly be undertaken, despite the fact that folk art typically lacks stylistic unity.

Second, only Gombrich attaches to the definition the secondary criterion of expressiveness. This is an important condition. It has already been argues in the section on usage in ordinary language that without such a condition, it is possible to use the term in a vacuous manner.

Third, Gombrich's definition is compatible with a focus on either the product or on the technical processes that result in the product (see the previous discussion on style as applied to an object or an activity). However, modern art historians tend to focus on the product, as they argue that process often fails to discriminate among diverse products (for an exception see Focillon, 1948).[3] This tendency is reflected in Ackerman's and Schapiro's definitions. But whichever viewpoint is adopted, the product bears the style. Hence, style is deducible from the product.

Lifestyle

It is now time to define the word *lifestyle,* examine its properties, and use the preceding discussion to resolve the critical issues raised in Chapter 2.

---

[3] According to Focillon, "The examination of technical phenomena not only guaranteed a certain controllable objectivity, but afforded an entrance into the very heart of the problem, by presenting it to us in the same terms and from the same point of view as it is presented to the artist [1948, p. 36]."

Almost all sociologists will agree that lifestyle may be defined as "a distinctive, hence recognizable, mode of living." To this definition the condition of expressiveness (alternative choice) is attached, thereby insuring that usage is not vacuous (see the preceding discussion). In essence, this definition parallels Gombrich's definition of *style* and focuses attention on descriptive usage. In the latter definition, as in all others, descriptive, normative or idiosyncratic, formal or informal, style refers to a phenomenon that is eminently observable or deducible from observation.[4] Thus, it is also reasonable to require that lifestyle be eminently observable or deducible from observation. Furthermore, it follows that lifestyle is behavioral because, in the phrase "mode of living," a mode (manner or way) refers to a behavioral phenomenon (*Oxford English Dictionary,* 1961; *Webster's Seventh New Collegiate Dictionary,* 1972). Thus, lifestyle consists of expressive behaviors that are observable; as in art history and ordinary language, a focus on either the behavior (activity) itself or its product is justifiable.

These considerations lead to the following important conclusion: If it is agreed that it is reasonable to regard lifestyle as a distinctive and hence recognizable mode of living, attitudes, values, and behavioral orientations no longer qualify as candidates for inclusion in the domain of the content. These may be related to lifestyle, perhaps even causally, but that is a different issue.

It is not possible to derive the fundamental unit in lifestyle analyses from the definition itself. That is, a lifestyle could be meaningfully defined as a property of an individual, a group, or even a culture.[5] But sociological researchers have typically used the concept at the individual level, despite some assertions to the contrary. Researchers who assert that lifestyle is a group phenomenon typically base their conclusions on evidence that members of a given aggregate can be statistically differentiated from those of another aggregate, with respect to individually defined variables. There is nothing wrong with utilizing such types of evidence, but it does not

---

[4] By observable, I mean readily perceived, that is, clearly heard, felt, or viewed. Notice the implication of conspicuousness. This usage is consistent with definitions of the words "distinct" and "distinctive" (*Webster's Third New International Dictionary,* 1967).

[5] Previous researchers have attempted to apply the word style to culture, or to material items. The word itself, or similar words, have been used by anthropologists or historians to characterize civilizations, or, at a lower level of abstraction, artifacts (Kroeber, 1957, 1963). In this research, stylistic unity is often explicitly incorporated into definitions of style. For example, Kroeber defines style as "a system of coherent ways or patterns of doing certain things [1963, p. 66]." He proceeds to view civilizations and cultures as stylistic expressions and criticizes others (Mead, Benedict, Bateson, and Gorer) who have taken the same view for allowing the analysis to degenerate into psychological cliches. Additionally, he points out that such analyses are methodologically flawed.

imply the conclusion, which is a conceptual matter. The correct statement is that certain characteristics, for example, race, marital status, sex, education, are causes or correlates of lifestyle differentiation. In this vein, it should also be noted that such characteristics embody behavioral expectations, and perhaps normative behavior, but not expressive behavior.

Thus, when researchers speak of a middle-class lifestyle, they generally mean that the members of the middle class seem to share what are regarded as lifestyle elements to a greater extent than they share these elements with upper- or lower-class individuals. In this context, the term *middle class* when joined to the word *lifestyle* functions as a descriptive label derived from empirical analysis.

Analytically, it is clear that there is no need for these types of labels (see the discussion of Baroque style). Furthermore, in the preceding context, the application of the label confounds conceptualization with empirical analysis in a manner that is analogous to confusing period style with theoretical style. That is, in the absence of a one-to-one correspondence, the application of the label itself is not just confusing and inappropriate; it also distorts, by means of gross oversimplification, the nature of descriptive reality.

It may still be possible, although it is not necessary, to utilize meaningful descriptive labels (modern and traditional, for example) if lifestyle elements configure in such a manner that only a few of the multitude of possible combinations are realized, that is, unless the level of stylistic unity is high, descriptive reality cannot be imparted by well-chosen labels.[6] This itself can be viewed as an empirical issue.

It is important that the empirical character of stylistic unity in lifestyle analyses be recognized.[7] Recall that stylistic unity is not a necessary property of a lifestyle, according to my definition. Many previous researchers have studied lifestyle elements one at a time, although they appear to be interested, if only implicitly, in stylistic unity. Inferences regarding stylistic unity have been made on the basis of this strategy, by stringing the separate conclusions together with a series of commas. Needless to say, there is no basis for such inferences. Multivariate density functions cannot be inferred from marginal density functions. Other researchers have simply assumed the existence of stylistic unity. Both types of researchers would be forced to the logical conclusion that lifestyle does not exist in the absence of stylistic unity.

In this study, the distinction between stylistic unity and lifestyle is

---

[6] The emphasis on description may well detract from more important tasks, for example, understanding the sociological sources of lifestyle differentiation.

[7] A more detailed discussion of this point can be found in Chapter 8.

maintained, both conceptually and throughout the empirical analysis. One of the empirical analyses focuses exclusively on lifestyle differentiation. The other analysis focuses primarily on stylistic unity, which is viewed as a proximate cause of a lifestyle.

While it is helpful to know that lifestyle can be viewed as an individual property consisting of observable and expressive behaviors that may or may not exhibit stylistic unity, it is not at all clear which behaviors best indicate lifestyle.

This raises a dilemma that can only be resolved by allowing secondary criteria to influence the choice of behaviors. Others have already been criticized for using ad hoc sets of indicators that stem from specific research concerns. The criterion of convenience is unacceptable.

Art historians are not particularly helpful in the resolution of this issue. Ackerman argues that the elements must facilitate an interesting story. Focillon (1948) and Wölfflin (1932) allow abstract theoretical concerns to structure the focus. (I say abstract theoretical concerns to distinguish these from empirical concerns or from theoretical issues arising in a more circumscribed context, like those mentioned in Chapter 2.) Presumably, the two approaches are somewhat associated. The approach I take is somewhat more general than either one of these. Since I wish to synchronically differentiate individuals within the post–World War II American population, I want to examine those behaviors that are "significant" in modern American life. This requires a historical argument that is made in the next chapter.

CHAPTER 4

Lifestyle, Consumption, and the American Experience: A Historical Sketch

In the preceding chapter, it is argued that lifestyles can be meaningfully conceptualized as sets of expressive, observable behaviors defined over individuals. Criteria for identifying those behaviors that best index lifestyle have yet to be formulated, although it has been argued that it is not enough merely to select ad hoc behaviors of particular interest as some prior researchers have done. Selecting behaviors in an ad hoc manner does not allow for the development of a broad concept applicable to a variety of questions at diverse points in time, or even at a single point in time.

A reasonable method of selection is to choose behaviors that are not only expressive and observable, but of primary a priori significance within a given "historical reality." The implications of utilizing the condition of spatio-temporal salience as a secondary criterion are severalfold. Most importantly, a broad and general context is provided. Lifestyle becomes a concept with both specific content and social meaning, a concept that can be usefully employed in other research activities. The advantages of this should be obvious. On the other hand, the approach does have its disadvantages. Whereas the abstract concept of lifestyle (sets of expressive, observable behaviors) need not change over time and space, the particular behaviors selected as spatio-temporally salient are by no means fixed. Were we to study lifestyles in feudal England, as well as contemporary America, the behaviors selected on the basis of the secondary criterion need not bear a resemblance across studies. Nor are the relevant behaviors always clear, as during periods of major transition.

Since the setting for this study is contemporary America, those phenomena that are of primary importance in the American experience are discussed. To facilitate the discussion and to demarcate rough timepoints for which the subsequent observations hold, a historical argument is required. Contemporary American life is best understood by understanding American history, that is, by understanding the sequences of ongoing events that combined over a period of time to produce a contemporary social reality distinctly different from that which existed a mere 30 years ago.

Following the historical sketch, that demonstrates the salience of consumption in American life, three issues are addressed. First, the relationship between consumption and expressiveness, second, the relationship between work and expressiveness, and finally, the relationship between consumption and leisure are considered.

The argument that I make leads to a simple conclusion: Americans are a society of consumers. Consumption is an expressive activity that includes much of and shapes the totality of American life in a very profound manner. It is not just that Americans live in a society in which activities are increasingly consumed at a cost. Beyond this, it is the fact that Americans attach so much intrinsic importance to this activity that allows the conclusion that lifestyles are created predominantly through consumption.

The Historical Argument[1]

Between 1860 and 1900 many of the patterns shaping twentieth-century life first emerged in discernible form. On the eve of the Civil War,

[1] The validity of the historical argument rests upon the assumption that much of consumption reflects induced, as opposed to intrinsic, demand. The consumption mentality could be generated in some other fashion, so that the conclusion of the argument might be correct, independently of the structure of the argument. But if the argument is improperly structured, much of the historical evidence is irrelevant, and the linkage between consumption and the psyche has yet to be demonstrated, in which case some other argument for the saliency of consumption must be generated.

Therefore, the argument that demand originates with the consumer must be considered. Those who claim consumption stems from the exertion of independent, individual prefer-

America was a predominantly rural nation. Slightly more than 80% of the nation's inhabitants lived in rural settings. The number of places classified as urban (population of 2500 or more) by the U.S. Census was less than 400, and only nine American cities had populations in excess of 100,000. New York was the only American city with a population larger than 1,000,000, and in what is now the city of Los Angeles fewer than 6000 people resided.[2]

A large part of the population was therefore engaged in agricultural pursuits; data from the census of 1870 indicates that 53% of all gainful workers were so occupied. Only about 20% of all gainful workers were employed in the manufacturing and mechanical industries, and fewer than 10% were employed in the trade industry. Large-scale technology had not yet arrived on the American scene in massive proportions, productivity was low by subsequent standards, and only within the finance and transportation industries was there evidence of much concentration (Dowd, 1974).

Americans worked long hours (DeGrazia, 1962), believed in the value of such activity, and earned little by current standards. They were typically undereducated, though not quite illiterate (Taeuber and Taeuber, 1975, p. 186). By modern standards, Americans were provincial and lacked the ability to communicate or travel easily across vast amounts of space.

Between 1860 and 1900, the forces that generated the initial conditions for the rise of the consumption society contributed to a drastic

---

ences operating in the marketplace point to the fact that a fair portion of market research is conducted precisely to discover what consumers desire (Katona, 1964). Secondly, consumers want to know and take steps to compare brands against one another when considering product purchases. That is, consumers attempt to make "rational" choices in order to consume efficiently. In addition, the advertising record indicates that quite a few products have been unsuccessful, despite large advertising campaigns; witness the Edsel.

These claims, although by and large correct, miss the point entirely and do not at all reflect upon the validity of the argument for induced demand. The argument, as given here, is neither ahistorical nor product or brand specific. The ahistorical argument conditions on the link between consumers and the specific marketplace at a fixed time point, ignoring the process by which people are conditioned to desire a multitude of goods and services in the first place. Induced demand is not a specific, but rather a general phenomenon; neither the mix of goods at a particular time, nor the fact that consumers wish to purchase wisely, and in fact, reject some products or brands entirely, vitiates the induced demand argument in the least. By addressing themselves to the link between consumers and a product- or brand-specific marketplace at a given time, critics of the induced demand hypothesis have failed to grasp or illuminate the content of the argument at all.

[2] The demographic information cited in the next few pages is taken from three sources. These are (a) Glaab and Brown, 1967; (b) *Historical Statistics of the United States, 1789–1945*, published by the U.S. Census Bureau; and (c) Taeuber and Taeuber (1975).

transformation of American society. Fueled by land speculation and over-extension of the railroad networks, dramatic urban growth occurred in the period between 1870 and 1900. In conjunction with post–Civil War technological advances, speculation contributed to the depressed economic conditions of the period. These factors, in turn, paved the way for the wholesale emergence of the large corporate firm. In the face of declining prices and the advent of large-scale technology, the necessity of avoiding intense price competition (which reduced declining profits even further) eventually culminated in the great mergers of 1897–1905, during which "over 5300 industrial firms came under the control, finally, of 318 corporations, the most advanced and powerful firms in the economy [Dowd, 1974, p. 71]." The American economic system would never again be the same. In due time, neither would the American public.

In short, by 1900 the earlier characterization of American life was no longer true. Somewhat less than 40% of all gainful workers were now occupied in agricultural pursuits, and approximately 25% were engaged in the manufacturing and mechanical industries. A few of the wealthier Americans owned automobiles and telephones; as of yet, there were no radios. But the majority of Americans were by no means considerably better off than before. Though not as uneducated as previously, Americans managed to retain many of their provincial attitudes and acquire a host of others.

Over 30,000,000 people now lived in more than 1700 urban places, and in the 38 cities with populations larger than 100,000, over 14,000,000 people resided. The percentage of the population residing in urban places had doubled in 40 years, and the frontier era was at an end. Mass transit was common in the cities, as were traffic jams. America was well on its way to becoming an urban nation.

In 1910 a technological innovation, the assembly line—a logical outgrowth of urbanization and capital concentration—was introduced into the American economic system by Ford. The innovation was so successful that within 5 years, the amount of productive labor required to assemble a chassis had dropped to approximately 15% of the original time (Ewen, 1976, p. 23). But whereas it led to dramatic increases in per capita productivity, the advent of mass production significantly changed the character of work for those involved, whose numbers were rapidly increasing. Work became more efficient, but also more fragmented and tedious. And as intrinsic work satisfaction declined, the potential for labor unrest increased.

Even before the advent of mass production, social control of workers was never far from the minds of the corporate leaders and their managers. A docile, or at least not hostile, work force was needed to comply with production demands. The attainment of such a goal, it was felt, would not only further enhance productivity, but would quell potentially revolutionary labor unrest and lead to the stabilization and acceptance of social roles within a hierarchical order defined by those at the summit. In the later nineteenth century, when the issues were focused on working conditions and the number of weekly hours, the typical response to the movements advocating the implementation of change was armed suppression. By 1910, the more liberal corporate leaders advocated less violent strategies (at least as a first order means) for the ensurance of a stable work force. Not wishing to grant any significant changes, the companies (more accurately, a few of the larger companies) developed programs ostensibly concerned with the general "welfare" of the workers. In actuality, the primary emphasis of the programs was industrial discipline (Ewen, 1976, p. 15).

But the implementation of these programs (which foreshadow the development of the human relations school) appeared to be an insufficient response to the advent of mass production. Following World War I, labor unrest intensified dramatically and membership in various radical organizations rose. In conjunction the two not unrelated events engendered a wave of "retaliatory raids, firings, repression, and massive deportation of immigrant workers and radicals [Ewen, 1976, p. 9]."

Social control was not the only problem facing employers. The increase in per capita productivity that resulted from the new technology had boosted total production so much that expanded markets were now needed to drain off excess production. World War I was over and Say's Law could not automatically be counted on to work.

By the early 1920s it was clear that these two interrelated problems demanded a satisfactory solution. At that time, wages began to rise at an unprecedented rate. Simultaneously, hours worked per week began to drop. For those affected by such changes, and this by no means included all or even the majority of the population, the advent of discretionary income constituted a qualitative break with the past.

If workers could be convinced to spend this "excess" income within the system, the excess production problem could be solved. If workers could also be convinced that consumption is a primary goal (in particular, a more salient dimension of experience than work itself), social control could be maintained predominantly by manipulating wages. And, although increasing wages increases production costs, these costs can always be passed on to the consumer by the large corporation. Clearly this is a more appealing strategy than granting workers a significant voice in other aspects of the production process.

The successful implementation of the dual strategy hinged on convincing the workers (*a*) to consume and (*b*) to rank order this activity as more important than work itself. Given the values of a majority of Americans in 1920 and the labor unrest within the country at that time, it was not at all clear that the strategy could be successfully implemented. Americans traditionally believed in their work and displayed some adherence to the Protestant Ethic, of which frugality was a corollary. Indeed, thrift was an important doctrine within the system, having been espoused and emphasized by mainstream ideological leaders for some time. In order to quickly make Americans into consumers par excellence, a complete restructuring of the traditional set of beliefs was called for. To the advertising industry, at that time a nascent concern, fell this important task.[3]

The industry responded by focusing on means of demand creation, both abstract and concrete. Early advertising methods were, to be sure, somewhat crude by comparison with contemporary market research. But the task at hand was not to discover which types of people buy a particular brand of detergent. Indeed, the scope of the task that faced the industry was much broader.

To make people buy it is not enough to grant the means and the products and hope that the linkage will follow. Members of the advertising industry realized this at an early stage. First, the existing negative attitudes to consumption had to be destroyed. Second, strong positive attitudes had to be created.

The industry used two complementary approaches to generate the consumption psyche en masse. First, it appealed to those human needs that were regarded as instinctual and powerful, such as gratification, sex, love, play, prestige. By associating product ownership and need gratification, the advertisers repeatedly encouraged the individual to find satisfaction in the acquisition of goods and services (positive reinforcement). Second, the industry encouraged consumption as a method of obtaining social acceptability (negative reinforcement). Immigration, and the differences between immigrants and Americans, had made the public extremely sensitive to social convention and the ostracism engendered by the failure to conform. Advertisers went to work on this American anxiety, asserting the existence of a link between consumption and conformity; the latter phenomenon they called "civilization." In essence, the advertisers argued that the acquisition of acceptable goods was a means of overcoming class

[3] Prior to the 1920s, advertising was by no means widely accepted by the major corporations as an efficient distributive strategy. According to Ewen (1976): "Between 1918 and 1923, a greater percentage of articles in the advertising trade journal, "Printer's Ink," were devoted to ways of convincing "ancient" corporations that advertising was a given of modern industrialism than were devoted to advertising and merchandising techniques [p. 32]."

and ethnic barriers. Consumption was the way to be an American. Ads produced in this fashion, Ewen (1976) notes "were geared to make people ashamed of their origins and, consequently, the habits and practices that characterized them as alien [p. 43]." Fortunately, such individuals could buy their way out.

In tandem with the efforts of the advertising industry, two other forces contributed to the emergent link between life satisfaction and consumption. The first of these is the development of the motion picture,[4] and the second is the expansion of credit.

In 1922, 40 million tickets were sold each week to movie goers (Mowry, 1965, p. 4). As the costs of film production skyrocketed throughout the decade, producers aimed for larger and larger audiences, cultivating the mass taste that they had helped to bring about.

The content of the pictures, described below, stems in part from the trivial character of work itself.

> Because the majority of the movie audience had no desire to be reminded of their shabby homes and their dreary, monotonous work, most pictures dealt with carefree individuals engaged in exciting adventures and surrounded by frivolous luxuries. The typical heroine wore expensive clothes, furs, and elegant jewels, and either lived in a stately mansion or flitted between the deluxe hotels of the world; the hero, usually without visible means of support, was as splendidly accoutred, drove the fanciest automobile, and pursued the most attractive young women. . . . The movie credo was one of sustained consumption, not production. And continually reiterating this theme, the industry became midwife to the birth of the leisure-seeking, pleasure demanding, materialistic consumer society of modern America [Mowry, 1965, pp. 5–6].

The advertising industry, then, in part, merchandised and reified the aspirations and ambitions created and nurtured by the movie industry.

But the subjective link between satisfaction and consumption was given objective form by the heads of the major corporations, who encouraged the expansion of consumer purchasing power. Although wages had increased, it remained the case that major durables (in particular, automobiles) required substantial outlays. The acquisition of such items required either long term saving (which is still practiced extensively in Europe, according to Katona (1971)) or the extension of installment credit to the potential consumer. In America, the latter practice became widespread in the 1920s. The automobile industry took the lead in encouraging this development and in the process added a few new wrinkles to ensure

---

[4] Mowry (1965, p. 6), in fact, claims that the movie industry may have been more instrumental in the production of the mass consumption market than the advertising industry, as it offered powerful visual stimuli, something the advertising industry could not yet do.

that a higher proportion of new, as opposed to used, products would be sold in the future. According to Dowd (1974):

> By 1924 new car buyers were no longer the focus of the auto industry's attention; their numbers had begun to shrink. What was needed was stepped-up replacement, and a large used-car market to support it. In turn, this led to what has since become the hallmark of consumer goods production and distribution: deliberate product obsolescence, extensive advertising, and consumer finance. General Motors took the lead in all three; advertising, yearly model changes, trade-ins, and living in constant debt were thereby elevated to what many take to be the American way of life [p. 101].

Shortly thereafter "home appliances, radio sets, furniture, and even such luxuries as jewelry were being sold on the installment plan [Mowry, 1965, p. 7]." At the end of January, 1929, total installment credit outstanding stood at over $2,600,000,000, while noninstallment credit outstanding stood at almost $3,000,000,000. Of the former component, over $1,100,000,000 of the total represented automobile installment credit (Klein, 1971; Tables C-12 and C-3).

It appeared that the consumption economy was well underway. But since approximately two-thirds of the population was still effectively excluded from the means of continuous participation (Soule, 1947), it would perhaps be more accurate to say that the consumption economy was off to a flying start. Future years would witness the incorporation of previously excluded sectors of the population as the economy continued its rocket-like expansion.

The crash of 1929, and the subsequent worldwide depression put a stop to economic growth, sending the American economy into a severe tailspin from which it did not recover until World War II broke out. In that period, the unions made gains, and significantly, the motion picture industry continued to thrive. The advertising industry was forced to cut back on its campaign to impress consumption upon the American psyche and focused its attention on the motif of temporary sacrifice.

The war's end was accompanied by a mild recession, after which business boomed again. Wages were higher, and increasing, and industry operated more efficiently than it had ever operated in the past. The service sector was expanding rapidly, and the corporations had regained their former power. Advertisers now had access to a newer and better medium, the television, and a new set of social circumstances (the Cold War, and slightly later, McCarthyism) with which to encourage conformity. As the cities grew more crowded, dirtier, and in general, less attractive, Americans were constantly reminded that the good life existed in the suburbs. Housing loans were now easier to obtain (incidentally, mortgages on homes are not included in the consumer credit figures), and the focus of the expanding housing market shifted to the suburbs, the new center of private construction. In short, the time for consolidating the consumption economy and extending its scope had finally arrived.[5]

The automobile industry responded to the times by making credit easier to obtain and allowing for the extension of the repayment period. As before, cars were built to last only a certain period of time, and psychological obsolescence was induced by the designers' annual model changes. In January, 1950, automobile installment credit stood at $4,705,000,000. By January, 1955, the appropriate figure was over twice as high; by January, 1960, the figure was almost four times that of the 1950 figure. Throughout this period, between 400,000 to 600,000 new cars were registered most months.

The figures for total installment credit outstanding show a similar trend over this 10-year period, rising from approximately $12 billion in January, 1950, to nearly $39 billion in January, 1960.

In addition, the use of credit cards, which existed prior to World War I, first became significant in the 1950s. Unlike the earlier cards, these were usable at a variety of establishments for a variety of purposes. Circa 1958 the banks instituted a new policy: The balance on a card could be paid off over time, subject to interest charges (Mandell, 1972, p. 5). Credit card use in America grew, until in 1970 it was estimated that 50% of all American families used credit cards. A substantial portion used the cards as a vehicle for consumption beyond current means (Mandell, 1972).

It was during the 1950s then that the consumption economy and the consumption mentality became "real" for a large proportion of the American public. By the end of that decade, this point was widely recognized and popularized eloquently by Galbraith in *The Affluent Society* (1958). It is not accidental that this book was hailed as the most important piece of the decade.[6]

In the 1960s, Americans were even richer. Having now enjoyed the "good life" for more than a decade, Americans took certain things for granted. Increasingly, they consumed experiences, both within the Amer-

[5] Suburban expansion helped to consolidate the consumption economy in several respects. Beyond the obvious (selling new homes), the expansion of the living territory beyond the existing routes of the mass transit systems increased the demand for automobiles. Significantly, it was during this period that the two-car family emerged. Not only did Americans increase their stock of major consumer durables (refrigerators, televisions, cars, etc.) during this time; in addition, suburban living, as it developed in America, required the private, as opposed to commercial, ownership of a host of other major goods, including such items as washing machines and dryers. In short, suburban life touched off a new wave of demand and a new set of needs, above and beyond those which previously existed.

[6] Similar observations have been made about other countries; in particular see Lefebvre (1971).

ican service sector, which continued to boom, and abroad, as Americans traveled and vacationed, consuming culture.

A consumption mentality appeared to be well entrenched, even though its increasing visibility began to attract more critics. In the later 1960s and early 1970s, the consumption economy came under strong internal attack. Nevertheless, the system continued to thrive, in part because American society was structured so as to require the private consumption of a wide variety of goods and services. But this is only a partial explanation. The consumption mentality was well ingrained, even in the minds of its critics,[7] and advertisers easily manipulated this audience by playing to it:

> Appropriating the lingo and styles of the New Left, the counterculture, feminism, neo-agrarianism, ethnicity, drug-vision and other phenomena, the advertising industry, seeking markets, has generated a mass culture which reflects the spirit but not the cutting edge of this resistance. While advertising of the twenties spoke against the deprivations of scarcity, an increasing amount of today's advertising and product imagery speak to the deprivations of what has been called "abundance." . . . . Ads mirror the widespread judgment that mass-produced goods are junky and unhealthy. Products are advertised as if they contain this anticorporate disposition—praised for their organic naturalness and their timeless quality [Ewen, 1976, p. 219].

What really changed during the later 1960s were specific preferences, as particular goods and classes of goods came to have altered social meaning. In the aggregate, this merely required the production of a somewhat different mix of specific goods and more product differentiation.[8]

Consumption and Expressiveness

The historical argument is complete. That is, the salience of consumption has been established. Before the broader argument that consumption best indexes lifestyle is complete, several issues must be considered. First, since lifestyle is expressive, it must be demonstrated that consumption is expressive. Second, it must be demonstrated that consumption better indexes lifestyle than plausible alternatives, such as work and leisure. In this section the relationship between consumption and expressiveness is considered.

[7] This point is also made by Aronowitz (1973, pp. 122–123).

[8] Product differentiation may be viewed as a phenomenon that helps consumers match specific self or desired self images with a given product, beyond the link established by desire for the product itself. For example, for the modern automobile consumer, the generalized notion of a car is an abstraction devoid of specific content; the consumer purchases a Ford or a Mercedes, a wagon or a sports car, but never just a car.

Consumption is expressive if the consumer is free to choose what he or she consumes. But the degree of choice is always relative. In Soviet society, governmental decisions about the allocation of resources impose restrictions upon the range and form of that which is offered. That is, potential consumption is restricted by decisions of the state. But the state does not stop there. In the face of scarcity, the state is partially responsible for the distribution of consumption items as well. Of course the overarching role of the state is moderated somewhat by the fact that any state must contend with the problem of legitimation, that is, the state must at least satisfy some consumer demands. By and large, however, consumption in Soviet society is not an officially recognized goal. Consumption is secondary to many other things, and at the individual level, consumption is not expressive, but severely constrained. Many products are difficult to obtain under any circumstances, and those that are available are not well differentiated.

Contrast this with the situation in the United States. Here the private and state sectors of the economy are at least formally separated. Governmental decisions influence, but do not determine to nearly the same extent that which is offered. This makes for a diverse marketplace. Both the range and form of that which is offered is quite extensive. At the individual level, the only real restriction in America is the presumed ability to pay at some point in the present or future. Therefore, consumption in American society is much more expressive than in Soviet society. This should hardly come as a surprise. On the other hand, consumption in America is not nearly so expressive as one might imagine (as is made particularly clear in Edward Bellamy's *Looking Backward*).

At the individual level, the individual qua organism needs food to survive. According to Maslow (1954) hunger, when it exists, becomes the overwhelmingly dominant motivational force underlying action. But this explains neither the quantity nor the qualitative content of the individual's tastes, save at a subsistence level. Similarly, with respect to shelter, the second level in Maslow's hierarchy, the organism needs shelter, but not specifically a hut, a mobile home, an apartment, condominium, or a home mortgaged to the hilt.

It has long been recognized that under normal circumstances the individual needs self-esteem. Self-esteem can be generated in almost any fashion—a job well done, a hobby, or the ownership of a Cadillac, to mention but a few possible sources. Although self-esteem can be generated in many ways, and indeed, probably is, the historical argument indicates that, in America, self-esteem is partially rooted in the possession of goods by virtue of the significance attached to such by their owners. The symbolic meaning of goods may well differ across individuals (no doubt, some people would be ashamed to possess a Cadillac), and the amount of self-esteem caught up in consumption varies over individuals, but this is not at issue.

The point is this: The individual consumes in part because he must. But consumption in America, even at the most elementary levels, is interlaced with stylistic manifestations. These represent the expressive content of otherwise instrumental means. They are indicative of different tastes and preferences, conditioning on income. Furthermore, different tastes and preferences are generated in part by variations in individual need structures.

It appears that consumption in America is expressive. That is, there is a great deal of choice for those with the income to live beyond subsistence. There is one other reason that consumption is expressive, which stems from the subjective attitudes Americans hold about consumption, rather than the objective conditions previously considered.

The primary rule in consumption is that the individual must pay, or suffer the possibility of sanction at some point. Beyond this rule, there are no others (save exceptions such as drugs and prostitution) that are hard and fast, and everyone is entitled to choose his consumption bundle. Furthermore, the individual is not only entitled to choose whatever mix he or she pleases but may do so for any number of reasons, or combinations of reasons, consistent or inconsistent. One need not even explicitly justify (except perhaps to a few others) his or her reasons or have reasons at all. For example, it is just as reasonable to drive a Mercedes for its snob appeal as for its quality or its looks. For the wealthy, it is just as reasonable to eat hamburgers and drink Coke as it is to eat Châteaubriand and drink Dom Perignon. It is true that an individual's choices may be ridiculed and subjected to invidious comparisons, but neither poor choice nor bad taste comes under the realm of sanction. Consumption is sacrosanct, and no one questions the right of an individual to consume in the manner he sees fit.

Work and Expressiveness

Potential critics might think work better indexes lifestyle than consumption by virtue of the criterion of salience. Although the relative importance of work-related aspects of life, as opposed to consumption, is amenable to debate and empirical analysis, salience is not the primary criterion by which work is excluded from the domain of content.

First, the work situation is structured, with built-in constraints for most workers. Those who are autonomous, it may cogently be argued, have merely internalized the norms of the work environment (Bowles and Gintis, 1976) and thereby supervise themselves. The criterion that life-style, like style, refers to an expressive phenomenon forces attention on phenomena in which a clearly definable dimension of choice is present. As previously noted, choice is always a matter of degree. Nevertheless, it is not at all clear that work, at a given point in an individual's life, reflects a great deal of choice.

While this argument is sufficient for the exclusion of work from the domain of content, it should also be noted that many people view work instrumentally. The rewards that stem from the work activity are signifi-cant, but their significance does not lie in the work itself, but in the fact that the rewards have social meaning, or are convertible into objects that have meaning. That is, for many persons, work is less salient than consumption.

Leisure and Consumption

One more argument demands attention. That is the apparently rea-sonable contention that the fact of declining hours in the work week is as important (if not more important) as the rise in consumption because it represents a quantum jump in the amount of leisure time Americans have at their disposal. The presumed increase of leisure time, as manifested by a set of leisure time activities, certainly qualifies as an expressive, observ-able behavior. Furthermore, Exhibit 4.1, adapted from DeGrazia (1962, p. 441), seems to bear out the assertion that Americans have more leisure time.

However, not all nonwork time is leisure time. There is also subsis-tence time and free time. Unfortunately, the difference between leisure time and free time, although conceptually useful, is difficult to measure; therefore, in the discussion that follows, leisure time and free time are combined under the grouped category of free time. The argument below, which seriously questions the existence of more free time in contempo-rary America, follows DeGrazia (1962) closely. The starting point is the 31-hour difference between 1850 and 1960 in Exhibit 4.1. Initially, De-Grazia adds 2 to 2.5 hours per week for fringe benefits, which include "paid vacations, holidays, and sick leave [p. 66]." There is then a differ-ence of 33 hours per week to explain.

Exhibit 4.1, DeGrazia points out, fails to reflect the incidence of part-time work. When part-time workers are excluded from the 1960 cal-culations, it is found that full-time workers in nonagricultural pursuits work an average of 46.4 hours per week, while those engaged in agricul-ture work an average of 60 hours per week. Similar calculations for 1850 cannot be made, but DeGrazia reasons that the incidence of part-time work then was small enough to comfortably ignore. The net effect of this restriction is to make the average difference closer to 25 hours. A conservative estimate for moonlighting in 1960 brings the difference to 24 hours.

EXHIBIT 4.1

Length of Average Work Week in Agriculture and in Nonagricultural Industries, 1850–1960

Year	All Industries	Agriculture	Nonagricultural Industries
1850	69.7	72.0	65.7
1860	67.8	71.0	63.3
1870	65.3	70.0	60.0
1880	63.8	69.0	58.8
1890	61.7	68.0	57.1
1900	60.1	67.0	55.9
1910	54.9	65.0	50.3
1920	49.4	60.0	45.5
1930	45.7	55.0	43.2
1940	43.8	54.6	41.1
1941	44.2	53.2	42.2
1942	45.2	55.3	43.1
1943	47.3	58.5	45.1
1944	46.2	54.4	44.6
1945	44.3	50.6	43.1
1946	42.4	50.0	41.1
1947	41.7	48.8	40.5
1948	40.8	48.5	39.6
1949	40.2	48.1	39.0
1950	39.9	47.2	38.8
1951	40.4	47.9	39.4
1952	40.5	47.4	39.6
1953	40.0	47.9	39.2
1954	38.9	47.0	37.9
1955	39.7	46.5	38.9
1956	39.5	44.9	38.8
1957	39.1	44.2	38.6
1958	38.6	43.7	38.1
1959	38.5	43.8	38.0
1960	38.5	44.0	38.0

Sources: 1850–1930: agriculture and nonagricultural industries from J. Frederic Dewhurst and associates, America's Needs and Resources: A New Survey, Twentieth Century Fund, New York, 1955, Appendix 20-4, p. 1073; all industries is average of other two columns weighted on the basis of percentage of gainfully occupied in agriculture and in nonagricultural industries as shown in Historical Statistics of the United States, 1789-1945, U.S. Bureau of the Census, 1949, Series D6-7, p. 63.

Eight and one-half hours for traveling to and from work in 1960 (the calculation assumes that this work-associated activity is more like work than free time, and that travel to and from work was not an issue in 1850) make the average difference between 15.5 and 16 hours per week. Another 5 hours for work around the house, and 2 hours for helping with household chores brings the difference to 8.5 hours per week. A similar set of calculations, DeGrazia argues, can be made for women, both for those who work and those who do not. For both groups of women, the story ends up much the same as for men. For a recent study that confirms such assertions, see Vanek (1974).

Beyond this set of calculations, it must be added that free time was much more extensive at other historical points. Despite the common view that widespread free time is a corollary of the movement beyond subsistence, the fact remains that the average peasant in feudal society had significantly more free time than his or her modern American counterpart (Bloch, 1961).

So much for the extent of free time. It should be clear that the argument for leisure cannot rest upon a quantitative assessment of free time. Yet this itself is the primary argument for the salience of leisure in contemporary society.

One further observation is in order. The utilization of free time often involves prior or simultaneous consumption. In American society, this has increasingly become the case as a wide variety of activities have come under the economic umbrella, and as new marketable activities have been created.

According to DeGrazia, the juxtaposition of higher wages and shorter work hours, in conjunction with the given economic and social conditions, created the free-time problem. Traditionally, utilization of free time was not problematic. But in urban, industrial societies that is no longer as true. Businessmen and advertisers offered commercial recreation as a

Sources continued

1940-1952: Dewhurst and associates, op. cit., Appendix 20-1, pp. 1064-1069.

1953-1960: U.S. Bureau of the Census, Current Population Reports: Labor Force, Series P-50, Nos. 59, 67, 72,85, and 89; Bureau of Labor Statistics, Employment and Earnings, Annual Supplement, Vol. 6, No. 11, May 1960, plus preliminary unpublished data for 1960 from B.L.S. The averages published by the Census were adjusted downward to reflect zero hours of work for those "with a job but not at work."

partial solution to the free-time dilemma; commercial sporting activities and the movies are relatively early forms. Free-time articles were increasingly offered, for example, radios. Besides the direct commercialization of free time, there are labor-saving appliances, such as cars, washing machines, vacuum cleaners. These, proponents argue, help to minimize the amount of time spent accomplishing the necessary but routine and mundane tasks of everyday life, leaving more time for other activities.

Thus, free time and consumption are highly associated: If you want to know what people do with their free time, look at their consumption bundle. Of course, examination of the consumption bundle will not tell us precisely how time is allotted across free-time activities. For this type of information, time budgets are needed. But, as DeGrazia and others point out, time budgets are insensitive both to multiple activities simultaneously conducted and to the meaning of the activities themselves. For example, if a housewife irons and talks on the phone at the same time, it is not immediately clear how the time is to be partitioned. As an example of the second point, consider the person who chooses to sleep an extra hour on his or her day off, not because the organism requires it, but because the activity is relaxing or soothing; the typical time budget study allocates this hour to subsistence time, that is, that time necessary for maintenance of the organism.

Empirical examination of the utilization of free time also bears out the contention that it is highly associated with consumption. For Americans, in 1957, DeGrazia (1962) lists the following activities as typical:

> watching television; listening to the radio; listening to records; reading newspapers, magazines, books; working around yard or in garden; pleasure driving; going to meetings or organizational activities; attending lectures of adult school; visiting; going out to dinner; going to the theater, concerts, opera, movies; participating in sports (bowling, riding, skating, fishing, swimming, golf); sightseeing; amusement parks; attending sports events; placing pari-mutuel bets; spending time at the drugstore; playing cards; engaging in special hobbies (photography, stamp collecting); keeping pets; and playing slot machines [p. 105].

DeGrazia takes the list as support for the contention that "the previous lists built on expenditures excluded important free-time activities [p. 104]." Although the contention has some merit, perusal of the list itself indicates that almost all these activities would show up, either directly or indirectly, in a relatively careful expenditure study, as most of the activities cited either directly or indirectly require consumption.

On the surface, it appears that consumption adds to free time and leisure. But, according to DeGrazia, the utilization of free time and the artificial creation of more free time detracts from free time itself. The magnitude of free-time expenditures drives people to work longer and harder so that they can make more money with which to enjoy their free time and purchase goods to increase the stock of free time itself.

The net result, as DeGrazia (1962) indicates, is perverse: "I have nothing against the cycle. But while it is spinning around, to hope for leisure is useless. Consumption gobbles time up alive [p. 223]."

So far, the argument in this section has emphasized two points. First, consumption tends to subsume leisure. Second, leisure is not as extensive as one might initially think. Consumption is therefore more salient than leisure; this is not to say that leisure is unimportant. As it stands, the argument is incomplete. If consumption is a consistently better index of lifestyle, it must be the case that leisure either fails to satisfy one of the two primary criteria (observability and expressiveness) or else consumption satisfies both primary criteria at least as well as leisure. Both consumption and leisure are expressive. Because consumption tends to subsume leisure, it follows that it must be at least as expressive. Furthermore, even apart from the argument that consumption subsumes leisure, consumption in America is more observable than leisure (Veblen, 1966). The argument that consumption better indexes lifestyle than leisure does is now complete.

Summary

I began this chapter by pointing out that even with the constraints already imposed on the domain of content, it is not clear which phenomena best index a lifestyle. In order to resolve this issue, I then imposed the secondary criterion of spatio-temporal salience, thereby sacrificing spatial and temporal generality for analytic and conceptual generality. It is not my contention that this is the only reasonable criterion to employ; it is merely argued that this is a solution to the problem that is superior to prior ad hoc solutions, because it imparts general meaning to the concept of lifestyle, thereby allowing for an integration of the concept into disciplined sociological thought.

The historical sketch (there is no pretense to a detailed historical argument, as this alone would require several volumes), in conjunction with the discussion of the relations between consumption and expressiveness, work and expressiveness, and leisure and consumption leads to the conclusion that consumption is the activity that best captures what is meant by lifestyle.

Individual variations in lifestyle have not yet been discussed. The primary reason lies in the assumption that the specific processes generating variation either from or within a meaningful context are best understood after an initial understanding of the context itself has been achieved. Since this has now been accomplished, it is time to consider the variation within its context, and the manner in which this is generated.

CHAPTER 5

Toward a Sociological Theory
of Lifestyle Differentiation

This chapter initiates a new line of inquiry, addressing the sources of individual variation in lifestyles. The argument is made that lifestyle differentiation stems from variations in the positions individuals occupy within the social structure. Other theories of lifestyle differentiation and consumption are also considered, in particular, the sociological theory of alternative lifestyles, and economic theories of consumption are discussed. It is shown that the sociological theory of lifestyle differentiation subsumes the sociological theory of alternative lifestyles. The relationship between the theory of lifestyle differentiation and economic theories is somewhat more complex, but it is fair to say that the two theories are not incompatible, and that in the absence of price variation, the sociological theory is often more general.

Where Does Lifestyle Come From?

It has already been established that consumption is expressive, that is, it allows for a wide variety of choice. Furthermore, choices may be made for any number of reasons, all of which are legitimate. In view of this, it might be argued that consumption is basically unstructured, save for the constraint imposed by the rule that consumption must be paid for, and the constraints imposed by an individual's needs. That is, two individuals with identical needs and equal means might be expected to consume in rather different ways. But is this variation idiosyncratic or structured, if not logically structured? Furthermore, if the variation is not idiosyncratic, it is of interest to give an account of the process by which differentiation is generated.

In addressing this question, the first observation that needs to be made is obvious: The individual, although unique, is inherently social, i.e., the mind is not disjoint from the external world. Attitudes, perceptions, and behavior stem from a dynamic interplay of ego and alter, subject and object, the I and the Me.[1] According to Mead, the I is "the response of the organism to the attitudes of the others; the 'me' is the organized set of attitudes of others which one assumes [1934, p. 175]."

That is, the uniqueness of a lifestyle comes from the I, the socially patterned part from the Me. Both I and Me are intimately shaped by the totality of an individual's experience, the set of ordered sequences of social experiences to which the individual is subjected. Although this is a theoretically useful observation, the complexity of individual experience, so phrased, defies analysis. The key to simplification lies in Mead's observation that the individual

> reacts or responds to himself in terms of the attitudes others have toward him. His self-appraisal is the result of what he assumes to be the appraisal by others. The "me" is the self as conceived and apprehended in terms of the point of view of significant others and of the community at large [Coser, 1977, p. 338].

The individual, then, operates on himself, but not in a vacuum; the manner in which he does so depends upon significant others and the community at large. Self-reflexiveness can occur because the perceptions of the other are organized in a fashion that the individual is capable of perceiving and internalizing.

---

[1] By grouping together these different theories, I do not mean to assert that they are all alike, or for that matter, that Mead's theoretical structure is not fundamentally different. Indeed, it is much different. As Blumer points out:

> Mead saw the self as a process and not as a structure. Here Mead clearly parts company with the great bulk of students who seek to bring a self into the human being by identifying it with some kind of organization or structure. . . . Such schemes which seek to lodge the self in a structure make no sense since they miss the reflexive process which alone can yield and constitute a self [1969, pp. 62–63].

Presumably, the organized perceptions of others are more easily perceived and more compelling to the individual when he enters into prolonged association with the perceiver(s). Perceivers may be acting as reference individuals or members of reference groups, or some combination of the two.

Organized bodies of people who are significant referents, and who satisfy the criterion of prolonged association with one another can be said to constitute a group. There are many such groups, so that the individual cannot be in prolonged association with the members of all groups. His or her set of social referents are therefore likely to be derived from those groups with whom he or she is in prolonged contact. Furthermore, the individual is most likely to be engaged in prolonged association with members of a group when the individual is a member of the group. But the strength of the derived referents depends not only upon the individual, but upon the character of the group itself (see Merton, 1968, pp. 364–373).

In societies that are structurally differentiated on numerous salient axes (for example, the U.S.), it would be surprising to discover that individuals are members of only one group. It would be only slightly less surprising to discover that individuals use only one of their membership groups as a reference group. The usual case is that the individual uses several reference groups. He or she can either attempt to average the inputs from each group or selectively sort inputs from the various groups, taking some here, some there. In fact, the individual probably does both. However, when the individual perceives a reference group unfavorably, that perception will generally lead to the development of alternative attitudes and values that do not conform to those perceived as operative within the group itself. Therefore, it is expected that such individuals will exhibit alternative behavior in situations and facets of life in which association with other members of the group is not involved.

Technically, the set of referents that an individual maintains need not require membership in, or recognition of, a reference group. Collectivities, that is "people who have a sense of solidarity by virtue of sharing common values and who have acquired an attendent sense of moral obligation to fulfill role expectations [Merton, 1968, p. 353]" are also referent sources, as are social categories, defined as "aggregates of social statuses, the occupants of which are not in social interaction. These have like social characteristics—of sex, age, marital condition, income, and so on—but are not necessarily oriented toward a distinctive and common body of norms [Merton, 1968, p. 353]."

Finally, there is no reason to believe that an individual's referents must come from such tangible sources at all. Referents may even include mass media elements, a proposition for which there is a fair amount of support, or fictitious characters in an F. Scott Fitzgerald novel.

Now that the question of referents has been addressed, it is of some import to consider the overarching structural context in which a set of referents is generated.

Social Structure and Referent Generators

The referents that an individual generates, although diverse and subject to infinite gradation, tend to be highly structured by conditions to which he is subject. Indeed, were this not the case, society would exhibit much more chaos than order, and the maintenance of society would be more problematic than it is. In this section the manner in which collectivities, roles, and status-sets generate distinct referents is considered.

Individuals have statuses, or positions, that they occupy in a social system. With each status is associated a role that is composed primarily of a set of structured expectations that the individual should fulfill in order to enact the role properly.

In any society, there is some internal differentiation. Therefore it is expected that individuals will occupy positions on a variety of structurally differentiated axes. Since each position on an axis is associated with a corresponding role, individuals will normally be expected to enact several roles. In complex societies, the tendency for an individual to hold several positions is increased by the greater number of saliently differentiated axes. This fact, in conjunction with the increased amount of differentiation within an axis means that in complex societies there will also exist more distinct positions and combinations of positions than in simpler societies.

The enactment of a role requires that the individual in the position behave, at some level, conformably with the expectations of those he encounters in the performance of that role. Since these others are likely to hold a multiplicity of other roles, with different role demands, it is not surprising that the individual is often unable to conform to the frequently competing demands made by those in his or her "role-set." (A role-set is defined by Merton as "that complement of role relationships which persons have by virtue of occupying a particular social status [1968, p. 423]."

Several forces intervene between the conflicting demands and eventual role enactment. First, the demands made by those in the role-set are differentiated along dimensions of involvement of role partners, and the differential power of role partners (power in the Weberian sense). In addition, occupants of the role have access to mechanisms that insulate "role-activities from observability by members of the role-set [Merton, 1968, p. 428]," and the occupants are often able to make role partners realize that their demands conflict with those made by other role partners. Since tenants in similar positions tend to have similar problems or to have experienced similar problems, they tend to support one another, both formally and informally. This encourages greater role articulation.

In addition, because individuals in similar positions tend to have somewhat similar experiences as a function of these positions, they tend to interact most with and share such experiences with others who are likely to understand these, that is, with others in similar positions. It is not necessary that individuals interact in this fashion. But it is likely that they will do so for two reasons. First, social interaction is structured so that it is easier to interact continuously in social spheres to which one has frequent access. Second, such interactions are likely to prove comfortable and satisfying. Therefore, others with whom similar positions are shared are likely to become referents, even when the set of all such persons itself is not a reference group. In other words, a reference group is likely to be generated from some subset of all the position holders.

Just as conflicting expectations may be generated from a multiplicity of role partners in the role-set, conflicting expectations may be generated by virtue of holding multiple statuses. In that case, the generators are not role partners, but the properties within each role. When taken across positions, the conjunction of properties may prove inconsistent. By this I do not mean logically inconsistent, although that may also be the case.

Serious inconsistencies are mitigated through a variety of mechanisms. First of all, individuals tend to progress through somewhat orderly status sequences (Merton, 1968, p. 437). By this it is meant that individuals change roles in a progression which (a) the individual can prepare for (anticipatory socialization) and (b) in such a manner that small progressions do not generate extremely inconsistent conjunctions. As for logically inconsistent conjunctions, Merton points out that "those reared as Christian Scientists and committed to this faith do not ordinarily become physicians [p. 437]." That is, self-selection contributes to the orderliness of the status sequence.

Inconsistent conjunctions, when they occur, tend to be removed in a variety of ways. Besides the fact that an individual can often remove himself from one or more of the positions engendering such a conjunction, a new social definition of the conjunction itself may arise, particularly if the conjunction occurs with any great frequency. For example, 20 years ago, the simultaneous holding of the two positions mother and worker led to a negatively composed conjunction. Now the two positions are frequently maintained jointly, and the character of the conjunction has been redefined so as to be at least neutral.

Many conjunctions are neutrally composed, that is, composed of properties that are not consistent or inconsistent with respect to one another. Furthermore, conjunctions can be, and often are, positively rather than negatively composed.

The upshot of this discussion is simple. Although individuals hold more than one role, there are mechanisms that make certain conjunctions unlikely and minimize the saliency of other particular conjunctions beyond that attached to the separate properties associated with different positions. What this implies is that within a position, there are common experiences that operate on the holders, not without respect to their other statuses, but in addition to these. That is, the role behaviors associated with positions are viewed as more or less additive operators on the individual, with a few exceptions that will be considered shortly.

It has already been stated that individuals are more likely to associate with others in similar statuses. Extension of this assertion leads to the conclusion that individuals who occupy similar status-sets, when these exist with some frequency, are more likely to associate with those in similar status-sets, though not to the exclusion of others with whom one or more positions are similar. Therefore, individuals with similar status-sets (similar to social categories) or similar subsets of status-sets will also tend to form patterned associations and utilize such associations as a referent source.

A similar set of remarks applies to members of collectivities, although membership in a collectivity is not always a status per se. When membership in a collectivity is highly salient (for example, race in the U.S.), it may well be the case that this referent source does not operate additively. For example, being black or white may fundamentally condition the experiences and role enactment associated with the position of lawyer.

Finally, there are other types of systematic phenomena that operate on the individual's experience but that are not easily subsumed under the concept *position* or the concept *collectivity*. For example, an individual's lifestyle is conditioned by whether or not he lives in a city or a small town. One does not in general purchase theater tickets, and therefore attend the theater, in a small town. There are no such tickets to buy. To put the matter quite simply, there are different stimuli from which to choose in the city. In the same vein, it might be pointed out that region is also a fundamental condition. For example, individuals in Florida do not have much opportunity to snow-ski or purchase many winter coats. Nor do individuals in Wisconsin have much opportunity to surf on Lake Michigan.

Even after the consideration of structural phenomena that systematically channel the process of referent generation, the individual remains idiosyncratic. For example, role distance no doubt differs for individuals in similar positions. Whereas some occupants of positions interact primarily with others of similar status, there are other occupants who refuse to do so, save for the interaction that is minimally necessary to fulfill role demands. Such persons, it is expected, will maintain a different set of referents.

Before the operationalization of the sociological theory is explicated, it is important to consider its relationship to other theories of lifestyle differentiation and consumption. In this fashion it becomes clear that, by and large, the competing theories are either subsumed by, or not at odds with, the sociological theory. First, I consider the sociological theory of alternative lifestyles. Next I consider economic theories of consumption and their relation to the sociological theory of lifestyle differentiation.

Lifestyle and Alternative Lifestyles

In the past 10 or 15 years, sociologists have begun to examine (explicitly) "alternative lifestyles." At present, these constitute the focus of sociological research on lifestyles, which is primarily descriptive.

In terms of the theoretical structure elaborated in this chapter, alternative lifestyles arise when an individual's significant referents are exclusively generated subculturally. That is, the property of membership within the subculture is the only salient characteristic the individual possesses. Such is the case with members of certain religious sects. In this instance, consumption may not be a good index of lifestyle.

Less extreme, but nonetheless salient, are cases where subcultures operate on their members by fundamentally structuring the set of relevant social experiences, but not to the exclusion of the effects of other positions. In such cases, which are more common than the extreme cases, the process of lifestyle differentiation operates as it does for individuals whose lifestyles are not generated subculturally, save that the process interacts with subculture, that is, reference class or subpopulation.

By implication, any empirical analysis in order to be correct should deal with these issues. In the first case, where lifestyle might require a different index, the only explanatory variable is subcultural affiliation. In the second, the analyses need to be generated within the relevant reference classes.

Conceptually, the issue is not at all difficult. The only real problem lies in the collection of data. For example, sect membership is not a typical survey item. However, the failure to ascertain these pieces of information need not hinder the implementation of any empirical inquiry. Despite a great deal of undue attention, the relative frequency of these "alternative lifestyles" is not great, that is, should not affect subsequent calculations.

In other words, sociologists have written a great deal about an imperceptible fraction of the population, thereby failing to discuss lifestyle differentiation within the majority of the population. This is unfortunate for a variety of reasons, not the least of which is the fact that this focus has detracted from attempts to build a more encompassing theory of lifestyle differentiation.

Economic Work on Consumption

Consumption has long interested both sociologists and economists. Within the former discipline, interest may be traced to LePlay's concern with the standard of living in nineteenth century Europe. Briefly, LePlay maintained, among other things, that studies of consumption shed light on both familial structure and social organization, that the type and level of consumption is indicative of social well-being, but that the values underlying a manner of consumption are more effective indicators of well-being.

Motivated by LePlay's work and cognizant of the import of familial composition and rural–urban differentials, Zimmerman (1929) showed that type of investment varies with class and rural–urban status. He also showed that consumption tradeoffs are substantively different for rural and urban families (Zimmerman and Black, 1924). In this vein, both he and Loomis (1934) argued: "The commercialized farmer accommodates to a decreased ratio of workers to consumers during the growth period of the family by adapting land and capital resources so that acres tilled are distributed more evenly per capita than acres owned [Zimmerman, 1936, p. 54]." On the more pragmatic side, Zimmerman and Black (1927) published standard of living scales for village, urban, and rural families based on the concept of the male adult equivalent. Similarly, Kirkpatrick (1923) published separate cost-consumption unit scales for a variety of expenditures for rural families.

In economics, interest in consumption can be traced back to the works of Ernst Engel, a student of LePlay, and the Austrian marginalists. In modern economic work, with which we are primarily concerned, the conventional starting point is the consumer's tastes and preferences, as manifested over points (vectors) in a J-dimensional commodity set X, assumed to be divisible, unbounded from above, and bounded below by the vector **0**, which is contained in **X**. The preferences are assumed to be weakly ordered.[2] Furthermore, it is assumed that "the set of bundles not preferred to x and the set of bundles to which x is not preferred are both closed in X, for any x [Phlips, 1974, p. 7]." In conjunction, the conditions guarantee for the ith consumer the existence of a continuous utility function u_i from R^J to R^1. It is also assumed that more is better than less, i.e., $u_i(x) \geq u_i(x^\circ)$ if $x \geq x^\circ$, and that the utility function is quasi-concave and twice differentiable.

Next, the economist assumes that the consumer seeks to maximize his utility subject to the budget constraint $\Sigma_j p_{ij} x_{ij} = y_i$, where p_{ij} is the price of the jth commodity to the ith consumer, x_{ij} is the quantity of the jth commodity purchased by the ith consumer, and y_i is total expenditure, denoted income. Optimization of the utility maximization problem yields the system of direct demand equations $x_{ij}^* = g_{ij}(p_{i1}, \ldots p_{iJ}, y_i)$, $j = 1, \ldots, J$, where the asterisk is used to indicate that the quantities are optimal.

Let $U_k, k = 1, \ldots, K$ constitute a partition of the set of consumers such that the elements (consumers) in U_k have identical utility functions, that is, identical tastes and preferences. The demand equations can then be rewritten as

$$x_{ij}^* = \sum_{U_k} g_{kj}(p_{i1}, \ldots, p_{iJ}, y_i) I_{U_k}, \qquad j = 1, \ldots, J,$$

where I is an indicator function on U_k. In a suitably restricted cross section, prices do not vary, so the demand equations reduce to $x_{ij}^* = \Sigma_{U_k} g_{kj}(p_1, \ldots, p_J, y_i) I_{U_k}, j = 1, \ldots, J$. In this special case, estimation of the system $p_j x_{ij}^* = \Sigma_{U_k} h_{kj}(y_i) I_{U_k} + \epsilon_{ij}, j = 1, \ldots, J$, where ϵ_{ij} is an item by consumer disturbance, yields the effect of income on the expenditure for the jth item, $j = 1, \ldots, J$, holding prices at the level $(p_1, \ldots, p_J)$. Equations of this form are called Engel curves and have been the object of extensive investigation. Engel curve estimation is considered in the next chapter.

Recently, an economic theory based on the human capital literature has been advanced (Michael, 1972). In this theory, the household is viewed as a small firm that produces commodities. The commodities are assumed to be produced in accord with a homogeneous production function of degree one in the direct inputs time and goods. The other input is a

[2] A "weak ordering" exists if preferences are comparable and transitive. That is, for any two points x° and x' in X, the consumer can establish whether x° is more or less preferred to x', or whether the two bundles are equally preferred. Further, if x' is preferred to x°, and x^2 is preferred to x', then x^2 is preferred to x°.

fixed level of human capital, indexed by education. In turn, the commodities are inputs in the utility function. Thus, education is explicitly introduced into the analysis, and its effects reflect efficiency in nonmarket production; it is hypothesized that education increases nonmarket productivity, just as it increases market productivity.

The Relationship between Economic Theories of Consumption and the Sociological Theory of Lifestyle Differentiation

The sociological theory of lifestyle differentiation is compatible with a focus on various aspects of consumption, including expenditures. In this study, only expenditures are considered, because of data limitations. Therefore, it is important to establish the relationship between the economic theories of consumption and the sociological theory of lifestyle differentiation, as the latter applies to expenditures, for two reasons. First, with prices constant, both theories will yield similar systems of equations, with subtle differences in interpretation that supersede the semantic differences of the two disciplines. Second, in the general case (when prices are allowed to vary), the relationship between the theories change, and it is seen that both are incomplete because each ignores the other. However, neither theory is incompatible with the other, indicating that integration and synthesis might prove fruitful for both disciplines.

In the economic theory tastes and preferences exogenously determine the preference relations from which the utility function is derived. In the sociological theory, lifestyle differentiation, as indexed by consumption, is engendered by differences in tastes and preferences. These in turn are produced by social structural differentiation, the exogenous set of variables in the sociological analysis. Thus, when prices are fixed, the sociological theory subsumes the economic theory because tastes and preferences are an explanandum, rather than an explanans, and because consumption indexes lifestyle, which is more general than consumption itself. As in the general case, the theories are abstractly compatible. The economic theory does not suggest that sociological factors are irrelevant, and the sociological theory is not incompatible with utility maximization theory.[3] Therefore, it is possible to draw upon prior economic work to implement a more effective test of the sociological theory than would otherwise be the case.

---

[3] No doubt a small minority of sociologists would object to this statement and question some of the assumptions underlying the theory, for example, comparability or transitivity.

When prices are fixed, the sociological theory is also more systematic than the economic theory. Factors other than income are an integral part of the theory itself. Economists dodge the issue by allowing the utility maximization problem to be partition specific. But when they assume that the utility function is identical for all individuals, as is often the case, the introduction of other sources of variation into the right hand side of the Engel curve is ad hoc, though necessary for unbiased estimation of the income effects and for reduction of the error variance. In the sociological theory introduction of these sources comes directly from the theory itself. In addition, sociological wisdom suggests that race and age interact with the parameters of the Engel curve. That is, sociological theory suggests that the utility function is not constant over race or age.

Despite the abstract compatibility of the theories, and the fact that both will lead to similar systems of equations when prices are fixed, the two theories differ in emphasis. In the economic theory, the effects of income are of primary import. The other variables are to be controlled for. In the sociological theory the income effects are interesting only in relation to the effects of the other variables, whose interpretation stems from a coherent theory.

Once prices are allowed to vary, the two theories no longer have the same relationship with one another. The sociological theory has little to say about the effects of changes in the prices, although this is a potentially interesting sociological problem. In economic theory, this issue is of primary concern (Brown and Deaton, 1972; Parks, 1969; Christensen et al., 1975). As before, the economic theory is devoid of sociology. In this more general case, it is clear that neither theory is complete. It is probable that consideration of sociological factors would change the estimates of those parameters that interest the economist, just as it is probable that the effects of the sociological factors depend upon prices.

These relations no longer hold for the comparison with the human-capital-based theory, because the sociological theory does not explicitly incorporate time, and because education is viewed as a source of variation in tastes and preferences, not nonmarket productivity. If the efficiency theory is correct, both it and the sociological theory are incomplete whether or not prices vary.

CHAPTER 6

Implementing the Theory: Data and Methods

This chapter initiates the third logical part of this study, the empirical implementation and testing of the theory that has been constructed in the previous chapter. More specifically, the aim in this chapter is to provide an overview of the data and methods used to test the theoretical construction. One warning is in order. Strictly speaking, the hypothesis that lifestyle differentiation is produced by variation in the structure of social roles is not tested. The link between consumption and lifestyles is a logical link, in no way subject to empirical disconfirmation.

With this caveat explicit, the issues that must be addressed in this chapter may be set out. First, the abstract measurement of the social structural variables must be considered. Second, the dimensionality and measurement of consumption must be discussed. Third, economists have analyzed consumption data for quite some time, and there is much to be learned from this body of literature. Of particular interest are the specification of consumption relationships and the measure of income used as an explanatory variable. After considering these issues, the data and estimation procedures utilized are introduced, and a few of the important empirical results are reviewed. Many of the details are reserved for future chapters, however.

Indexing the Causal Factors

Associated with any formalized role is a position (status or title) that implicitly connotes the essence of the role itself. Hence, an individual's place in the social structure may be indexed by the titles he or she holds. Since very little solid information on lifestyles is available, and since there is no reason to suspect otherwise, it is assumed that the salient statuses that need to be delineated are those that are germane to the differentiation of social identity.

Following Davis (1949) the statuses may be categorized as either ascribed or achieved. Initially, the individual receives certain statuses that provide the basis for early socialization. Sex, age relations, and kinship status are universal examples. No less important in some heterogeneous societies are race, ethnicity, and religion. Additionally, all societies recognize some form of achievement as a basis for further differentiation. In some societies, achieved statuses come to replace the ascribed statuses in general importance, although the replacement process is never complete. Although salient achieved statuses vary from society to society, they may nonetheless be systematically linked to the structure of society. Since it is not the purpose here to link statuses with structures, it should suffice to point out that in modern Western societies marital status, parenthood, educational attainment, occupational attainment, and income are among the most important of the achieved statuses. In line with classical sociological interest in the stratification system, this work focuses primary attention on the last three achieved statuses.

However, all the statuses mentioned above, except for ethnicity and religion, are considered. The implicit assumption is that net of the other statuses, these are not of primary importance. Two other independent variables are considered. First, rural–urban variation must be taken into account. Second, regional variation must be considered. The primary reason for inclusion of these variables is that lifestyle chances are assumed to depend upon these variables, as indicated in the preceding chapter. A secondary, but no less important reason is the fact that prices may vary by these variables; the importance of this consideration should become clear shortly.

Consumption

The word *consumption* has been used in an abstract sense to clarify the relationship between it and, in the American context, the concept of *lifestyle*. For the subsequent empirical work in this study, such abstract usage will not do. In order to empirically implement the theory, consumption must be operationalized.

Two issues must be addressed in conjunction with the operationalization process. The most important conceptual issue involved in utilizing consumption to index lifestyles is the isolation of those aspects (items or qualities) of consumption that are germane to lifestyle from those that are not. Since lifestyles are both expressive and subject to observation by others, only those aspects of consumption that best satisfy these criteria should be considered. In the previous chapter, it was argued that consumption itself is basically expressive, so it remains to isolate visible consumption from that which is not as visible.

Unfortunately, this is no easy task; it is impossible to implement this conceptual distinction other than crudely. At the outset, it must be recognized that the distinction is ideal typical. Underlying the types is a continuum. Any classification scheme must necessarily utilize an arbitrary cutoff point on the continuum, thereby ignoring the degree to which the item qualifies or fails to qualify for inclusion.

But this is the least problematic issue. The categorization of most goods and services depends upon the consumer, as the items in question cannot be said to possess such properties except in their utilization. Thus, the problem is actually a person–item interaction. Even this conceptualization of the problem is too simpleminded. It ignores the fact that the "other" is by no means homogeneous. Strangers observe consumption to a lesser degree than friends and neighbors, who, in turn observe less than the immediate family. Conceptually, the problem is similar to that encountered in the observation of interaction: There is both a frontstage and a backstage, as well as various regions in between. Those who are privileged to observe the most intimate details (those who are backstage) have access to all other regions. Next are observers who have access to all but the most intimate details, and so forth.

These issues are clearly amenable to empirical analysis and demand attention. In this study, this is not forthcoming. First, the issues have not yet been studied, and there is no ideal data with which to do so. Second, an undertaking of this sort would clearly be substantial as well as somewhat tangential. In this work, attention is focused on consumption items that are not clearly definable as primarily frontstage or backstage, etc. However, a fair amount of attention has been directed toward the exclusion of items or components of items that would appear to be observable to only the very few. For example, medical expenditures are not examined. Although other items that are studied are by no means homogeneous in their visibility, it should be clear which items are more observable than others, empirical proof notwithstanding. For example, "food at home" is subject to observation, but is less observed by others than furniture in the home, which in turn is less subject to observation than an individual's usual mode of dress, etc.

A second important issue is that in practice, the individual need not be the unit of analysis in consumption data. Yet lifestyle is viewed as a property of the individual. Although the consumer unit (defined later in this chapter) may in fact consist of an individual, it would severely restrict the scope of this analysis to ignore consumer units consisting of more than one person. Two problems are thereby raised. First, can it be claimed that a lifestyle is a property of a family? Logically, the answer is no. It is the case, however, that the family does have strong tendencies toward the sharing of a lifestyle, and it may even be claimed that the amount of shared overlap is sufficiently great to justify the assertion that the family (at least its adult members) does appear to lead a common lifestyle. Although this might be somewhat less true of the entire family when there are children present, these members of the family unit are subordinate, dependent upon parental choices in most aspects of life. In this sense, children cannot be said to choose a lifestyle, and the parents can be said to have chosen a lifestyle for the family.

With these considerations in mind, the assumption is made that the familial unit shares a lifestyle. This solves the empirical problem of disaggregating consumption into components due to particular family members, but it clearly raises another problem. Which are the salient statuses, those of husband or those of wife? This exploratory study, like many studies in the fertility literature, uses the household heads' statuses in the estimation of statistical models. Although the strategy is imperfect at best, its use is partially justified by the fact that the strategy is conventional and appears to work elsewhere, and by the fact that marriage partners are typically homogamous.

Of course, none of the solutions to the problems raised above are in any way absolute. Most of the issues are empirical, whereas the justifications are speculative because there are no facts to fall back on.

It must also be recognized that consumption is a multidimensional phenomenon. Only then can the limitations of this work, which focuses on expenditures, be properly explicated.

The first distinction economists make is that between consumption as it refers to the use of a good and consumption as it refers to the expenditure on a good for some given time period (Branson, 1972, p. 191). In the first usage, the consumption during a given period is the amount of use of the good in question. In general, this value, expressed in dollars, differs from the expenditure (rents are an exception). When expenditures are undertaken solely for replacement purposes, and the period of utilization is the same as the period of expenditure, the two values are equal.

The distinction is an important one and highlights the potential importance of timing and turnover in expenditures. Since it is safe to assume that a large proportion of expenditures on consumer durables are not undertaken solely for replacement purposes, turnover rates, to the extent that these vary by the causal factors previously outlined, constitute an important sociological dimension of consumption.

A related dimension of consumption is captured by the concept of inventories. Whereas economic work has focused primarily on expenditure systems, consumption inventories, in which the quantities of a durable good are counted, are sociologically significant. For example, it is perhaps of more interest to know how many cars are owned by a family than it is to know that in some time period the family spent a certain number of dollars on cars. Since expenditures (on a homogeneous good) are the product of price and quantity, utilization of expenditure information indicates neither how many cars the family purchased, nor the purchase price.

Goods are rarely homogeneous. Product differentiation, either by brand name or class is therefore important to understanding consumption behavior. To return to the automobile example, knowledge of price and quantity is clearly insufficient to classify an automobile as domestic or foreign, old or new, large or small, red or blue, luxury or nonluxury, Ford or Chevrolet. Yet because of the symbolic attitudes toward cars that are commonly held in this society, these are the very attributes of a good or service that might interest a sociologist most.

Finally, the structure of consumption must be considered. Which goods and services are complements? Which are substitutes? How do goods and services received and/or used relate to one another beyond their logical complementarity and substitutability? How do consumers order their priorities, thus giving rise to observed consumption?

Unfortunately, these issues cannot be considered here in their full complexity, either conceptually or empirically. The reason for this will become clearer when the data and methods that are actually used in this study are described. For now it should suffice to point out that utilization of the abstract concept of consumption leaves much to the imagination, and no empirical implementation is likely to do the problem justice.

Engel Curve Analyses

In this study, expenditures alone are examined, since information on other dimensions of consumption was not available with these data at the time the analysis was conducted. Such information would have to be obtained from other data sets, and the available existing sets are undesirable from other standpoints, such as failure to measure the independent variables and insufficient number of observations.

Since economists have worked with expenditure data extensively, it pays to consider the empirical literature. Only Engel curve estimation is considered.

Allen and Bowley (1935) estimate linear curves of the form $y_{ij} = \alpha_j + B_j y_i + \epsilon_{ij}$, where y_{ij} is the expenditure of the ith consumer on the jth commodity, y_i is the sum of the y_{ij}, or total expenditure, ϵ_{ij} is a consumer by item stochastic term, and α_j and B_j are the parameters of the jth equation. Although this system if estimated by ordinary least squares has nice properties, that is, $\Sigma_j \alpha_j = 0$, $\Sigma_j B_j = 1$, the model suggests that inferior (superior) goods are associated with increasing (decreasing) income elasticities as the level of income drops (rises).[1] Hence, the specification is unacceptable and is probably instrumental in explaining the poor fit to the data.

Aware of these shortcomings, Prais and Houthakker (1955), in what is considered by many to be the classic consumption study, additionally fitted models of the form $\log y_{ij} = \alpha_j + \beta_j \log y_i + \epsilon_{ij}$, $y_{ij} = \alpha_j + \beta_j \log y_i + \epsilon_{ij}$, $y_{ij} = \alpha_j - \beta_j/y_i + \epsilon_{ij}$, and $\log y_{ij} = \alpha_j - \beta_j/y_i + \epsilon_{ij}$, where the notation is as previously described. These functions, by satisfying (a) and (b), have the following advantages over the linear form:

> (a) for many commodities, there exists a level of income below which these commodities are not consumed; (b) in many cases, there is also a saturation level which acts as an upper limit, whatever the level of income; (c) the adding up criterion implies that all commodities cannot display a saturation level, for otherwise total income would not be entirely allocated above a certain level [Phlips, 1974, p. 110].

In the empirical work, Prais and Houthakker found that the functional form $\log y_{ij} = \alpha_j + \beta_j \log y_i + \epsilon_{ij}$ best fit the data, with the exception of food items.

The authors also recognized the need for introducing an index of family size into the analysis. Furthermore, they compute different estimates for the working and middle-class subpopulations; formally, this is equivalent to partitioning the observations into sets U_1 and U_2, with utility functions u_1 and u_2, respectively.

Since this study, an issue that has received a great deal of attention concerns the measurement of y_i, the variable on the right hand side of the equation. In the earlier work, y_i was typically taken to be total expenditures or income. As Summers (1959) shows, use of the first measure yields biased coefficients when ordinary least squares estimation is used because

---

[1] For definitions of the terms *inferior goods* and *superior goods*, see page 74.

y_i and y_{ij} are endogenous and determine one another. Current economic wisdom suggests that the appropriate right hand side variable is a measure of long-run household income (permanent income), as consumers are assumed to adjust their expenditures in accord with their long-run income (Friedman, 1957; Ando and Modigliani, 1963). Thus, use of yearly income leads to biased estimates of the permanent income coefficient (Friedman, 1957).

In the typical cross-sectional data set, measures of permanent income are unavailable. Furthermore, without at least several years of data, hypothetical measures are difficult to construct. Friedman (1957) suggests and Liviatan (1961) shows that if the data are grouped by income into classes and the mean expenditure is regressed on the mean consumption, a consistent estimate of the permanent income coefficient is obtained. Additionally, use of this procedure allows the truncation problem to be side-stepped. The problem itself arises because certain types of items are purchased infrequently, and in a 1-year survey a substantial proportion of the sample will have 0 values on such items. The problem is discussed in Tobin (1958) and Heckman (1974, 1976). In this procedure, the mean expenditure on an item can be interpreted as a yearly average, that is, as the product of the probability of purchasing with the purchase price; within group homogeneity is assumed. For these reasons, grouping, as suggested by Friedman (1957) is utilized in this study.

Use of this method leads to a multivariate system of equations with identical explanatory variables, and variances that are inverse to the known number of observations within a cell. Hence, the system may be estimated by applying weighted least squares to each equation (Zellner, 1962; Michael, 1972).

The Data

The data utilized in this study are the interview records from the 1972–1973 Survey of Consumer Expenditures, conducted by the Bureau of Labor Statistics (BLS), in conjunction with the Bureau of the Census. Two hundred and sixteen primary sampling units, 162 of which were chosen by probability sampling were selected, and the sample of addresses was taken from the 20% tape of the 1970 Population Census. The survey universe includes the civilian noninstitutional population, the institutional population residing in doctors' and nurses' housing within general hospitals or boarding houses, and Armed Forces personnel residing off base. The following are excluded: students in dormitories or in fraternity or sorority housing, prisoners, residents of monasteries or ships, and individuals inhabiting living quarters that consist of five or more unrelated individuals. The sampling unit is the consumer unit (c.u.), which closely corresponds to the Census concept of "household." Specifically, a c.u. is constituted by a financially independent person living either in a household with others, a hotel, home or boarding house, or by two or more people who typically reside together, pool income, and share expenses. However, never married children living at home are not treated as a separate c.u., regardless of the financial arrangements involved.

Unlike prior expenditure surveys conducted by BLS, the interview and diary records were obtained from different c.u.'s, making it impossible to merge the two data sources. However, the interview data was collected quarterly over an interval of 15 months and therefore allows for a more accurate assessment of the value of expenditures than did previous surveys.

The BLS reports that the "quarterly survey obtained detailed data for 60 to 70% of total family expenditures [Carlson, 1974, p. 17]." This represents expenditures on approximately 2600 detailed items and includes data on assets, liabilities, and components of c.u. income. Additionally, relevant household information (race, sex, age, education, occupation, family size, etc.) were collected.

In this analysis, the data was combined across survey years. A multiplier of .941 was applied to the 1973 income and expenditures data, this deflator constituting a crude adjustment for inflation.

Ten approximately equal disposable income groups were cross-classified by four education classes by four occupation groups, for a total of 160 potential cells. In order that the grouping be efficacious, it is minimally necessary that the cells have enough observations to permit reliable parameter estimation. In this analysis, it is assumed that the effects of the independent variables interact with race (blacks versus others) and head's age (age less than 25, age 25–64, age 65+), so that there are six subpopulations of interest. While the total sample size is large (after deleting c.u.'s with incomplete data on income and/or head's race, $n = 18198$), the subsample sizes are not large enough in all subsamples to permit the required analysis. There are only 1155 other heads less than 25, and 116 black heads in this age group. In the age group defined as 65 and over, there are 2248 others and 301 blacks. Finally, in the 25 to 64 age group there are 11,832 others and 1346 blacks. However, after deleting observations with unreported educational achievements and marital status, as well as c.u.'s whose heads are not currently working or failed to report occupation, the six numbers are, respectively, 864, 71, 636, 62, 10,176, and 978. The large attrition in the sample size for observations aged 65+ is undoubtedly due to the occupational criteria used in the selection procedure; it is unfortunate that B.L.S. did not ask heads of such c.u.'s the last typical occupation held. The salience of occupational status to this analysis necessitates the availability of occupational data.

Given the method of analysis chosen, only the subsample of 10,176 nonblack heads aged 25–64 was judged sufficiently large. While this limits our ability to make meaningful comparisons, it is not clear, given the constraints imposed by the structure of the data, that there is a better solution to the problem than this. In other words, only the nonblack subsample aged 25 to 64 will be examined. This is unfortunate and necessary, but it should be remembered that this subpopulation is numerically predominant by far. Furthermore, the focus of this study is analytical rather than descriptive. Total population estimates are not necessary, and the ability to make inferences about the effects of the independent variables is limited only by the inability to make comparisons.

The basic independent variables in the analysis are transformations of head's marital status, head's age, location, total consumption (in the light of the discussion regarding the estimation of the permanent income coefficient, this variable is hereafter referred to as income), head's education (see Appendix A) in years of completed schooling, and head's occupational status (see Appendix B), measured in terms of Duncan SEI scores (Duncan, 1961; Featherman, Sobel, and Dickens, 1975). These are more thoroughly described in Exhibit 6.1. Similarly, Exhibit 6.2 presents acronyms and definitions for the dependent variables. The dependent variables are constructed by summing over the expenditures on specific items and transforming the sums. The specific items are listed in Appendix C. In Exhibit 6.2 notice that the variables *Theatre* and *Sports* are excluded from subsequent analyses. Reasons for this are given in the next chapter.

Estimation

In this study, three different statistical techniques are utilized. First, weighted least squares is used to estimate the expenditure system. Second, oblique, unrestricted maximum likelihood factor analysis is used to uncover the structure of stylistic unity. Third, a multiple indicator multiple cause (MIMIC) model is estimated by maximum likelihood procedures (LISREL program) in an attempt to assess the effects of the social structural variables on stylistic unity. The procedures are best discussed within a more empirical and substantive context, because their use is closely tied to the context itself. To discuss them now would be confusing and tedious. However, there are several other points that are best considered now.

For estimating the expenditure system, consideration of the economic

EXHIBIT 6.1
Independent Variables

---

*Region -- South is omitted percentage
   R1 -- percentage Northeastern
   R2 -- percentage North Central
   R3 -- percentage Western

FAMSIZE -- log(average family size)

HMSTATUS -- percentage unmarried

Location -- Outside SMSA's is omitted percentage
   L1 -- percentage in central cities of size 400,000+ (size
      refers to SMSA)
   L2 -- percentage outside central cities of size 400,000+
   L3 -- percentage in SMSA's of size 50,000 - 399,999

HINCOME -- log(total consumption)

HEDUC1 -- log(head's education)

HSEI -- log(head's SEI)

HEDSEI -- HEDUC1 X HSEI

HEDON -- HEDUC1 X HINCOME

HSEON -- HSEI X HINCOME

HAGE -- head's age

---

    *Northeast: Connecticut, Maine, Massachusetts, New Hampshire,
      New Jersey, New York, Pennsylvania, Rhode Island, Vermont;
    North Central: Illinois, Indiana, Iowa, Kansas, Michigan,
      Minnesota, Missouri, Nebraska, North Dakota, Ohio, South
      Dakota, Wisconsin;
    South: Alabama, Arkansas, Delaware, District of Columbia,
      Florida, Georgia, Kentucky, Louisiana, Maryland, Miss-
      issippi, North Carolina, Oklahoma, South Carolina,
      Tennessee, Texas, Virginia, West Virginia;
    West: Alaska, Arizona, California, Colorado, Hawaii, Idaho,
      Montana, Nevada, New Mexico, Oregon, Utah, Washington,
      Wyoming.

literature proves extremely useful. Nevertheless, the analysis is exploratory because the sociological theory of lifestyle differentiation does not suggest the exact manner in which the independent variables (in particular the socioeconomic variables) differentiate lifestyle. In conjunction with a high degree of collinearity among these variables, the need for stable

EXHIBIT 6.2
Dependent Variables

FOODHOME -- log(food at home)

ALCOHOL -- log(expenditures on alcohol)

HOUSING -- log (expenditures on housing)

TEXTILES -- log(expenditures on household textiles)

FURNITUR -- log(expenditures on household furniture and floor covers)

DECORAT -- log(expenditures on household decorations)

CASCLOTH -- log(expenditures on casual clothing)

DRSCLOTH -- log(expenditures on dress clothing)

PERSCARE -- log(expenditures on personal care)

VACATION -- log(expenditures on vacation)

CLUBS -- log(expenditures on membership fees for clubs and organizations)

TV -- log(expenditures on television)

MUSIC -- log(expenditures on musical equipment)

CAMP -- log(expenditures on major camping, health and sports equipment)

READING -- log(expenditures on reading materials)

GIFTS -- log(gifts to persons outside household)

*THEATRE -- log(subscriptions to theater, concert, opera, and others)

*SPORTS -- log(expenditures for subscriptions for season's tickets to sporting events)

---

*Excluded from subsequent analysis

parameter estimates in the 17 equations, and a reluctance to rely upon arbitrary statistical conventions, the empirical problem becomes considerable, though not intractable.

The analytical strategy that is brought to bear on the problem is best described as exploratory and sequential. In order that the reader may judge the analysis, it must therefore be set out in great detail, and because the analysis is sequential it must also be explicated sequentially. Furthermore, because the first set of substantive conclusions rests upon the final system of expenditure equations, the data analysis itself, while substantively motivated, is influenced predominantly by statistical, rather than sociological, considerations.

When attention is turned toward the consideration of stylistic unity and its relation to the structural variables, a similar problem arises. Stylistic unity, if it exists, is viewed as a proximate cause of a lifestyle. That is, if stylistic unity exists, the lifestyle items are manifestations of this underlying structure. In this sense, lifestyle consists of components that reflect the form and existence of stylistic unity. In turn, it is argued that social structural differentiation causes differentiation in stylistic unity. In order to assess the effects of the structural variables it is necessary to know the form of stylistic unity. But stylistic unity is conceptualized as an empirical phenomenon, and the sociological theory of lifestyle differentiation does not address itself to the form of stylistic unity. Therefore an exploratory statistical analysis oriented to uncovering the form of stylistic unity is a necessary first step. Only after this preliminary analysis has been conducted can we consider the effects of the structural variables on stylistic unity. This requires a more general exploratory analysis in which the results from the first analysis are consistently incorporated. As before, in order that the reader may judge the analysis, it is explicated sequentially, in great detail.

The second point is this: In many of the models, there are interactions between education, occupational status, and income. While the interactions are of great import, it is helpful to consider the total effects of the variables, defined in this study as the partial derivative of the dependent variable with respect to the independent variable of interest. When interaction effects are present, the estimated partial depends upon levels of other variables. By varying the levels and inspecting the changing partials, it is possible to obtain new insights into the relationships between the socioeconomic variables. In order that the interpretation of the partials and changes in the partials be correct, statistical tests must be performed, both for the partials and for the differences between the partials. An example should suffice to clarify and illustrate these points. Suppose the model is given as (1) $y = X_1B + \gamma_1\text{HINCOME} + \gamma_2\text{HEDUCl} + \gamma_3\text{HSEI} + \gamma_4\text{HEDSEI} + \gamma_5\text{HEDON} + \gamma_6\text{HSEON} + \epsilon$, i.e., $y = X_1B + X_2\Gamma + \epsilon$, where X_1 contains observations on the socioeconomic variables (see Exhibit 6.1 for definitions), X_2 contains observations on the other variables, and ϵ is a vector of stochastic elements. Additionally, it is assumed that (2) $(X'_1, X'_2)'$ has full rank and (3) $(\epsilon \mid X) \sim N(0, \sigma^2 I)$. Under these assumptions, the coefficient matrix $(\hat{\mathbf{B}}', \hat{\boldsymbol{\Gamma}}')'$ has a $N((\mathbf{B}', \boldsymbol{\Gamma}')', \sigma^2((X_1,X_2)'(X_1,X_2))^{-1})$ distribution. The fact that linear combinations of multinormally distributed random variables are normally distributed is also used, as is the fact that the residual sum of squares, divided by σ^2, has a χ^2_{n-k} distribution, where n is the number of observations, k the number of independent parameters estimated.

Now consider the partial derivative of y with respect to HINCOME. This is given as $\partial y/\partial \text{HINCOME} = \gamma_1 + \gamma_5 \text{HEDUC1} + \gamma_6 \text{HSEI}$, estimated as $(\partial \hat{y}/\partial \text{HINCOME}) = \hat{\gamma}_1 + \hat{\gamma}_5 \text{HEDUC1} + \hat{\gamma}_6 \text{HSEI}$. This illustrates that the partial with respect to income depends on levels of status and education. In order to test that the partial takes on some specific value, say h_0, under some null hypothesis, the standard deviation of the partial, which is easily computed, is necessary. Then, using the facts above, as well as the independence of numerator and denominator in the following expression, $[(\partial \hat{y}/\partial \text{HINCOME}) - h_0]/\text{s.d.}\,(\partial \hat{y}/\partial \text{HINCOME})$ has a t distribution under the null, with $n - k$ degrees of freedom. It is also of interest to consider differences between partials at various levels of the variables. Suppose the partial with respect to income is computed at two levels of status and education, HSEI_1 and HEDUC1_1, and HSEI_2 and HEDUC1_2. The difference between the partials, $(\partial \hat{y}/\partial \text{HINCOME})|_2 - (\partial \hat{y}/\partial \text{HINCOME})|_1$ is easily reexpressed as $(\text{HEDUC1}_2 - \text{HEDUC1}_1)\hat{\gamma}_5 + (\text{HSEI}_2 - \text{HSEI}_1)\hat{\gamma}_6$. From this expression, it should be clear how to compute the variance of the difference between partials, and from the explication above, it should be clear how to test hypotheses about the value of the differences under some null hypothesis.

Before abandoning the partials entirely, it is important to indicate that they are elasticities, percentage changes in the unlogged dependent variable produced by a 1% increment to the unlogged independent variable under question. To see this, remember that y is the log of some variable, say y^*; similarly, x is the log of some variable, say x^*. Define Δ as the difference operator. Then, holding constant the levels of the variables which do not involve x,

$$\Delta y \approx (\partial y/\partial x)\Delta x; \quad \text{that is,} \quad \log(y_2^*/y_1^*) \approx (\partial y/\partial x)\,|_{x_1} (\log(x_2^*/x_1^*)).$$

Further reexpression yields

$$\log\left(1 + \frac{y_2^* - y_1^*}{y_1^*}\right) \approx \frac{\partial y}{\partial x}\bigg|_{x_1}\left(\log\left(1 + \frac{x_2^* - x_1^*}{x_1^*}\right)\right)$$

and neglecting terms of order greater than one in the Taylor expansion of

$$\log\left(1 + \frac{y_2^* - y_1^*}{y_1^*}\right) \quad \text{and} \quad \log\left(1 + \frac{x_2^* - x_1^*}{x_1^*}\right)$$

yields the approximate equality

$$\frac{\Delta y^*}{y_1^*} = \frac{\partial y}{\partial x}\bigg|_{x_1}\left(\frac{\Delta x^*}{x_1^*}\right) \quad \text{or} \quad \frac{\Delta y^*/y_1^*}{\Delta x^*/x_1^*} = \frac{\partial y}{\partial x}\bigg|_{x_1},$$

which shows the result.

Recall that the dependent variables are logged expenditures on items (goods). In economic parlance, goods with income elasticities less that 0 are called *inferior,* and goods with income elasticities greater than 0 are called *superior.* Furthermore, if the income elasticity is less than one, the item is often called a necessity, whereas, if the income elasticity is greater than one, the item is called a "luxury." This somewhat arbitrary and conventional nomenclature is utilized in this study. Additionally, luxuries are often referred to as *strongly superior,* and necessities are often referred to as *weakly superior,* provided that the income elasticity is descriptively greater than 0. If the income elasticity is not statistically different from one, the item is viewed as *normally superior, or normal.*

By partial analogy, items with status elasticities greater than 0 (less than 0) are called status superior (status inferior). If the status elasticity for an item is not significantly different from 0, that item is said to be normal with respect to status. The same conventions are adopted in the discussion of the elasticities of education.

CHAPTER 7

Social Structure and Lifestyle: A Preliminary Analysis

In this chapter an expenditure system is estimated, and the effects of the independent variables are assessed. Particular attention is paid to the effects of the socioeconomic variables.

The starting point is the weighted least squares regressions of the dependent variables on the location variables $L1$, $L2$, $L3$, the region variables $R1$, $R2$, $R3$, the family size variable FAMSIZE, marital status (HMSTATUS), head's age (HAGE), and income (HINCOME). This is justified by the primary interest in the effects of the socioeconomic variables, net of the other effects. However, HINCOME is included in this basic model (hereafter referred to as the basic model or model 1) because it makes little sense to estimate the equations without controlling for some measure of income. The basic model, in order to provide a meaningful context for comparison, must be meaningful itself.

The abstract notion that educational attainment, occupational status, and income are especially germane to the differentiation of lifestyle does not help to indicate the manner in which these variables influence the Engel curve. Above and beyond the main effects of these variables, or even in lieu of the main effects, it is not difficult to imagine that income (status or education) conditions the manner in which education and/or status (income) operates. Indeed, this is hinted at in various parts of the text. Therefore the interaction between income and education (HEDON), and the status by income interaction HSEON are potentially relevant; a similar argument applies to the status by education interaction HEDSEI. For this reason, various combinations of education (HEDUC1), occupational status (HSEI), HEDSEI, HEDON, and HSEON are added to and compared with the basic model. This is elaborated upon in the text.

After choosing functional forms for the equations that constitute the system, coefficients and elasticities are tested for significance. Attention is directed to patterns of significance both within variables across equations and within equations across variables. For certain purposes, the signs and magnitudes of the coefficients or elasticities are of interest, but the underlying interest in social process, as manifested in an arbitrary and changing form, often makes the consideration of significance itself more fundamental than the interpretation of sign, etc.

Some Preliminary Results

For the cross-classification, as described in the previous chapter, one cell contains no cases so that there are, in effect, 159 rather than 160 observations, an average of 64 cases per cell. The range is between 1 and 530. Only seven cells contain fewer than 10 cases, and in the weighted analyses, the weights are the square root of the number of cases within a cell[1] multiplied by a proportionality constant. Thus these cells, as they are sufficiently few in number, need not create considerable concern, since the estimation procedure assigns low weights to them.

For the 19 expenditure variables, the number of cells with entries of 0 or less than 1 is first tabulated. The results are displayed in Exhibit 7.1. The procedure followed in this study is to replace 0 values with the arbitrary value of 1 (since $\lim_{x \to 0^+} \log x$ is unbounded from below) and to regress the logged expenditures on the vector of explanatory variables. Since this procedure effectively ignores potential selectivity problems (see the references in the last chapter), use of the procedure in the equations for expenditures on subscriptions to the theater, concerts, the opera, etc. (THEATRE) and expenditures on season's tickets for sporting events (SPORTS) is not warranted. Hence, these variables are excluded from

---

[1] If the model is given by (1) $\mathbf{y} = X\mathbf{B} + \boldsymbol{\epsilon}$, (2) X is full rank, (3) $(\boldsymbol{\epsilon} \mid X) \sim N(0, \sigma^2 W)$, where W is a known positive definite matrix, it may be transformed to (a) $W^{-1/2}\mathbf{y} = W^{-1/2}(X\mathbf{B} + \boldsymbol{\epsilon})$, (b) X is full rank, (c) $(W^{-1/2}\boldsymbol{\epsilon}|X) \sim N(0, \sigma^2 I)$. Ordinary least squares applied to the transformed problem yields estimates of the form $\hat{\mathbf{B}} = (X' W^{-1} X)^{-1} X' W^{-1} \mathbf{y}$. These are BLUE. In the present context, W, hence $W^{-1/2}$ is a diagonal matrix. In this study, it is the elements of $W^{-1/2}$ that are spoken of as the weights, rather than the elements of W^{-1}.

EXHIBIT 7.1
*Number of Cells with Expenditures in [0, 1]**

	Number	Percent (=N/159)
1. FOODHOME	0	0.0
2. FOODAWAY	0	0.0
3. ALCOHOL	2	1.3
4. HOUSING	0	0.0
5. TEXTILES	0	0.0
6. FURNITUR	1	0.6
7. DECORAT	2	1.3
8. CASCLOTH	0	0.0
9. PERSCARE	1	0.6
10. VACATION	1	0.6
11. CLUBS	4	2.5
12. TV	4	2.5
13. MUSIC	13	8.2
14. CAMP	7	4.4
15. READING	0	0.0
16. GIFTS	1	0.6
17. DRSCLOTH	1	0.6
18. THEATRE	133	83.6
19. SPORTS	95	59.7

*Technically, the acronyms for the expenditure variables in this exhibit should be changed, as the dependent variables are in logged form. Since this is likely to be confusing, the same acronyms are used in the exhibit.

further analyses. It is assumed, reasonably, that the selectivity issue is not problematic elsewhere.

In Exhibit 7.2 means and standard deviations (appropriately weighted) of the dependent and independent variables are presented. If the antilog of the means on logged variables is taken, the geometric mean of the unlogged variable is obtained. Its value is less than or equal to the value of the arithmetic mean.

Exhibit 7.3 presents the regression coefficients and F ratios for the explanatory variables in the basic model (model 1). The HINCOME coefficient is tested against the null hypothesis that its population value is 1, that is, the null hypothesis is that the item in question is normal, the alternative that the item is a luxury or a necessity.

There is little point in dwelling upon the results from the basic model. It is useful, however, to point out several features of the system. First, the income (HINCOME) coefficient differs from 1 in 15 of the 17 equations, using a .05 significance level. The age (HAGE) coefficient is significant in

EXHIBIT 7.2
Means and Standard Deviations of Dependent and Independent Variables

	Mean	S.D.
Dependent		
FOODHOME	7.2933	.3018
FOODAWAY	6.0536	.4552
ALCOHOL	4.4449	.5198
HOUSING	7.4704	.3833
TEXTILES	4.0143	.4992
FURNITUR	5.2225	.6166
DECORAT	2.7953	.9080
CASCLOTII	5.1306	.4489
DRSCLOTH	4.7997	.6711
PERSCARE	4.6458	.4042
VACATION	5.5018	.7309
CLUBS	3.0306	1.0700
TV	3.8959	.5110
MUSIC	2.9097	.8416
CAMP	2.7048	.9715
READING	3.9690	.5318
GIFTS	5.0919	.5034
Independent		
R1	.2229	.0546
R2	.2956	.0802
R3	.2150	.0751
L1	.2007	.0663
L2	.3701	.1120
L3	.1472	.0473
FAMSIZE	1.2000	.2365
HMSTATUS	.1814	.2056
HINCOME	9.1069	.3471
HAGE	43.3795	4.1260
HSEI	3.6362	.5677
HEDUC1	2.4663	.2747
HEDSEI	9.0506	2.0916
HSEON	33.2002	5.8024
HEDON	22.5033	2.9686

14 of 17 equations. The family size (FAMSIZE) and marital status (HMSTATUS) coefficients are significant six times. In the casual clothing (CASCLOTH) equation both coefficients are significant, but this is the only equation where this occurs. While this may seem unusual, the correlation between the two variables is .92, reflecting the fact that the family size variable is generally 0 for the unmarried, and greater than 0 other-

wise. It also appears that the location and region variables do not contribute substantially to the explanatory power of the basic model, at least not when the effects are separately considered. Nonetheless, these variables are retained; it is premature to drop them from the analysis.

Adding Variables to the Basic Model

As previously indicated, the processes by which education, occupational status, and income are presumed to influence the Engel curve are complex. Hence it is a priori difficult to argue for one or another augmentation of the basic model. Since the addition of five variables to the basic model is under consideration, this leaves 31 possible models under which the basic model is nested. Each model must be considered across 17 equations. This is an enormous task, and any strategy based on consideration of all alternatives is unlikely to lead to a definite set of models, since conventional statistical criteria do not unambiguously lead to clear choices. These criteria are useful in distinguishing between alternative functional forms only in certain restricted and well-specified situations, for example, if there are two models to compare, one of which is nested under the other. If there are a variety of models, such a strategy breaks down quickly. A simple example should suffice to illustrate this point. Suppose there are three models, A, B, and C, A nested under B nested under C. It is not clear what conclusions can be reached when the comparison of C to A is significant, the comparison of B to A is not, and the comparison of C to B is not significant. Other cases that would make interpretation difficult can be constructed with this situation.

When there is no clear hierarchy of variables and models, as there is in the preceding example, matters can become more complicated. Here it can be argued that since three of the variables considered for addition to the basic model are interactions between terms that are either already in the model or candidates for inclusion, the conventional strategy of attaching primacy to the main effects should be adopted. Interactions should therefore be considered only after the main effect parameters have been estimated. While such a choice would simplify matters somewhat, it will still not resolve all the difficulties. Most importantly, this choice is a convention and merely that. It is arbitrary, and unless dictated by the theory, it is not any more meaningful than testing for main effects, net of the interactions. In some instances, it does not even make sense, and while it might be argued that it is parsimonious to adopt this convention, there is no reason to expect that the processes that operate in the real world are parsimonious as well. Hence this strategy is unacceptable.

EXHIBIT 7.3
Basic Model WLS Regressions with F Ratios in Parentheses

Dependent	Constant	R1	R2	R3	L1	L2	L3	FAMSIZE	HMSTATUS	HINCOME*	HAGE
FOODHOME Adj.R².949	3.050	.162 (2.143)	-.001 (.000)	-.156 (2.153)	.067 (.313)	.134 (2.162)	.196 (2.010)	.685 (87.331)	-.128 (2.551)	.301 (348.089)	.014 (75.012)
FOODAWAY Adj.R².918	-6.538	-.055 (.068)	.051 (.111)	-.169 (.692)	.022 (.009)	-.006 (.001)	-.163 (.379)	-.243 (3.004)	.167 (1.119)	1.453 (40.051)	-.007 (5.880)
ALCOHOL Adj.R².5974	-5.624	1.455 (7.378)	.757 (3.740)	1.651 (10.315)	-1.061 (3.337)	-.443 (1.005)	-.048 (.005)	-.557 (2.465)	-.109 (.079)	1.238 (1.717)	-.236 (9.155)
HOUSING Adj.R².860	-2.180	-.200 (.732)	-.159 (.867)	.314 (1.970)	-.162 (.409)	-.067 (.120)	-.365 (1.567)	-.189 (1.500)	.425 (6.353)	1.190 (3.969)	-.021 (37.787)
TEXTILES Adj.R².879	-8.692	-.099 (.124)	-.381 (3.430)	-.176 (.423)	.297 (.946)	.357 (2.371)	.537 (2.323)	.300 (2.580)	.417 (4.215)	1.328 (11.866)	.001 (.025)
FURNITUR Adj.R².813	-9.589	-.422 (.949)	.027 (.007)	-.439 (1.114)	.028 (.004)	-.245 (.469)	.123 (.052)	-.394 (1.885)	-.283 (.818)	1.791 (29.020)	-.017 (6.942)
DECORAT Adj.R².786	-20.872	.653 (.916)	-.488 (.959)	-.132 (.041)	-.105 (.020)	.009 (.000)	.058 (.005)	-.116 (.066)	1.088 (4.886)	2.772 (58.912)	-.037 (13.798)
CASCLOTH Adj.R².936	-6.627	-.158 (.728)	.132 (.954)	.130 (.536)	.590 (8.675)	.342 (5.045)	.374 (2.616)	.288 (5.530)	.351 (6.913)	1.184 (8.697)	.005 (3.898)
DRSCLOTH Adj.R².924	-13.439	-.175 (.341)	-.913 (17.316)	-.662 (5.264)	.164 (.254)	.211 (.728)	.073 (.037)	-.367 (3.402)	.239 (1.212)	2.120 (121.187)	-.008 (3.421)

Variable	Adj.R²											
PERSCARE	.861	-6.198	-.279 (.728)	-.069 (.954)	-.557 (.536)	.408 (8.675)	.505 (5.045)	.651 (2.616)	.205 (5.530)	.349 (6.913)	1.010 (8.697)	.013 (3.898)
VACATION	.911	-13.848	.438 (1.526)	.161 (.384)	.784 (5.296)	-.539 (1.959)	-.242 (.685)	-1.387 (9.756)	-.947 (16.220)	.069 (.072)	2.349 (126.117)	-.019 (13.637)
CLUBS	.793	-25.992	1.376 (3.026)	-.296 (.263)	.322 (.180)	-.750 (.765)	-.595 (.832)	-.399 (.163)	-1.767 (11.365)	-.050 (.008)	3.562 (91.617)	-.027 (5.294)
TV	.353	1.048	.946 (2.008)	.515 (1.117)	.624 (.948)	-.135 (.035)	-.708 (1.655)	-1.489 (3.175)	.471 (1.148)	-.627 (1.693)	.349 (8.312)	-.017 (3.287)
MUSIC	.475	-12.970	-.796 (.645)	1.836 (6.439)	1.734 (3.326)	-1.154 (1.153)	-.930 (1.295)	-1.619 (1.703)	.267 (.166)	1.171 (2.680)	1.899 (7.190)	-.043 (8.785)
CAMP	.769	-11.227	-.025 (.001)	.491 (.785)	1.939 (7.099)	-.126 (.024)	-.423 (.458)	.135 (.020)	-.092 (.034)	-1.521 (7.714)	1.730 (8.092)	-.042 (14.552)
READING	.925	-7.796	.086 (.133)	-.639 (13.685)	.401 (3.115)	.007 (.001)	.135 (.476)	-.292 (.971)	-.869 (30.665)	-.237 (1 920)	1.576 (51.625)	-.033 (91.453)
GIFTS	.742	-8.573	.411 (.978)	.330 (1.182)	.471 (1.399)	-.576 (1.637)	.020 (.003)	-.091 (.031)	-1.323 (23.107)	-.528 (3.097)	1.565 (16.127)	.022 (12.705)

*For HINCOME, $H_0 : B_{HINCOME} = 1$

N = 159

Degrees of freedom for F ratios = 148

Having rejected typical regression strategies, it is not immediately clear how to add variables to model 1. This problem is exacerbated by the fact that the expenditure system has 17 equations; the system can be constrained to have identical explanatory variables or fitting can be done on an equation-by-equation basis. The first choice suffers from the defect that no one functional form, even among the constrained forms examined here, is likely to be uniformly best for all the dependent variables. The second choice suffers from the defect that it necessitates an inordinate amount of analysis to uncertain end.

Finally, both choices suffer from the fact that there are often several forms fitting the data equally well. However, it appears that the first choice is more desirable conceptually. If this approach proves inadequate, it can be abandoned subsequently.

Since conventional strategies are arbitrary, the approach adopted here is both eclectic and sequential. In essence, various alternatives to model 1 are estimated and compared with model 1 by means of conventional strategies where appropriate. Considerations early in the analysis are allowed to influence decisions at later steps. Like the more conventional strategies, this one is arbitrary, though not capricious so long as reasonable substantive and statistical decisions are made throughout the analysis. Additionally, this strategy has the advantages that it is flexible and tied closely to the data. Its primary disadvantage is that in order for the reader to judge the analysis, it must be spelled out in great detail.

Data Analysis

In Exhibit 7.4 is presented the correlation matrix (weighted by the elements of W^{-1}) for the variables income (HINCOME), occupational status (HSEI), education (HEDUC1), and the interactions HSEON, HEDSEI, and HEDON. Several of the correlations are particularly large, especially the correlation between HEDON and HEDUC1 and that between HSEI and HSEON. There is reason to be concerned about the effects of potential multicollinearity on the regression hyperplane when variables as highly correlated as these are incorporated into the same equation. In the extreme case the variance–covariance matrix of the explanatory variables does not possess a unique inverse; hence the coefficients are not unique. In less extreme cases, the inverse will exist but may have large diagonal elements, hence large standard deviations of the coefficients. When this occurs, the explanatory variables in question are likely to have insignificant coefficients. One approach is to omit one or more of the highly correlated variables from the equation. The approach

EXHIBIT 7.4
Correlations Among the Socioeconomic Variables

	HINCOME	HSEI	HEDUC1	HEDSEI	HSEON
HSEI	.436				
HEDUC1	.451	.532			
HEDSEI	.502	.916	.822		
HSEON	.602	.981	.570	.922	
HEDON	.664	.572	.966	.834	.652

adopted here is somewhat different; the issue is not prejudged. Except in the extreme case, multicollinearity is treated as an empirical issue. If it becomes necessary to omit variables, so be it; but there is no reason to do so before examining the data.

Initially, HSEON is not entered into equations containing HSEI. Since HEDON and HEDUC1 are highly correlated, this set of variables must be approached with some caution. It turns out subsequently that the correlation between HEDUC1 and HEDON is not particularly problematic.

If F ratios for the five variables omitted from model 1 are calculated, it can be seen that in 6 of 17 equations, HEDSEI would enter the equation next in a forward stepwise regression. In 5 equations, HSEI would enter, and in 3 equations HSEON or HEDON would next enter.

Let model 2 consist of the basic model with the addition of the variable HEDSEI. Exhibit 7.5 presents the F ratios for the comparison between models 2 and 1, as well as other comparisons. In the equations for housing expenditures (HOUSING), household textiles (TEXTILES), household decorations (DECORAT), membership fees for clubs and organizations (CLUBS), expenditures on camping, health and sports equipment (CAMP), and reading materials (READING), the inclusion of HEDSEI leads to a significant increment in the regression sum of squares at the .05 level. Net of the interaction, it is reasonable to ask whether there are effects of education (HEDUC1) and occupational status (HSEI). Model 4 in which these additional regressors are added to model 2 addresses the question. First, there are significant incremental effects in 9 of the 17 equations, including the equations for DECORAT, CLUBS, CAMP, and READING. The other 5 equations in which there are significant incremental effects ($\alpha = .05$) are food at home (FOODHOME), food purchased

EXHIBIT 7.5

Comparisons of Some Alternative Models by Means of F Ratios

	2→1	3→1	4→1	4→3	4→2	5→1	5→4
FOODHOME	1.460	.567	2.647	6.773	3.219	3.459	5.637
FOODAWAY	.015	2.903	3.776	5.345	5.655	3.927	4.134
ALCOHOL	2.308	1.231	.822	.000	.093	.752	.552
HOUSING	12.451	20.545	15.021	3.173	15.108	11.197	.029
TEXTILES	4.803	2.907	2.286	1.043	1.028	7.529	.683
FURNITUR	3.886	2.307	1.528	.004	.366	2.175	4.021
DECORAT	19.814	11.045	8.748	3.741	2.952	6.525	.028
CASCLOTH	3.652	2.370	1.788	.634	.859	1.364	.125
DRSCLOTH	32.254	16.597	11.362	.916	.938	8.751	.942
PERSCARE	6.850	5.150	7.928	12.662	8.134	7.407	5.157
VACATION	7.058	3.098	2.639	1.692	.456	4.032	7.837
CLUBS	29.724	15.607	10.756	1.045	1.227	9.482	4.811
TV	1.077	1.125	2.479	5.123	3.164	2.877	3.923
MUSIC	.016	.212	1.591	4.338	2.362	1.185	.001
CAMP	.008	3.329	3.661	4.133	5.488	3.963	4.598
READING	46.497	25.275	16.895	.354	3.705	13.827	3.690
GIFTS	.043	.132	.205	.372	.861	.441	1.149
Reference Distribution	$F(1,147)$	$F(2,146)$	$F(3,145)$	$F(1,145)$	$F(2,145)$	$F(4,144)$	$F(1,144)$

1. BASIC MODEL (Exhibit 7.3)
2. BASIC MODEL + HEDSEI
3. BASIC MODEL + HEDUC1 + HSEI
4. BASIC MODEL + HEDUC1 + HSEI + HEDSEI
5. BASIC MODEL + HEDUC1 + HSEI + HEDSEI + HEDON

away from home (FOODAWAY), dress clothing (DRSCLOTH), personal care expenditures (PERSCARE), and expenditures on televisions (TV). Next, model 4 is compared with model 3 in which occupational status (HSEI) and education (HEDUC1) are added to model 1. This comparison assesses the contribution of the interaction net of the main effects of HEDUC1 and HSEI. The contribution is significant for the equations for FOODHOME, FOODAWAY, PERSCARE, TV, expenditures on musical equipment (MUSIC), and CAMP. Finally, model 4 is compared with model 1. This comparison indicates that model 4 has significantly greater explanatory power at the .05 level for the equations for FOODAWAY, HOUSING, DECORAT, DRSCLOTH, PERSCARE, CLUBS, CAMP, and READING.

The last three comparisons indicate the tendency for the main effects to augment the interaction effects in the same equations in which the interactions significantly augment the main effects. Furthermore, there is a tendency for the group of all three to significantly increase the explanatory power over model 1 in those equations. The data also exhibit the following tendency: in those equations for which model 2 does not "explain" the data better than model 1, this tends to be true of models 3 and 4 as well, and model 4 does not tend to "explain" the data better than model 2.

Suppose that model 4 is proposed as a tentative, intermediate alternative to model 1. If HEDON is added to model 4, model 5 "explains" the data better than model 4 for the variables FOODHOME, FOODAWAY, household furniture (FURNITUR), DRSCLOTH, PERSCARE, VACATION, CLUBS, TV, and CAMP, that is, for 9 of the 17 equations. Furthermore, this model "explains" the data better than model 1 for the equations FOODHOME, FOODAWAY, HOUSING, TEXTILES, DECORAT, DRSCLOTH, PERSCARE, vacation expenditures (VACATION), CLUBS, TV, CAMP, and READING, i.e., in 12 of the 17 equations. Again, and not surprisingly, model 5 tends to be better than either models 4 or 1 in the equations previously identified.

Comparison of the F ratios corresponding to the variables HEDSEI, HSEI, and HEDUC1 for the individual coefficients in models 4 and 5 (Exhibits 7.6 and 7.7) points to a rather strange occurrence. For example, consider the dependent variable READING. In model 4, the F ratio for HEDUC1 is .062. In model 5, the F ratio for HEDUC1 is 4.338 and that for HEDON is 3.690. This occurs in other equations as well. Also, if HEDUC1 is significant in model 4, both it and HEDON tend to be significant in model 5. Now consider the dependent variable FOODAWAY. In model 4, the F ratio for HEDUC1 is insignificant, but the F ratios for HEDSEI and HSEI are both significant. But, in the model 5 equation for FOODAWAY the F ratios for HEDUC1 and HEDON are significant, whereas the F ratios for HSEI and HEDSEI are now insignificant. This occurs in the CAMP equation also.

The reason these occurrences are surprising stems from the large correlation between HEDON and HEDUC1. It would be reasonable to suspect that with two variables so highly correlated, it would be difficult to

86 | 7. Social Structure and Lifestyle: A Preliminary Analysis

EXHIBIT 7.6
F Ratios for HEDSEI, HEDUC1, and HSEI in MODEL 4

	HEDSEI	HSEI	HEDUC1
FOODHOME	6.773	6.241	4.367
FOODAWAY	5.345	6.540	2.035
ALCOHOL	.000	.060	.006
HOUSING	3.173	2.874	.380
TEXTILES	1.043	.664	.065
FURNITUR	.004	.091	.003
DECORAT	3.741	2.141	.282
CASCLOTH	.634	1.317	.614
DRSCLOTH	.916	.000	.326
PERSCARE	12.662	16.249	13.051
VACATION	1.692	.885	.624
CLUBS	1.045	.129	.091
TV	5.123	6.184	4.444
MUSIC	4.338	4.664	3.338
CAMP	4.133	5.233	1.195
READING	.354	1.019	.062
GIFTS	.372	.461	.231

d.f. for denominator of F ratio are 145

find significant effects of either variable, net of the other. The fact that this is not the case may necessitate an explanation.

Residual plots appear to be a useful way of looking into this matter. In Exhibit 7.8, weighted standardized residuals are plotted against HEDON, as defined in the weighted design space. That is, after transformation of dependent and independent variables to correct for heteroscedasticity, the standardized OLS residuals from the newly defined problem are plotted against the weighted values of HEDON. The dependent variable in question is FOODAWAY, and the model from which the residuals are defined is model 4. If there is a linear effect of HEDON, it should show up in the plot. Instead, inspection of the plot does not reveal a discernible linear effect, and three rather large values of the independent variable are notable. While the residuals for these three values do not appear to be unusually large relative to the others, it must be remembered that least squares minimizes the function $(y - XB)'(y - XB)$. Partition the subscripts corresponding to the observations so that those that do not correspond to these large values are in the set A, while those that do are in the set A^*. Then

$$(y - XB)'(y - XB) = (y - XB)'(y - XB)I_A + (y - XB)'(y - XB)I_{A^*}$$

where I is an indicator function defined on the appropriate sets. In the regression problem, the contribution of elements in A^* is disproportionate to the number of elements in A^*. That is, in this minimization problem, elements in A^* unduly influence the regression hyperplane. From the plot, by analogy, it may be seen that these three observations then force a line to tilt in their direction.

The heuristic argument above suggests that the analysis treat these

EXHIBIT 7.7
F Ratios for HEDSEI, HSEI, HEDUC1, and HEDON in MODEL 5

	HEDSEI	HSEI	HEDUC1	HEDON
FOODHOME	12.304	11.722	3.664	5.637
FOODAWAY	.752	1.101	5.178	4.134
ALCOHOL	.154	.374	1.214	.552
HOUSING	1.966	1.745	.002	.029
TEXTILES	1.704	1.285	.579	.683
FURNITUR	1.288	.712	3.825	4.021
DECORAT	2.930	1.719	.004	.028
CASCLOTH	.227	.583	.249	.125
DRSCLOTH	1.768	.289	.707	.942
PERSCARE	3.273	4.739	8.657	5.157
VACATION	6.933	5.470	6.698	7.837
CLUBS	.099	.803	4.374	4.811
TV	8.963	10.152	2.332	3.923
MUSIC	2.985	3.175	.153	.001
CAMP	.328	.582	5.378	4.598
READING	2.382	.709	4.338	3.690
GIFTS	.004	.000	1.311	1.149

d.f. for denominator of F ratio are 144

EXHIBIT 7.8

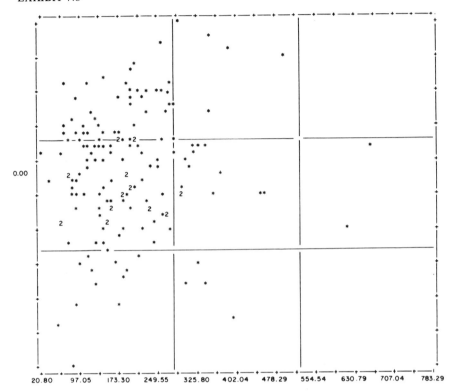

points as outliers, and either (*a*) systematically deweight them, (*b*) leave them or a subset of them out of the analysis, or (*c*) fit a parameter for these points. However, a plot of these same residuals against the squared weights (Exhibit 7.9) indicates that the large weights correspond to those points that have been identified as outliers. Since the weights are the square roots of the number of individual cases within a cell normalized by a proportionality constant, the outliers are those points in the crossclassification with the highest "density," that is, they constitute a substantial fraction of the individual level data. Therefore, the fact that these points are allowed to influence the regressions heavily should no longer cause concern. That is, it is no longer appropriate to consider these observations outliers.

While HEDON and HEDUC1 often operate in the fashion just described, this is not always the case. Consider the expenditures on alcohol

(ALCOHOL) equation. Examination of models 4 and 5 indicates that the addition of HEDON does not substantially alter the conclusions reached about the effects of education on the consumption of alcohol. However, the augmentation may create a multicollinearity problem.

One more point needs to be considered. Since HEDON and HEDUC1 operate in such an unusual fashion, it seems reasonable to suspect that HSEI and HSEON might operate similarly, particularly for items that appear to be related more to status than to education, for example, compare the F ratios for models 4 and 5 for the dependent variable TEXTILES.

It should be apparent that the strategy that leads to the estimation of model 5, in light of the quirks exhibited by the data itself, yields inadequate parameter estimates. This occurs because the analysis of patterns in the data, which will ensue after a more adequate estimation of the system, relies heavily on relationships among various coefficients and/or linear and

EXHIBIT 7.9

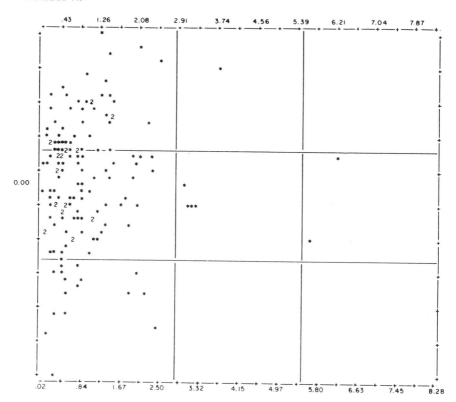

stochastic combinations of the coefficients. If the coefficients are unstable (excessively large standard errors), then the ability to make inferences about the patterns will be severely constrained.

Therefore, it seems appropriate to abandon the criteria of fitting one functional form for all equations and to utilize all that has been learned about the data so far to add in the variables more intelligently. In light of the current information, model 5 is regarded as adequate for the equations FOODHOME, PERSCARE, VACATION, and TV. Net of the variables in model 5, HSEON would not enter the model with a significant coefficient, at the .05 level; nor would application of a forward stepwise regression procedure to model 1 lead to a model with HSEON as a regressor.

No augmentation of variables to model 1 ever improves the GIFTS or MUSIC equations, so model 1 is regarded as adequate for these dependent variables. This leaves 11 equations to consider in greater detail.

Inspection of the F ratios in Exhibit 7.7 indicates that for the variables FOODAWAY, FURNITUR, CLUBS, CAMP, and READING, it might be appropriate to consider adding HEDUC1 and HEDON to model 1 and assess whether or not such an intermediate model yields an adequate representation of the data. Refitting with this intermediate model is satisfactory for the variables FOODAWAY and CAMP. In both cases, addition of variables to the intermediate model does not improve the fit, and in both cases a forward stepwise regression procedure produces this model. This leaves the CLUBS, READING, and FURNITUR equations to be considered. For these equations, Exhibit 7.10 reports the F ratios for the included and omitted variables from both the intermediate model and a model that includes all five variables. From the exhibit it is clear that the intermediate model performs poorly in the CLUBS and READING equations because a status effect exists. The F ratios for the omitted variables are ˙descriptively similar, so that it is not initially clear which variable should be added to the model first. If the largest F ratio is chosen, as in forward stepwise regression, HSEON would be added to both equations. For the variables CLUBS and READING, HSEON is added to the intermediate model. Net of this addition, there are no significant incremental effects of HSEI or HEDSEI in either equation. Similarly, for the variable FURNITUR, HEDSEI is added to the intermediate model.

The equations for ALCOHOL, HOUSING, TEXTILES, DECORAT, CASCLOTH, and DRSCLOTH require discussion. From Exhibit 7.7, it is clear that HEDUC1 and HEDON do not jointly operate in the same fashion as in the other equations described in that exhibit, excepting GIFTS. This could be because neither HEDUC1 nor HEDON contribute significant increments, net of a set of appropriate status-related variables, or it may be the case that one or the other variable contributes

EXHIBIT 7.10

F Ratios for HEDUC1, HEDON, HSEI, HSEON, and HEDSEI in MODELS A* and B**

	HEDUC1	HEDON	HSEI	HSEON	HEDSEI
CLUBS (A)	2.517	3.572	16.798	17.064	16.011
READING (A)	4.150	2.882	22.687	24.625	23.061
FURNITUR (A)	3.498	3.430	3.806	3.660	4.396
CLUBS (B)	2.769	3.281	.177	.584	.200
READING (B)	4.548	3.952	.629	.295	2.002
FURNITUR (B)	2.194	2.506	.347	.853	1.647

*MODEL A is the BASIC MODEL + HEDUC1 + HEDON
**MODEL B is the BASIC MODEL + HEDUC1 + HEDON + HEDSEI + HSEON + HSEI
d.f. for A is 146
d.f. for B is 143

to the explanatory power of the appropriate baseline model. A specific possibility is that HSEI and HSEON operate jointly, as HEDUC1 and HEDON sometimes operate; if HSEI and HSEON are added to model 1, it is found that such a model is adequate for the variables ALCOHOL and CASCLOTH. Net of the model that includes these variables, no other omitted variable has a significant F ratio. But this strategy does not work well for the other equations. Hence we return to model 1.

In the TEXTILES equation, the largest F ratio for an omitted variable is HEDSEI. If HEDSEI is added to model 1 and the F ratios for the remaining omitted variables are considered, it is found that no other variable enters the model at the .05 level. Hence this model is accepted for the TEXTILES equation.

For the variable DRSCLOTH, inspection of Exhibit 7.11 indicates that HSEON next enters in a forward stepwise regression. No other variable significantly augments the intermediate model that includes HSEON.

For the variable DECORAT, Exhibit 7.3 reveals that net of HEDSEI and HSEI, the effect of HEDUC1 is not significant. From inspection of the F ratios for variables omitted from model 1, it is clear that HEDSEI enters the equation next in a forward stepwise regression. Net of the intermediate model that includes HEDSEI as an additional explanatory variable, HSEI (as would HSEON) significantly augments the regression sum of squares. However, since the F ratio for HSEI is largest, this variable is next entered. Net of the intermediate model containing the

EXHIBIT 7.11

F Ratios for the Omitted Variables HSEI, HEDSEI, HSEON, HEDUC1, and HEDON under MODEL 1

	HSEI	HEDSEI	HSEON	HEDUC1	HEDON
ALCOHOL	2.440	2.308	1.942	.215	.248
HOUSING	1.301	12.451	1.813	41.395	42.418
TEXTILES	1.997	4.803	2.205	4.535	4.422
DECORAT	9.052	19.814	9.747	14.880	15.178
CASCLOTH	4.761	3.652	4.104	.179	.123
DRSCLOTH	32.429	32.254	32.806	2.463	2.259
MUSIC	.346	.016	.261	.038	.082

d.f. are 148

variables HSEI and HEDSEI, no variables contribute additional explanatory power. Therefore, the intermediate model is accepted. An intermediate model containing HEDSEI and HSEON would also be acceptable. As in some of the other cases in which the largest omitted F ratio is used as a criterion, more than one model appears to be defensible.

Finally, the equation for HOUSING is considered. HEDON is entered, using the largest F criterion. Net of the new model, no omitted variable contributes additional explanatory power. Therefore, this representation of the data is accepted as adequate.

Having fit the equations, it is reasonable to ask whether this process should continue. Two considerations are relevant. First, in the equations there appear to be some variables, or sets of variables, that rarely have significant effects, for example, the location coefficients. Second, the initial analysis had identical explanatory variables in each of the equations. In that case, ordinary least squares (OLS) on the weighted data applied equation by equation produces the same estimates as would an iterative generalized least squares procedure (GLS) no matter what the form of the variance–covariance matrix of the disturbances. This situation no longer applies.

In considering the first point, it is wise to remember that the fitting process was carried out to discover how the socioeconomic variables other than HINCOME, net of the variables in model 1, influence the Engel curve. Therefore, model 1 may be regarded as misspecified only by its exclusion of the five socioeconomic variables. The intermediate models that include subsets of these variables constitute the "proper" specification of the equations. Thus, statistical tests on the coefficients lead to the acceptance or rejection of the theory that produces the model itself. While variables with statistically insignificant coefficients can be dropped from the model, and the model can then be reestimated, there is no need to do so, since this step is unnecessary for testing the theory.

The second point must now be considered. Is OLS, applied to the weighted data, an adequate estimation procedure? The issue, as generally presented, hinges on the improvement in efficiency that GLS would give, since both OLS and GLS estimators are generally unbiased and consistent[2] (Kakwani, 1967). Theil (1971) shows that when the equations in a system contain identical explanatory variables, OLS and GLS produce the same results. Furthermore, if the variance–covariance matrix of the cross-equation disturbances is diagonal, OLS and GLS produce the same results in the population. He also shows in an analysis of a two-equation case that gains in efficiency from GLS are greatest when the explanatory variables in the two equations are uncorrelated and the disturbances from the equations are highly correlated. If the disturbances are not highly correlated, OLS may be preferable to GLS, even when the explanatory variables in the two equations are uncorrelated. In addition, if the explanatory variables in the first equation can be expressed as a linear combination of the variables in the second, there is no gain in efficiency from estimating the parameters of the first equation by GLS, rather than OLS.

---

[2] Technically, this statement is not true. OLS is unbiased when the model is linear, properly specified, X has full rank, and $E(\epsilon \mid X) = 0$. OLS is consistent when the sequence $1/n(X_n'X_n)$ converges and when $V(\epsilon \mid X) = \sigma^2 I$.

With GLS, the situation is more complicated. Let

$$
y = \begin{pmatrix} y_1 \\ \cdot \\ \cdot \\ \cdot \\ y_p \end{pmatrix}, \quad
X = \begin{pmatrix} X_1 & 0 & \cdots & 0 \\ 0 & X_2 & & 0 \\ \cdot & & \cdot & \cdot \\ \cdot & & & \cdot \\ \cdot & & & \cdot \\ 0 & 0 & & X_p \end{pmatrix}, \quad
B = \begin{pmatrix} B_1 \\ \cdot \\ \cdot \\ \cdot \\ B_p \end{pmatrix}, \quad
\epsilon = \begin{pmatrix} \epsilon_1 \\ \cdot \\ \cdot \\ \cdot \\ \epsilon_p \end{pmatrix}.
$$

Let the model be given by $y = XB + \epsilon$, X full rank, $E(\epsilon \mid X) = 0$ and $V(\epsilon \mid X) = \Sigma \otimes I$, where Σ is the variance–covariance matrix for the ith observation, $i = 1, \ldots n$. Let $S = \{S_{kj}\}$, $k = 1, \ldots p, j = 1, \ldots p$, where $S_{kj} = e_k'e_j/n$, and ϵ_k and ϵ_j are vectors of OLS residuals from the kth and jth equations. Kakwani shows that the GLS estimator of B, given by $(X'(S^{-1} \otimes I)X)^{-1}X'(S^{-1} \otimes I)y$ is unbiased so long as $f(\epsilon_{i1}, \ldots \epsilon_{ip}) = f(-\epsilon_{i1}, \ldots -\epsilon_{ip})$, $i = 1, \ldots n$. Sufficient conditions for consistency (Theil, 1971, p. 399) are (a) the sequence $(1/n)(X_n'(\Sigma^{-1} \otimes I_n)X_n)$ converges, (b) $\text{plim}_{n \to \infty} (1/n)(X_n'((S_n^{-1} - \Sigma^{-1}) \otimes I_n)X_n = 0$, (c) $\text{plim}_{n \to \infty} (1/\sqrt{n})(X_n'(S_n^{-1} - \Sigma^{-1}) \otimes I_n) \epsilon_n) = 0$, (d) for P square such that $P'P = \Sigma^{-1} \otimes I$, the entries in the random vector $P\epsilon$ are independent and identically distributed.

In the present situation, it should be clear that variables in different equations are highly correlated, for example, all the equations contain ten identical explanatory variables, and the additional five variables that occur in combinations in some equations are themselves highly correlated. Also (data not shown), the correlations between the residuals is not unduly large.

These observations appear to indicate that it may be just as well to estimate the system of equations by OLS. There is also another reason why this is the case, and this reason is sufficient in and of itself.

The fitting procedure may allow explanatory variables that do not belong (belong) in an equation to enter (to be deleted from) the analysis. Therefore, one or more of the equations in the system is probably misspecified. OLS estimation of the system clearly localizes specification error to the particular equation that is misspecified, while GLS allows the specification error in an equation to affect the parameter estimates in the other equations. This is the most important reason for using OLS, applied to the weighted data.

Interpreting the Results

An interpretation of the results must not degenerate into an equation-by-equation explanation of the effects of the explanatory variables. Rather, an explanation must seek to establish relationships among the coefficients and variables both within and across equations, that is, the patterns among coefficients are at issue.

The consumption items are viewed as indexing lifestyle and therefore constitute an observable form that is assumed to be generated by the social structural variables and a stochastic term. The form itself is somewhat elusive, arbitrary, and less fundamental than the process itself. At the macro-level, changes in the form are induced by factors other than those studies here, for example, technology and foreign trade. This is not an issue that concerns us. Irrespective of such changes, it could also be the case that an explanatory variable is salient to the differentiation of a lifestyle item at two times; at time 1, it has a positive coefficient, at time 2 a negative coefficient. The significance of the coefficient is more important, since this indicates whether the variable is important, that is, yields information about the process. The sign reveals the arbitrariness of the form itself, which can change from day to day, despite the fact that the same explanatory variables differentiate the lifestyle. A simple example should clarify this point. Suppose there exists some item that is positively associated with education, net of the other variables. Suppose the item diffused through the population, and the educated stopped buying that item, say, because it lost its "snob appeal." Then, at the second time, the item would be negatively associated with education. At both times, educational differentials are important in explaining the variation in the item, despite the descriptive change in the form of the lifestyle.

The questions addressed in the analysis are of three sorts. First, the effects of the nonsocioeconomic variables must be addressed. Second, it is of interest to note the manner in which the introduction of the socioeconomic variables changes the initial conclusions about the effects of these. Third, and most importantly, the socioeconomic effects must be considered.

In the initial model (model 1 of Exhibit 7.3), the effects of age are significant in 14 of 17 equations. Given the relationship between age and the socioeconomic variables, inclusion of the latter should alter the initial conclusions. This does appear to be the case. In the final set of equations (Exhibit 7.12), the HAGE coefficients are now significant only seven times, for the variables FOODHOME, ALCOHOL, CASCLOTH, PERSCARE, MUSIC, CAMP, and GIFTS. The initial and final MUSIC and GIFTS equations are, of course, the same. Otherwise, it appears that the initial age effects are sometimes spurious and arise from the omission of important socioeconomic variables. In this vein, notice that in no case does the omission of the socioeconomic variables surpress any effects of age. If the primary import of age is biological, the age effects should tend to be significant and negative for both final and initial models in equations that refer to "activity-oriented" expenditures, for example, FOODAWAY, ALCOHOL, VACATION, CLUBS, and CAMP. Only the ALCOHOL and CAMP equations offer any support for this notion. Furthermore, the significant HAGE coefficients cannot be systematically related to inferior, normal, or superior dimensions of consumption. This leads to the conclusion that the partial elasticity of HAGE is sometimes significant, but not in any unambiguous fashion.

In the set of equations that have not been discussed, age is typically significant in the initial, but not in the final model. This could be very important. Since age does not appear to operate biologically, and since, in the final model "life cycle" variables are included, the insignificance of age may indicate a lack of period effects.

It is possible that the effects of HAGE are nonlinear, although unreported evidence suggests this is not the case. In this vein, it must also be remembered that the population to which these results apply is limited to nonblack households with heads aged 25–64. This amounts to truncating the distribution of HAGE at both tails, that is, at the two places where it is a priori expected that HAGE operates differently in the production of

EXHIBIT 7.12
WLS Regressions for Final Models with F Ratios in Parentheses

	FOODHOME	FOODAWAY	ALCOHOL	HOUSING
R1	.28972 (6.015)	-.20382 (.891)	1.32949 (6.443)	-.35983 (3.002)
R2	.00554 (.004)	-.15323 (.921)	.72909 (2.886)	-.01017 (.004)
R3	-.14663 (1.613)	-.22425 (1.218)	1.25408 (5.518)	.08696 (.187)
L1	.05459 (.215)	.06507 (.086)	-1.01609 (3.187)	-.04435 (.039)
L2	.12707 (1.978)	.07592 (.198)	-.36385 (.710)	-.26020 (2.273)
L3	.17149 (1.619)	-.17305 (.459)	.27259 (.166)	-.39244 (2.311)
FAMSIZE	.66219 (68.162)	-.18534 (1.817)	-.94327 (5.877)	-.14214 (1.079)
HMSTATUS	-.02320 (.070)	.18814 (1.371)	-.30272 (.633)	.05555 (.122)
HINCOME	-.08998 (.222)	2.46385 (65.914)	-.00851 (.000)	.67292 (40.485)
HAGE	.00709 (4.097)	-.00272 (.182)	-.02951 (14.325)	.00381 (.618)
HEDSEI	-.15690 (12.304)			
HSEI	.37789 (11.722)		-3.82198 (8.739)	
HEDUC1	-1.45573 (3.664)	3.96848 (8.880)		
HEDON	.20725 (5.637)	-.43469 (9.777)		.06906 (42.418)
HSEON			.40946 (8.223)	
CONSTANT	5.86918	-15.96226	6.81727	.01092
d.f.	144	146	146	147
Adj .R^2	.95626	.92395	.60126	.89031

EXHIBIT 7.12. *Continued*

	TEXTILES	FURNITUR	DECORAT	CASCLOTH	DRSCLOTH
R1	.11963 (.185)	-.58064 (1.630)	.45540 (.499)	-.10333 (.329)	-.00622 (.001)
R2	-.16869 (.563)	.14192 (.150)	.41856 (.666)	.18829 (1.626)	-.36448 (2.720)
R3	-.02012 (.005)	-.25400 (.306)	.14818 (.051)	.30265 (2.715)	-.11362 (.166)
L1	.36759 (1.470)	.20911 (.199)	.22625 (.108)	.59117 (9.115)	.33746 (1.288)
L2	.27839 (1.440)	-.28753 (.644)	-.46067 (.757)	.30497 (4.215)	.06886 (.093)
L3	.58938 (2.857)	.19885 (.138)	.23626 (.089)	.28846 (1.574)	.24845 (.526)
FAMSIZE	.48277 (5.697)	-.00819 (.001)	.50550 (1.152)	.45501 (11.552)	.15462 (.584)
HMSTATUS	.37373 (3.434)	-.35009 (1.072)	.43132 (.754)	.41886 (10.243)	.31963 (2.622)
HINCOME	1.13267 (76.286)	2.68670 (17.524)	1.68117 (30.616)	1.53577 (65.620)	1.64714 (176.850)
HAGE	.00617 (1.673)	-.00051 (.000)	.01186 (.669)	.00743 (7.676)	-.00511 (1.629)
HEDSEI	.03135 (4.803)	.05347 (4.396)	.32044 (16.110)		
HSEI			-.53550 (5.652)	1.2038 (7.324)	
HEDUC1		4.93214 (3.127)			
HEDON		-.53670 (3.409)			
HSEON				-.12679 (6.660)	.02504 (32.806)
CONSTANT	-7.73705	-19.56151	-14.82986	-10.3379	-11.05379
d.f.	147	145	146	146	147
Adj.R^2	.87948	.81879	.81618	.93968	.93741

continued on next page

EXHIBIT 7.12. *Continued*

	PERSCARE	VACATION	CLUBS	TV
R1	-.41305 (2.740)	.03773 (.010)	1.87011 (6.041)	.23675 (.109)
R2	-.06113 (.098)	.24112 (.670)	1.41823 (5.347)	.02558 (.002)
R3	-.55534 (5.187)	.84786 (5.318)	1.23861 (2.628)	.24741 (.124)
L1	.61317 (6.076)	-.38026 (1.028)	-.38736 (.246)	-.25462 (.126)
L2	.43550 (5.208)	-.28220 (.962)	-1.28961 (4.661)	-.48654 (.785)
L3	.65350 (5.269)	-1.28960 (9.023)	-.07054 (.006)	-1.46516 (3.197)
FAMSIZE	.52720 (9.684)	-.64679 (6.411)	-.85191 (2.572)	.15211 (.097)
HMSTATUS	.28376 (2.357)	-.25439 (.833)	-.37580 (.442)	-1.08232 (4.139)
HINCOME	1.67695 (17.303)	3.68776 (36.804)	-.37512 (.118)	2.77683 (5.727)
HAGE	.04538 (37.592)	.00989 (.786)	-.03500 (.025)	.00422 (.039)
HEDSEI	-.1709 (3.273)	.37509 (6.933)		.814133 (8.963)
HSEI	.5075 (4.739)	-.82211 (5.470)		-2.13801 (10.152)
HEDUC1	4.72602 (8.657)	6.26804 (6.698)	-9.54338 (4.195)	7.05993 (2.332)
HEDON	-.41868 (5.157)	-.77829 (7.837)	1.12568 (5.368)	-1.05110 (3.923)
HSEON			.04790 (17.064)	
CONSTANT	-15.96288	-25.92839	3.78179	-14.58127
d.f.	144	144	145	144
Adj.R^2	.88123	.91743	.83292	.38454

EXHIBIT 7.12. *Continued*

	MUSIC	CAMP	READING	GIFTS
R1	-.79583 (.645)	.47396 (.376)	-.02468 (.013)	.41072 (.978)
R2	1.83590 (6.439)	1.22722 (4.606)	-.28510 (2.602)	.32967 (1.182)
R3	1.73423 (3.326)	2.10238 (8.346)	.53214 (5.841)	.47126 (1.399)
L1	-1.15382 (1.153)	-.26336 (.108)	.24106 (1.147)	-.57630 (1.637)
L2	-.92951 (1.295)	-.73651 (1.449)	-.06843 (.158)	.01952 (.003)
L3	-1.61855 (1.703)	.16615 (.033)	-.20767 (.650)	-.09135 (.031)
FAMSIZE	.26732 (.166)	-.28739 (.341)	-.46166 (9.094)	-1.32283 (23.107)
HMSTATUS	1.17118 (2.680)	-1.6444 (8.165)	-.47734 (8.580)	-.52756 (3.097)
HINCOME	1.89937 (32.067)	-1.88016 (2.993)	1.43763 (20.934)	1.56451 (123.876)
HAGE	-.04280 (8.785)	-.05546 (5.929)	-.00791 (1.519)	.02157 (12.705)
HEDSEI				
HSEI				
HEDUC1		-13.89888 (8.493)	2.323461 (2.994)	
HEDON		1.53179 (9.467)	-.19751 (1.990)	
HSEON			.01605 (23.061)	
CONSTANT	-14.58127	22.07827	-9.97828	-8.57331
d.f.	148	146	145	148
Adj.R^2	.38454	.78586	.94383	.74210

lifestyle differentiation, forcing a nonlinear function over the entire distribution.

It has been argued that region and location effects should exist because these factors impose structural constraints on the degree and form of choice to which individuals are subject, and because prices may vary by location and region. The lack of location effects in either the basic or final models may stem from several sources. It is entirely possible that a quantity (price) effect exists but is balanced out by price (quantity) effects in such a manner that the same level of expenditures are produced. It is also possible that the price effect is relative, that is, prices vary, and income varies relative to prices, so that a constant effect on expenditures is found across locations.

Several other possibilities must also be considered. First, these measures may not adequately indicate the differential constraints imposed by locations; to some extent this is no doubt true. Second, while it is clear that access to opportunities differs across locations, it is easy to overestimate the extent to which this is the case. Finally, while opportunities may vary by location, it is not necessarily the case that individuals take advantage of these differential opportunities to the extent that an effect is observed. For example, residents of small towns do not have easy access to the opera or theatre, unless they are within reasonable driving distance of a larger place, whereas the residents of the larger place clearly have easier access. If the latter do not take advantage of the access differential, no differentiation emerges.

There are clear region effects in both the initial and final models, with a tendency for the effects to occur in the same equations, except CLUBS, for this set of variables. The effects, however, are not easily interpreted. There is no particular set of patterns that account for the significant effects across the equations, and thus it is difficult to make substantive conclusions. It is clear that region should be controlled for, however.

In model 1, the family size (FAMSIZE) coefficients are significant in 6 of 17 equations, and the marital status (HMSTATUS) coefficients are also significant in the same number of equations. In the final set of equations, family size is significant 8 of 17 times, marital status 4 of 17 times. In the CASCLOTH and READING equations both variables have significant coefficients in the final model. Inspection of the pattern of significant effects in initial and final models reveals some consistency. It is also clear that the significant marital status and family size effects discovered in the basic model are not always present in the final model. Furthermore, in some equations, significant effects due to these variables do not show up until socioeconomic factors have been controlled.

In the final model, the effect of marital status, when significant, is to increment marginal expenditures for the variable CASCLOTH and to decrease marginal expenditures on TV, CAMP, and READING. A consistent interpretation of the pattern of significance is not forthcoming. Among the significant coefficients, the results make sense, indicating in part that the recreational activities of the married may be somewhat more home-oriented.

The most interesting finding about HMSTATUS is its general lack of importance, indicating that it is not all that salient in the production of lifestyle variation. What does appear to be salient in this regard is FAMSIZE.

For FAMSIZE, there are significant effects in the equations for FOODHOME, ALCOHOL, TEXTILES, CASCLOTH, PERSCARE, GIFTS, VACATION, and READING. *Ceteris paribus,* increases in family size are accompanied by increases in FOODHOME, TEXTILES, CASCLOTH, PERSCARE and by decreases in ALCOHOL, VACATION, GIFTS, and READING. From Exhibit 7.12 it is clear that FAMSIZE, when significant, operates as expected. For weakly superior and normal goods, increases in family size are generally accompanied by increments to expenditures; for strongly superior goods, increases are generally accompanied by decreased expenditures. Thus, family size operates as a structural constraint on a fixed resource, the household income level, forcing shifts in the pattern of expenditures away from luxuries and toward those goods and services that are necessary or normal.

In essence, then, family size, rather than marital status produces lifestyle differentiation by forcing the shifts described in the pattern of expenditures. Net of FAMSIZE, HMSTATUS does not have clear effects on lifestyle differentiation. That is, marital status, in and of itself, does not appear to constitute a salient status, at least with respect to lifestyle differentiation.

Effects of the Socioeconomic Variables

In those models with interactions among the socioeconomic variables, a meaningful discussion of the main effects is precluded. In a model without interactions, the partial derivative of the regression function with respect to the variable in question is estimated by the regression coefficient of that variable. In equations of the form estimated here, the partial with respect to a variable often depends upon several regression coefficients, as illustrated in the previous chapter, and upon levels of the explanatory variables. The main effect parameter can be interpreted as the partial derivative of the regression function with respect to a variable only when the level(s) of the appropriate other variable(s) is (are) zero. However, as is the case in these data, when such a level is outside the range of the actual data itself, it need not make sense to render such an interpretation, and any such interpretation is artificial at best.

In Exhibits 7.13, 7.14, and 7.15, the estimated partials for the variables income (HINCOME), education (HEDUC1), and occupational status (HSEI) are presented, along with their standard deviations and t ratios, at particular levels of the appropriate explanatory variables. Since the means are stochastic, it is not quite appropriate to use the t distribution for testing statistical hypotheses. Therefore, the mean level is viewed as a fixed, chosen medium level. The low level is for a working-class head with $6400 and 8 years of education; the high level is for a middle-class professional worker with approximately $13,000 and 16 years of education.

On the basis of two tailed tests, with $\alpha = .05$, FOODAWAY, DECORAT, DRSCLOTH, CLUBS, MUSIC, and GIFTS are strongly superior, regardless of position in the socioeconomic hierarchy. Similarly, FOODHOME is always weakly superior, and FURNITUR, TEXTILES, TV, and READING are normal with respect to income. At the low level, HOUSING is weakly superior, ALCOHOL, CAMP, and PERSCARE are normal, and VACATION and CASCLOTH are strongly superior. At the middle and high levels, HOUSING and CASCLOTH are normal, PERSCARE is weakly superior, and ALCOHOL and CAMP are strongly superior. Finally, VACATION is strongly superior at the middle level, but normal at the high level.

The items HOUSING, TEXTILES, and DECORAT are always education superior. Similarly, FOODHOME, FOODAWAY, ALCOHOL, FURNITUR, CAMP, READING, GIFTS, CASCLOTH, DRSCLOTH, VACATION, CLUBS, TV, and MUSIC are normal with respect to education. PERSCARE is superior at the low level, but normal at the other levels.

FURNITUR, TEXTILES, DRSCLOTH, CLUBS, and READING emerge as status superior, irrespective of level. Additionally, at the low level, CASCLOTH and PERSCARE are superior; they are normal at the other levels. FOODHOME, FOODAWAY, HOUSING, MUSIC, CAMP, and GIFTS are status normal at all levels. DECORAT is normal at the low level, superior at the middle and high levels. VACATION is normal at low and middle levels, superior at the high level. Finally, ALCOHOL and TV are normal at the middle and high levels, but status inferior at the low level.

It is tempting to weave this mass of detail into a coherent story about the specific items and to extract from this general conclusions about the

EXHIBIT 7.13*

*Estimated Elasticities, Standard Deviations (s.d.), and t Ratios at the Low Level** of HSEI, HEDUC1, and HINCOME*

	Income, s.d., t	Education, s.d., t	Status, s.d., t
FOODHOME (d.f.=144)	.341, .072, -9.170	-.106, .222, -.478	.051, .029, 1.766
FOODAWAY (d.f.=146)	1.559, .110, 5.097	.141, .321, .440	0
ALCOHOL (d.f.=146)	1.207, .235, .883	0	-.235, .099, -2.365
HOUSING (d.f.=147)	.817, .090, -2.030	.605, .093, 6.514	0
FURNITUR (d.f.=147)	1.571, .245, 1.750	.390, .676, .058	.111, .053, 2.097
TEXTILES (d.f.=145)	1.133, .130, 1.023	.093, .042, 2.192	.065, .030, 2.192
DECORAT (d.f.=146)	1.682, .304, 2.242	.952, .237, 4.014	.131, .100, 1.308
CASCLOTH (d.f.=146)	1.159, .081, 1.968	0	.093, .036, 2.562
DRSCLOTH (d.f.=147)	1.722, .116, 6.241	0	.219, .038, 5.732
PERSCARE (d.f.=144)	.806, .152, -1.273	1.058, .468, 2.261	.152, .062, 2.452
VACATION (d.f.=144)	2.069, .229, 4.668	.588, .704, .836	-.042, .093, -.452
CLUBS (d.f.=145)	2.108, .407, 2.724	.317, 1.123, .283	.420, .102, 4.133
TV (d.f.=144)	.591, .465, -.879	.270, 1.216, .222	-.445, .178, -2.498
MUSIC (d.f.=148)	1.899, .335, 2.681	0	0
CAMP (d.f.=146)	1.305, .393, .777	-.481, 1.149, -.418	0
READING (d.f.=145)	1.075, .117, .635	.593, .322, 1.841	.141, .029, 4.795
GIFTS (d.f.=148)	1.565, .141, 4.016	0	0

*All calculations are rounded to 3 digits. For HINCOME the null value is 1; otherwise, it is 0.

**HSEI = 2.969388; exp{HSEI} = 19.479
HEDUC1 = 2.07944; exp{HEDUC1} = 8.0
HINCOME = 8.7598; exp{HINCOME} = 6372.84

EXHIBIT 7.14*

*Estimated Elasticities, Standard Deviations (s.d.), and t Ratios at the Middle Level** of HSEI, HEDUC1, and HINCOME*

	Income, s.d., t	Education, s.d., t	Status, s.d., t
FOODHOME (d.f.=144)	.421, .081, -7.115	-.139, .221, -.629	-.039, .026, -.354
FOODAWAY (d.f.=146)	1.392, .125, 3.138	.010, .313, .031	0
ALCOHOL (d.f.=146)	1.480, .221, 2.175	0	-.093, .092, -1.010
HOUSING (d.f.=147)	.843, .088, -1.785	.629, .097, 6.514	0
FURNITUR (d.f.=147)	1.363, .275, 1.313	.239, .653, .366	.319, .063, 2.097
TEXTILES (d.f.=145)	1.133, .130, 1.023	.114, .052, 2.192	.077, .035, 2.192
DECORAT (d.f.=146)	1.682, .304, 2.242	1.165, .290, 4.014	.255, .093, 2.762
CASCLOTH (d.f.=146)	1.075, .076, .981	0	.049, .034, 1.443
DRSCLOTH (d.f.=147)	1.738, .114, 6.482	0	.228, .040, 5.732
PERSCARE (d.f.=144)	.644, .172, -2.065	.292, .468, .623	.086, .055, 1.578
VACATION (d.f.=144)	1.768, .259, 2.963	.556, .709, .785	.103, .082, 1.259
CLUBS (d.f.=145)	2.573, .449, 3.504	.708, 1.094, .647	.436, .106, 4.133
TV (d.f.=144)	.185, .529, -1.540	.448, 1.355, .331	-.130, .156, -.832
MUSIC (d.f.=148)	1.899, .335, 2.681	0	0
CAMP (d.f.=146)	1.898, .447, 2.008	.051, 1.120, .045	0
READING (d.f.=145)	1.009, .129, .069	.525, .314, 1.673	.146, .030, 4.795
GIFTS (d.f.=148)	1.565, .141, 4.016	0	0

*All calculations are rounded to 3 digits. For HINCOME, the null value is 1; otherwise, it is 0.

**HSEI = 3.6362; exp{HSEI} = 37.947

  HEDUC1 = 2.4663; exp{HEDUC1} = 11.779

  HINCOME = 9.1069; exp{HINCOME} = 9017.298

EXHIBIT 7.15*

*Estimated Elasticities, Standard Deviations (s.d.), and t Ratios at the High Level** of HSEI, HEDUC1, and HINCOME*

	Income, s.d., t			Education, s.d., t			Status, s.d., t		
FOODHOME (d.f.=144)	.485,	.097,	-5.319	-.173,	.225,	-.772	-.057,	.031,	-1.855
FOODAWAY (d.f.=146)	1.259,	.023,	11.495	-.141,	.312,	-.452	0		
ALCOHOL (d.f.=146)	1.758,	.247,	3.071	0			.049,	.110,	.448
HOUSING (d.f.=147)	.864,	.123,	-1.101	.653,	.100,	6.514	0		
FURNITUR (d.f.=147)	1.199,	.325,	.612	.089,	.651,	.137	.148,	.007,	2.097
TEXTILES (d.f.=145)	1.133,	.130,	1.023	.135,	.062,	2.192	.087,	.040,	2.192
DECORAT (d.f.=146)	1.682,	.304,	2.242	1.383,	.119,	11.652	.353,	.093,	3.788
CASCLOTH (d.f.=146)	.989,	.086,	-.131	0			.005,	.040,	.130
DRSCLOTH (d.f.=147)	1.755,	.112,	6.733	0			.237,	.041,	5.732
PERSCARE (d.f.=144)	.516,	.205,	-2.361	.030,	.476,	.064	.034,	.065,	.521
VACATION (d.f.=144)	1.530,	.309,	1.716	.528,	.716,	.738	.218,	.097,	2.246
CLUBS (d.f.=145)	2.953,	.529,	3.689	1.099,	1.091,	1.008	.453,	.110,	4.133
TV (d.f.=144)	-.137,	.626,	-1.817	.635,	1.369,	.464	.119,	.185,	.643
MUSIC (d.f.=148)	1.899,	.335,	2.681	0			0		
CAMP (d.f.=146)	2.367,	.537,	2.545	.583,	1.175,	.496	0		
READING (d.f.=145)	.959,	.152,	-.268	.456,	.313,	1.459	.152,	.032,	4.795
GIFTS (d.f.=148)	1.565,	.141,	4.016	0			0		

*All calculations are rounded to 3 digits. For HINCOME, the null value is 1; otherwise, it it 0.

**HSEI = 4.31442; exp{HSEI} = 74.77
HEDUC1 = 2.7725887; exp{HEDUC1} = 16
HINCOME = 9.454; exp{HINCOME} = 12759.1

effects of the socioeconomic variables. For example, it might be noted that expenditures on ALCOHOL, CLUBS, and CAMP rise more rapidly with increases in income at the high level of the socioeconomic hierarchy than at the low level. For FOODAWAY, FURNITUR, and VACATION, the pattern is reversed. Apart from the specific effects on the items, this appears to indicate that net of the effects of education and occupational status, higher status people spend marginal increments to income differently than lower status people. That is, as income changes, differential placement in the socioeconomic order conditions the form of a lifestyle.

Above and beyond the fact that all of the conclusions are premature because it has not been ascertained that these income elasticities are statistically different from one another at the various levels, it is incorrect to argue in such a fashion, despite the temptation to do so. The specific conclusions, while interesting, are necessarily descriptive. Emphasis on these deflects attention from the primary task of isolating the structural sources of differentiation. Furthermore, the specific conclusions do not admit generalization. A coherent story is obtained by focusing on relations that appear to be significant, to the exclusion of those that are not. By failing to consider the latter, no valid general conclusions about the effects of the socioeconomic variables can be reached. Any general conclusion must rest upon the consideration of all the data, as opposed to a subset that is preselected precisely because its relations are statistically and substantively significant.

While it may seem otherwise, there are a plethora of general findings extractable from the mass of detail. First, it is clear that income differentiates consumption, hence lifestyle. Second, on the basis of two tailed tests at the .05 level, 13 of 17 items are normal with respect to education at the low level, and 4 are education superior. At the middle and high levels, 14 of 17 items are normal, 3 superior. Furthermore, HOUSING, TEXTILES, and DECORAT are education superior at all levels. That is, with the exception of these three items, the effects of education are generally statistically insignificant. Net of income and status, education appears to contribute only marginally to lifestyle differentiation. However, the effects of status are significant nine, six, and seven times, respectively, at low, middle, and high levels of the socioeconomic hierarchy. Net of changes in income and education, status is instrumental to the explanation of lifestyle differentiation, and it appears that status is most salient at the low level of the socioeconomic order.

It is also instructive to consider the manner in which the elasticities are related to one another. In Exhibit 7.16, under the rules described therein, the education and occupational status elasticities are crossclassified against one another. Inspection of the tables seems to warrant the

EXHIBIT 7.16

Elasticities of Education Crossclassified by Elasticities of Occupational Status at Different Levels* of the Socioeconomic Hierarchy

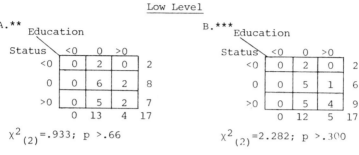

Low Level

A.**
Education

Status	<0	0	>0	
<0	0	2	0	2
0	0	6	2	8
>0	0	5	2	7
	0	13	4	17

$\chi^2_{(2)}$ =.933; p >.66

B.***
Education

Status	<0	0	>0	
<0	0	2	0	2
0	0	5	1	6
>0	0	5	4	9
	0	12	5	17

$\chi^2_{(2)}$ =2.282; p >.300

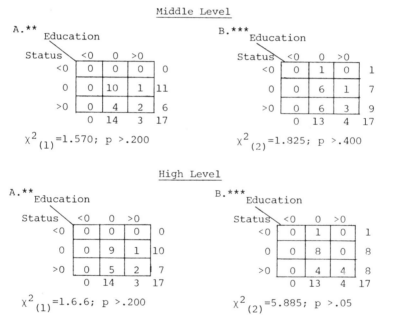

Middle Level

A.**
Education

Status	<0	0	>0	
<0	0	0	0	0
0	0	10	1	11
>0	0	4	2	6
	0	14	3	17

$\chi^2_{(1)}$ =1.570; p >.200

B.***
Education

Status	<0	0	>0	
<0	0	1	0	1
0	0	6	1	7
>0	0	6	3	9
	0	13	4	17

$\chi^2_{(2)}$ =1.825; p >.400

High Level

A.**
Education

Status	<0	0	>0	
<0	0	0	0	0
0	0	9	1	10
>0	0	5	2	7
	0	14	3	17

$\chi^2_{(1)}$ =1.6.6; p >.200

B.***
Education

Status	<0	0	>0	
<0	0	1	0	1
0	0	8	0	8
>0	0	4	4	8
	0	13	4	17

$\chi^2_{(2)}$ =5.885; p >.05

---

*Levels are defined as in the previous exhibits.

**A is based on a two tailed test of the status elasticity against the null that it is equal to 0. In both cases, the significance level is .05.

***As above, with the exception that the null hypotheses are rejected if the t-ratios have modulus greater than or equal to 1.

conclusion that the substantive effects of status and education are not associated, irrespective of level. Furthermore, χ^2 tests verify this conclusion, subject to the assumptions (a) that it is not problematic to view the marginals that are 0 as structural, and (b) that the small expected values in some cells under the null is not problematic.

In Exhibit 7.17, the education and income elasticities are crossclassified in three-by-three tables, at the low, middle, and high levels, under the rules described in that exhibit. Apart from the fact that it is of interest to search for patterns, there is a more specific reason for the exhibit. Michael (1972) has argued that the effects of education reflect "efficiency in consumption," rather than "tastes and preferences."

The argument implies that the education elasticities are less than 0,0, greater than 0 when the income elasticities are less than 1,1, greater than 1, respectively. In other words, the crossclassification matrix in the exhibit should be diagonal. In his analysis, Michael finds partial support for this argument. In economic parlance, our initial hypothesis is that education operates by producing changes in tastes and preferences. If the data fail to disconfirm Michael's hypothesis, the results are also consistent with the interpretation that hinges on tastes and preferences. That is, the hypothesis that it is changes in tastes and preferences that are reflected by differences in education can be confirmed by a variety of outcomes, including the case where the crossclassification matrix is diagonal. However, it has already been demonstrated that in these data the salience of education to lifestyle differentiation is marginal at all three levels.

As a consequence, it is not surprising to find that the results offer little support for Michael's theory. At most 5 of 17 entries lie on the diagonal of the crossclassification. Further evidence is obtained from the regression of the education elasticities on the income elasticities. At the low level the correlation between the elasticities is .008, which, with 15 degrees of freedom is not significantly different from 0. The regression coefficient is .006, the intercept .252. The results imply that when the income elasticity is less than -40.938, the education elasticity is less than 0; otherwise, it is greater. At the middle level, the correlation is .139 (not significantly different from 0), the regression coefficient .081, the intercept .162. If the income elasticity is less than -2.002, the education elasticity is less than 0, otherwise it is greater. If the income elasticity is 1, the education elasticity is predicted to be .173. Finally, at the high level, the correlation is .306 (not significant), the regression coefficient .186, the intercept .061. The education elasticity is predicted to be 0 when the income elasticity is $-.327$; when the income elasticity is greater, so is the education elasticity. If the income elasticity is 1, the predicted education elasticity is .247.

It must be noted that the "efficiency theory" does not specify that the

EXHIBIT 7.17

Elasticities of Education Crossclassified by Elasticities of Income at Different Levels* of the Socioeconomic Hierarchy

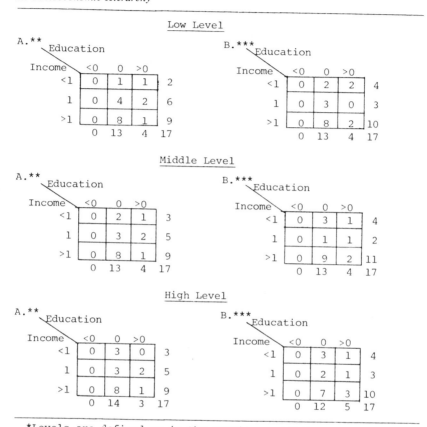

Low Level

A.**

Income \ Education	<0	0	>0	
<1	0	1	1	2
1	0	4	2	6
>1	0	8	1	9
	0	13	4	17

B.***

Income \ Education	<0	0	>0	
<1	0	2	2	4
1	0	3	0	3
>1	0	8	2	10
	0	13	4	17

Middle Level

A.**

Income \ Education	<0	0	>0	
<1	0	2	1	3
1	0	3	2	5
>1	0	8	1	9
	0	13	4	17

B.***

Income \ Education	<0	0	>0	
<1	0	3	1	4
1	0	1	1	2
>1	0	9	2	11
	0	13	4	17

High Level

A.**

Income \ Education	<0	0	>0	
<1	0	3	0	3
1	0	3	2	5
>1	0	8	1	9
	0	14	3	17

B.***

Income \ Education	<0	0	>0	
<1	0	3	1	4
1	0	2	1	3
>1	0	7	3	10
	0	12	5	17

*Levels are defined as in the previous exhibits.
**A is based on a 1 tailed test of the income elasticity against the null that it is equal to 1, crossclassified against the results from testing the education against the null that it is equal to 0. In both cases, the significance level is .05.
***As above, with the exception that the null hypotheses are rejected if the t ratios have modulus greater than or equal to 1.

relationship between the elasticities is linear, as has been assumed for purposes of estimating the regression line. Nonetheless, these descriptive calculations supplement the crossclassifications. Again, the evidence is unambiguous and offers little or no support for Michael's theory. At all three levels, the education elasticity is greater than 0 at a point where the income elasticity is less than 0, that is, at some point outside the range of the independent variable. Only for strongly superior goods is the prediction supported.

The models estimated here differ from Michael's in several respects, not the least of which is the inclusion of occupational status in this analysis. The relative salience of occupational status over education is not surprising if education is viewed as a means to the attainment of occupational status, the latter being the proximate cause of lifestyle differentiation. By implication, the effects of education are then indirect. With this in mind, proponents of the "efficiency theory" might argue for the same pattern between the income and status elasticities as was expected for the relationship between income and education elasticities. To address this hypothetical issue, Exhibit 7.18 is presented. At most 7 of 17 items are consistent with the predictions of the theory; certainly the support is stronger here, although marginal at best. Again, correlation coefficients, regression coefficients and intercepts are presented for the regression of the occupational status elasticities on the income elasticities. At the low level, the correlation is .412, significant at the .1 level. The regression coefficient and intercept are, respectively, .149 and −.160. The data imply that the status elasticity is 0 when the income elasticity is 1.069; if the income elasticity is less than this value, the status elasticity is predicted to be less than 0, otherwise, greater. At the middle level, the correlation is .587, the regression coefficient .142, the intercept −.100. At this level, the status elasticity is 0 when the income elasticity is .704; when the income elasticity is 1, the status elasticity is predicted to be .042. Finally, at the high level, the correlation is .457, the regression coefficient .087, the intercept −.011. The data imply that the status elasticity is 0 when the income elasticity is .130; if the income elasticity is 1, the implied value of the status elasticity is .076. Descriptively, the "efficiency theory" receives some support from the regressions, particularly at the low level, and somewhat less at the middle and high levels. The support is not that strong, but it would be a mistake to ignore it completely. It should be recalled that these results are entirely consistent with the more "natural" interpretation that occupational status is instrumental in differentiating tastes and preferences. Viewed in this fashion, the pattern indicates the tendency for the effects of status and income to complement one another. That is, a similar lifestyle change may be brought about by varying either levels of occupational status or income, and this appears to be the case at all levels of the stratification system, notwithstanding the fact that the tendency is most pronounced at the middle level. At the risk of some distortion, one might say that occupational status and income operate with some degree of interchangeability in the production of lifestyle.

EXHIBIT 7.18

Elasticities of Occupational Status Crossclassified by Elasticities of Income at Different Levels* of the Socioeconomic Hierarchy

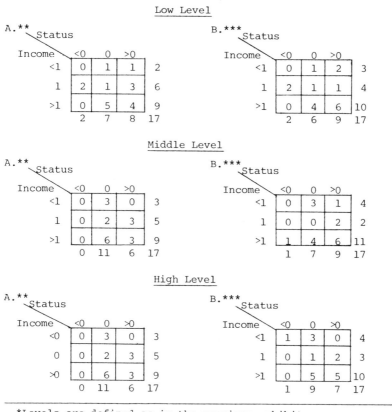

Low Level

A.**

Income \ Status	<0	0	>0	
<1	0	1	1	2
1	2	1	3	6
>1	0	5	4	9
	2	7	8	17

B.***

Income \ Status	<0	0	>0	
<1	0	1	2	3
1	2	1	1	4
>1	0	4	6	10
	2	6	9	17

Middle Level

A.**

Income \ Status	<0	0	>0	
<1	0	3	0	3
1	0	2	3	5
>1	0	6	3	9
	0	11	6	17

B.***

Income \ Status	<0	0	>0	
<1	0	3	1	4
1	0	0	2	2
>1	1	4	6	11
	1	7	9	17

High Level

A.**

Income \ Status	<0	0	>0	
<0	0	3	0	3
0	0	2	3	5
>0	0	6	3	9
	0	11	6	17

B.***

Income \ Status	<0	0	>0	
<1	1	3	0	4
1	0	1	2	3
>1	0	5	5	10
	1	9	7	17

*Levels are defined as in the previous exhibits.
**A is based on a 1 tailed test of the income elasticity against the null that it is equal to 1, crossclassified against the results from testing the occupational status elasticity against the null that it is equal to 0. In both cases, the significance level is .05.
***As above, with the exception that the null hypotheses are rejected if the t ratios have modulus greater than or equal to 1.

Another way to look at the relationships between income, education, and status is to examine the differences between elasticities at different levels of the socioeconomic hierarchy. In this regard, both statistically significant and substantively significant differences are of interest.

Exhibit 7.19 presents tests for differences between the three elasticities at the high and low levels of the socioeconomic hierarchy. Inspection of the first column reveals that the income elasticities are different at the two levels for 11 of the 17 differences, based on a two tailed test with a significance level of .05. This indicates that occupational status and/or education do tend to condition the relationship between income and lifestyle. In the second column, the education elasticities differ for 7 of the 17 differences, which indicates a slightly weaker tendency for income and/or status to affect the relationship between education and lifestyle. That is, propensities created by education tend to be less contingent on levels of status and/or income than propensities created by income are contingent on status and/or education.

Turning to the third column, the status elasticities are different for 11 of the 17 items, indicating that the effects of occupational status are conditioned by levels of income and/or education.

Singling out the statistically significant differences is preliminary to an examination of the substantive differences in elasticities. This issue is addressed in Exhibit 7.20. In this exhibit, the differences are crossclassified in accordance with the coding scheme used in the two previous exhibits. All significant differences (based on a two tailed test at the .05 level) are utilized; if a difference is insignificant, and the two point estimates of the elasticity are such that the entry lies off the diagonal, that item is excluded from the particular crossclassification. While levels of education and/or status condition the income elasticities, 11 of the elasticities have the same substantive interpretation at the two levels of the socioeconomic hierarchy. In six cases, they do not. At the low level the elasticity in the HOUSING equation is less than 1, but 1 at the high level. In the PERSCARE, TV, ALCOHOL, and CAMP equations, the elasticities are 1 at the low level; the first two are less than 1 at the high level, the second two are greater than 1 at the high level. Additionally, the elasticity for the CASCLOTH equation is greater than 1 at the low level, but 1 at the high level.

The education elasticities are remarkably consistent across levels, primarily because the effects of education are minimal or nonexistent in most equations at most levels of the socioeconomic hierarchy. At the low level, the elasticities are greater than 0 for the PERSCARE, HOUSING, DECORAT, and TEXTILES equations; at the high level, the elasticity in the PERSCARE equation is 0, but otherwise there is no change. In the context of the insignificance of the education effects, the exhibit reveals primarily the stability of insignificance. Finally, the status elasticities appear to change substantively 6 of 16 times, for the equations ALCOHOL, TV, DECORAT, VACATION, FOODHOME, and CASCLOTH. For the

EXHIBIT 7.19*

Differences Between Elasticities at the High and Low Levels of the Socioeconomic Hierarchy

	Income			Education			Status		
	Difference,	s.d.,	t	Difference,	s.d.,	t	Difference,	s.d.,	t
FOODHOME	.144,	.061,	2.374	-.067,	.059,	-1.132	-.109,	.031,	-3.508
FOODAWAY	-.301,	.096,	-3.127	-.301,	.096,	-3.127	0		
ALCOHOL	.551,	.192,	2.868	0			.284,	.099,	2.868
HOUSING	.048,	.007,	6.514	.048,	.007,	6.514	0		
TEXTILES	0			.042,	.019,	2.192	.022,	.010,	2.192
FURNITUR	-.372,	.201,	-1.846	-.301,	.205,	-1.465	.037,	.017,	2.097
DECORAT	0			.431,	.107,	4.014	.222,	.055,	4.014
CASCLOTH	-.171,	.066,	2.581	0			-.088,	.034,	2.581
DRSCLOTH	.034,	.006,	5.731	0			-.017,	.003,	5.731
PERSCARE	-.290,	.128,	-2.271	-1.029,	.126,	-8.178	-.118,	.065,	-1.809
VACATION	-.539,	.193,	-2.779	-.060,	.189,	-.317	.260,	.098,	2.937
CLUBS	.845,	.336,	2.515	.781,	.337,	2.317	.033,	.008,	4.133
TV	-.729,	.368,	-1.980	.365,	.361,	1.013	.564,	.188,	2.994
MUSIC	0			0			0		
CAMP	1.062,	.345,	3.077	1.063,	.346,	3.077	0		
READING	-.115,	.098,	-1.183	-.137,	.097,	-1.411	.011,	.002,	4.795
GIFTS	0			0			0		

*All calculations have been rounded to 3 digits. For the differences, the elasticity at the low level is subtracted from the elasticity at the high level.

EXHIBIT 7.20*

Crossclassification of Elasticities at the High and Low Levels of the Socioeconomic Hierarchy

Income

Low ╲ High	<1	1	>1	
<1	1	1	0	2
1	2	3	2	7
>1	0	1	7	8
	3	5	9	17

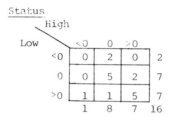

Status

Low ╲ High	<0	0	>0	
<0	0	2	0	2
0	0	5	2	7
>0	1	1	5	7
	1	8	7	16

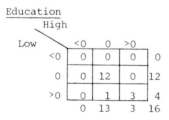

Education

Low ╲ High	<0	0	>0	
<0	0	0	0	0
0	0	12	0	12
>0	0	1	3	4
	0	13	3	16

*Levels are defined as in previous exhibits. In deciding which differences are significant a 2 tailed, .05 level test is utilized. All significant differences are used in constructing the tables in the exhibit; if a difference is insignificant, and the two point estimates of the elasticity are such that the entry in the table for that item lies off the diagonal, that item is excluded from the crossclassification. One tailed, .05 level tests are utilized to discern whether the income elasticities have values less than one or greater than one; the other elasticities are deviated about the value 0. If the null is not rejected, the elasticity is assumed to have the value 1 (income) or the value 0 (occupational status, education).

first two equations, the elasticity is less than 0 at the low level, 0 at the high level; for the next two, the elasticity is 0 at the low level, greater than 0 at the high level. Furthermore, in the FOODHOME equation, the elasticity is greater than 0 at the low level, less than 0 at the high level, while in the CASCLOTH equation, the elasticity is greater than 0 at the low level, 0 at the high level.

The educational differences have already been discussed. The status and income elasticities tend to be different at the low and high levels, and more than 50% of the time, when different, the manner in which these affect the detailed items changes substantively. From these observations, the general conclusion is straightforward. Net of the effects of education and occupational status (income and education), position in the stratification system conditions the manner in which income (status) differentiates lifestyle. Furthermore, the extent to which the substantive effects of the two variables are conditioned is roughly similar.

Summary

In this chapter, regressions for the 17 dependent variables are estimated; the fitting process is elaborated upon at some length, and a variety of issues are taken into consideration during this process. These are best addressed in the text itself. The equations themselves constitute the basis for all subsequent computations and conclusions.

Substantively, there appear to be significant age effects, but no clear pattern of effects emerges that does not defy unambiguous interpretation. In a similar vein, region effects are discovered, but a clear pattern does not emerge; the effects may indicate the presence of price variation across regions. On the more interpretable side, the family size effects, which often exist, operate in an orderly fashion. Increasing family size increments expenditures on necessities and normal items; decreasing family size increments expenditures on luxury items. Hence, family size constrains the manner in which the household income is disposed of: the greater the size, the greater the constraint.

On the other hand, there do not appear to be location or marital status effects. There are a variety of reasons why location effects might not exist, as described in the text. The preferred explanation is that they do not exist because potential access to differential opportunities is not capitalized upon. The lack of marital status effects may occur because family size is included in the equations. If this is the case, it indicates that marital status, in and of itself, does not differentiate among lifestyles. Rather, the constraints imposed by family size produce the variation.

Finally, the effects of the socioeconomic variables are examined at some length. Income and occupational status emerge with greater unconditional importance than education, as described in the text. The effects of status and the effects of education are not associated. However, the effects of status and the effects of income are positively related. That is, to some extent occupational status may be viewed as a substitute for income. To the same extent, income substitutes for status. For example, rich people with less status are able, by virtue of greater financial resources, to interact with and thereby attain a lifestyle similar to that of higher status persons. Education is basically normal, net of the other variables. Therefore, it is not surprising that the relation of substitutability with income does not hold for education. Nor is it surprising that Michael's interpretation of the education elasticities is rejected. Finally, differences between elasticities are compared at the high and low levels of the socioeconomic hierarchy. The effects of income, occupational status, and education are conditioned by level. In particular this is true of the status and income effects. That is, the marginal changes in lifestyle that result from increments or decrements to status and/or income vary by position in the stratification system.

CHAPTER 8

Social Structure and
Stylistic Unity

In this chapter, the issue of stylistic unity is addressed. Stylistic unity is conceptualized in terms of empirical patterns, and its existence is not taken for granted. It is itself an important concept (*a*) because it intervenes between social structure and the lifestyle variables, constituting the proximate cause of the observed lifestyle, and (*b*) because it, rather than the conglomeration of lifestyle variables, constitutes the basis for perception and evaluation of the lifestyle by others. It is also this elusive concept that most social theorists really attempt to address in discussions of lifestyle.

In order to discern the form and degree of stylistic unity, an unrestricted factor model for the 17 items is estimated by means of maximum likelihood. The scale free solution is rotated, and the factors are not constrained to be orthogonal. It is decided that a four factor solution is adequate, the first factor being a *general* factor, the second a *normal, everyday expenditures* factor, the third a *strongly superior entertainment* factor, and the fourth a *weakly superior entertainment* factor.

Standardized loadings less than .25 are assumed to be 0, and in this fashion a pattern matrix of free and fixed entries in the loading matrix is constructed. The factors are viewed as intervening variables, and an identified, linear structural equation model (in this case, a MIMIC model) is constructed to represent both the relationship between the factors and the items and the relationship between the structural variables and the factors. The model is discussed statistically and estimated by means of maximum likelihood. The initial solution is then modified to include several loadings previously assumed to be 0; following this, the model is modified to allow for correlated errors. Finally, estimates whose absolute values are less than their standard errors are dropped, and the model is reestimated.

The substantive conclusions are based upon this final model, and, as in the previous chapter, the effects of the three socioeconomic characteristics often depend upon levels of the other two. Accordingly, both the effects at particular levels and the differences between effects are examined. This yields a rather interesting set of conclusions about the manner in which the socioeconomic characteristics differentially generate variation in stylistic unity.

In light of the final model, the factors are reexamined, and it is concluded that there is an abstract organization of stylistic unity which, it is hypothesized, cuts across large blocks of time and space and is likely to persist in the future.

Lifestyle or Stylistic Unity?

While the initial hypotheses are tested in the preceding chapter, something seems to be missing in this characterization of the problem. Certainly, the results are not descriptively interesting. They tell us little about the actual manner in which people lead their lives, only that the manner appears to depend upon the places people occupy within the societal context. Of course, this is the most important issue at hand, and it has been argued that the description of lifestyles is not essential to an understanding of the more fundamental sources of differentiation. After all, the concrete form of a lifestyle may change in any arbitrary time period while the processes that differentiate among alternative forms persist. In this sense the form of a lifestyle is arbitrary and lacks immediate sociological meaning.

There is another sense in which this is not the case. In Chapter 3, following Hauser, a distinction is made between *style* and *stylistic unity*. By definition, a work of art possesses style. What it may or may not possess is stylistic unity, that is, *consistency* in the application of those formal elements that themselves constitute the style. Similarly, an individual with expressive opportunities possesses a lifestyle, which may or may not have the property that it is "coherent" in some sense.

In art, stylistic unity exists when the elements comprising style are combined in a manner that art historians believe is consistent. Consistency, then, is the essence of stylistic unity. Unfortunately, consistency is a property that is difficult to pin down, being neither logical nor necessary. Rather, it rests on shared perceptions that elements are patterned in a manner that makes some sort of esthetic sense.

In life, as opposed to art, consistency is even more elusive. Life is more fragmented than most works of art, and it is the rare individual whose life is governed by one overriding principle or set of principles, esthetic or otherwise. Furthermore, there is no well integrated community of trained observers who decide what is consistent and what is not. In short, other than those combinations that are excluded by logical necessity (and in life, these are few) one is left to wonder what is consistent and what is not.

The situation is not entirely hopeless. For example, most people would agree that it is not consistent to wear tennis shoes with a suit or to wear a plaid shirt with plaid pants. Since one is less likely to encounter an individual in a suit and tennis shoes than to encounter an individual wearing a plaid shirt and plaid pants, it would appear to be the case that the former behavior is more inconsistent than the latter.

The example, while it may seem facetious, illustrates two points rather well and allows us to proceed toward a formalization of the worldly analogue to artistic consistency. First, there is no logical reason why it should be consistent or inconsistent to wear or not wear such combinations of clothing. Secondly, and crucially, one behavior is more inconsistent than the other, because it occurs less frequently. This provides the key to "consistency" as it applies to the manner in which people carry out their lives. Consistency in this sense is synonymous with notions of empirically reoccuring patterns. That is, the patterns or combinations are consistent because they occur with sufficient frequency that they do not appear to observers as unusual. Patterns that appear irregularly are by and large inconsistent. Thus, it may be argued that stylistic unity within a lifestyle exists when the patterns of behavior that comprise that lifestyle are empirically common, that is, similar patterns are shared by a sufficient number of others, relative to all others.

It should be clear from this discussion that stylistic unity, as a property of a lifestyle, is amenable to empirical inquiry. Indeed, as conceptualized here, it is only through empirical analysis that questions regarding the existence, degree, nature, and concrete form of stylistic unity can be addressed, as the phenomenon is itself empirical.

Less clear are the reasons for interest in stylistic unity. Although justification is not required, there are a number of reasons for which sociologists should find this issue interesting.

The existence of stylistic unity has been assumed by previous researchers, who have unfortunately equated it with the lifestyle itself. (This is unfortunate because if stylistic unity does not exist, such authors are faced with the logical conclusion that lifestyle does not exist; our definitions do not suffer from these defects.) Presumably this occurs because observers mentally attempt to put together the patterns, in order to descriptively place the lifestyle and associate it with other characteristics. In other words, observers see the lifestyle first and then attempt to work backward to the patterns that generate the lifestyle. Thus, notions of consistency and inconsistency are implicitly introduced into the more common notions of lifestyle. This is not important because previous researchers have failed to make important distinctions, thereby falling into a logical trap. Rather, these observations are important because they indicate that descriptive reality, which is summarily mentally created, resides in the patterns observers distinguish.

It is upon this basis that individuals react to and evaluate one another. Furthermore, it is on the basis of perceived descriptive reality that observers associate the differentiation in lifestyles with either the variation in other characteristics or theories utilizing the concept.

For these reasons, it is important to address the question of stylistic unity. The argument about the process of observation indicates that stylistic unity, if it exists, is the proximate source of lifestyle. In other words, the lifestyle itself is a manifestation of stylistic unity. By intervening between social structure and lifestyle, variation in stylistic unity stems from differentiation within the social structure. The effects of social structure on lifestyle are then indirect, because they are channeled through stylistic unity.

Conceptually, stylistic unity has various dimensions. Two are considered here. First, the form of stylistic unity is addressed. Second, the extent to which stylistic unity exists is addressed, albeit indirectly. Conceptually, it should be clear from the outset that while both form and degree are of sociological interest, it is possible for changes in these characteristics to occur while the social structural variables that generate said characteristics retain the same pattern of salience. Thus, as in the previous chapter, the effects of the structural variables are of primary import, at least initially.

There are a variety of conceivable ways to empirically model stylistic unity. In this analysis, the form of stylistic unity is viewed as multidimensional. That is, several stylistic unity variables are allowed for. For the i th observation, this yields the following equation: $y_i = \Lambda_i(s.u._i) + \epsilon_i$, where $s.u._i$ is a k-dimensional vector of stylistic unity variables, ϵ_i and y_i are p-dimensional vectors of stochastic elements and expenditure items, and Λ_i a transformation from real k-space to real p-space, that is, from R^k to

R^p. If k is assumed constant for all i, and $\Lambda_i = \Lambda$ is constant for all i, the equation reduces to $y_i = \Lambda(\mathbf{s.u.}_i) + \epsilon_i$. In addition, it shall be assumed that Λ is a linear transformation. Since stylistic unity is a function of social structure, we may also write $\mathbf{s.u.}_i = \Gamma_i(x_i) + v_i$, where v_i is a k-dimensional vector of stochastic elements, x_i a q-dimensional vector of social structural variables, and Γ_i a transformation from R^q to R^k. It is assumed that $\Gamma_i = \Gamma$ for all i, and Γ is a linear transformation. Substituting the second equation into the first yields $y_i = \Lambda\Gamma(x_i) + (\Lambda v_i + \epsilon_i)$, the reduced form that was discussed in the preceding chapter.

Exploratory Factor Analysis

The model $\mathbf{y} = \Lambda(\mathbf{s.u.}) + \epsilon$ is now considered in greater detail. Suppose, without loss of generality, that $E(\mathbf{s.u.}) = E(\epsilon) = 0$, and $E((\mathbf{s.u.})(\mathbf{s.u.})') = \Omega$, a positive definite $k \times k$ matrix whose diagonal elements are 1, that is, Ω is the correlation matrix of the unobserved stylistic unity variables. Let $E((\epsilon)(\epsilon')) = \Theta$ be a nonsingular matrix with off-diagonal elements set to 0, and diagonal elements greater than 0, and let $E((\mathbf{s.u.})(\epsilon'))$ be the $k \times p$ 0 matrix. Then Σ_{yy}, the population variance-covariance matrix of the expenditure items, is given by $\Sigma_{yy} = \Lambda\Omega\Lambda' + \Theta$.

Notice that when $\mathbf{s.u.}$ is replaced by $M(\mathbf{s.u.})$, where M is a nonsingular linear transformation of order k, and Λ by $\Lambda M^{-1} = \Lambda^*$, $\Sigma_{yy} = \Lambda\Omega\Lambda' + \Theta$, as before. That is, there are an infinity of solutions Λ^* that generate the same Σ_{yy}. For the time being, suppose that the pattern of 0's in Λ is such that postmultiplication of Λ by any nonsingular matrix would alter the pattern; then Λ may be considered unique, given that a "suitable" Θ matrix exists. The equations, together with the assumptions on the form of Λ constitute a case of the "restricted" factor model (Lawley and Maxwell, 1971).

A priori, neither the value of k nor the form of Λ is known, as required by the restricted model. In practice, this situation is neither unusual nor intractable, so long as an exploratory approach is justifiable. That such an approach is justifiable follows from the previous discussion, in which the empirical character of stylistic unity is highlighted.

The exploratory approach taken here relies heavily upon the unrestricted factor model (Lawley and Maxwell, 1971). Assuming multivariate normality and using the method of maximum likelihood, the function $\log|\Sigma_{yy}| + \text{tr}(S_{yy}\Sigma_{yy}^{-1}) - \log|S_{yy}| - p$, where S_{yy} is the sample covariance matrix and p is defined as before, is to be minimized with respect to Λ and Θ for a given value of k, subject to the constraint that $\Lambda'\Omega^{-1}\Lambda$ is a diagonal matrix. The solution has the virtue that it is scale free (Timm, 1975). It may be proved (Lawley and Maxwell, 1971; p. 35) that the minimum value of the function, denoted here by f_k is such that $nf_k = -2 \log \lambda_k$, where λ_k is the likelihood ratio and n the sample size. Under H_k: there exist k factors, the test statistic $(n - (2p + 5)/6 - 2k/3)f_k$ has asymptotic distribution χ^2 with $1/2[(p - k)^2 - (p + k)]$ degrees of freedom. Thus we can sequentially test that the number of factors is $0, 1, \ldots, k$, stopping when an adequate significance level has been reached. The rotation problem remains. Several methods of attacking the problem are available. Here, the initial solution is analytically rotated in order to arrive at a solution that approximates a simple structure (Thurstone, 1947; Harman, 1967), using a direct oblimin rotation with $\gamma = 0$ (Jennrich and Sampson, 1966). After rotation, near 0 elements of $\hat{\Lambda}$ (loadings) are then assumed to equal 0, and an identified, restricted factor model is postulated. After this task is accomplished the full model with equations $y = \Lambda(\text{s.u.}) + \epsilon$ and s.u. $= \Gamma x + v$ can be reconsidered.

Exhibit 8.1 presents the correlation matrix for the 17 expenditure items. Maximum likelihood solutions for several values of k (recall that the solution is scale free, so that it does not matter whether the correlation matrix or the variance–covariance matrix is factored) are computed, and H_k is tested. For H_0, the test is that Σ_{vv} is diagonal. This can be rejected, indicating the existence of stylistic unity. For H_1 the test statistic has value 609.180, with 117 degrees of freedom and p value less than .001. For H_2, H_3, and H_4, the values are 234.212, 130.543, and 97.865, respectively, with degrees of freedom 103, 88, and 74. Under the appropriate reference distribution, the significance levels of the tests are less than .001, .005, and .05, respectively. While H_4 is technically rejected, it should be noted that when the sample size is moderately large, even small values of f_k lead to rejection of H_k. In Exhibit 8.2 the residual matrix $R - \hat{R}$ is given, $\hat{R}$ being the correlation matrix predicted by the fitted model under the four factor solution, R being the original sample correlation matrix. The diagonal elements are the elements of the diagonal matrix $\hat{\Theta}$, the maximum likelihood estimator of Θ.

It should be clear from the equation $\Sigma_{vv} = \Lambda\Omega\Lambda' + \Theta$ that the success of a factor model hinges on the ability to reproduce the off-diagonal elements in the variance–covariance matrix. In Exhibit 8.2, it should be noted that all the off-diagonal elements in the residual matrix are small, which means that despite the likelihood ratio test, the fit of the model is not at all bad. As a measure of fit consider the statistic

$$R^2 = 1 - \left[\sum_{i \neq j} (r_{ij} - \hat{r}_{ij})^2 \Big/ \sum_{i \neq j} r_{ij}^2 \right],$$

EXHIBIT 8.1
Correlation Matrix (Weighted by Elements of W^{-1}) for the 17 Expenditure Items

	FOODHOME	FOODAWAY	ALCOHOL	HOUSING	FURNITUR	TEXTILES	DECORAT	CASCLOTH	DRSCLOTH	PERSCARE
FOODHOME	1.000									
FOODAWAY	.702	1.000								
ALCOHOL	.427	.753	1.000							
HOUSING	.493	.857	.699	1.000						
FURNITUR	.688	.869	.638	.805	1.000					
TEXTILES	.762	.889	.642	.805	.868	1.000				
DECORAT	.557	.841	.652	.852	.851	.840	1.000			
CASCLOTH	.792	.922	.643	.819	.861	.932	.828	1.000		
DRSCLOTH	.693	.931	.682	.866	.889	.909	.870	.933	1.000	
PERSCARE	.825	.825	.483	.661	.771	.841	.693	.884	.847	1.000
VACATION	.595	.903	.708	.879	.853	.871	.863	.884	.912	.742
CLUBS	.548	.843	.690	.839	.776	.819	.854	.813	.884	.704
TV	.502	.467	.404	.411	.464	.501	.422	.474	.436	.353
MUSIC	.361	.619	.556	.666	.586	.576	.579	.606	.586	.441
CAMP	.697	.798	.667	.745	.756	.791	.744	.803	.779	.642
READING	.483	.869	.709	.908	.820	.820	.862	.818	.888	.658
GIFTS	.614	.807	.617	.747	.781	.806	.726	.828	.834	.761

EXHIBIT 8.1. *Continued*

	VACATION	CLUBS	TV	MUSIC	CAMP	READING	GIFTS
VACATION	1.000						
CLUBS	.865	1.000					
TV	.452	.361	1.000				
MUSIC	.642	.552	.341	1.000			
CAMP	.778	.714	.557	.538	1.000		
READING	.914	.882	.414	.612	.762	1.000	
GIFTS	.805	.746	.412	.500	.665	.752	1.000

where r_{ij} and $\hat{r}_{ij}$ are entries in the correlation matrix and the predicted correlation matrix, respectively. Clearly, $0 \leq R^2 \leq 1$. Under H_4, the value of this statistic is .99958, indicating that almost all the covariation in the correlation matrix is accounted for. In light of the earlier remarks about the likelihood ratio tests and the value of R^2 under H_4, the four factor solution is accepted as an adequate representation of the data.

Let $\hat{\Lambda} = [\hat{\lambda}_1, \hat{\lambda}_2, \hat{\lambda}_3, \hat{\lambda}_4]$ and define $v_i, i = 1 \ldots 4$ as $\hat{\lambda}'_i \hat{\lambda}_i$. In the orthogonal solution $(v_i/\Sigma_{i=1}^4 v_i) \times 100\%$ yields the percentage of explained variance due to factor i. In this vein it should be noted that factor 1 accounts for 88.6% of the explained variance, while factors 2, 3, and 4 account for 6.7, 3.5, and 1.1% of the explained variance. Together, the factors account for 82.4% of the variance.

Now the initial solution is rotated, as previously discussed; after 15 iterations the simplicity is 1.638. The rotated loadings (for the standardized solution) that exceed .25 in absolute value are presented in Exhibit 8.3. These are the loadings that are initially specified as nonzero when the full model is considered. If the evidence demands it, the specification shall be altered at that point. From Exhibit 8.3, it is easily seen that 41 loadings are set equal to 0. Furthermore, the diagonal elements of the matrix Ω are set equal to 1 for a total of 45 constraints. This is far in excess of the $k^2 = 16$ constraints that are necessary to identify the restricted model (Lawley and Maxwell, 1971, p. 13).

Focusing on the substantive interpretation of the rotated solution, it appears that factor 1 is a general factor, loading on all items save food at home (FOODHOME), expenditures on alcohol (ALCOHOL), and expenditures on television sets (TV). Note that the items household decorations (DECORAT), reading materials (READING), membership fees for clubs and organizations (CLUBS), housing expenditures (HOUSING), vacation

EXHIBIT 8.2[*]
Residual Correlation Matrix $R - \hat{R}$, from the Four Factor Model for the Data in Exhibit 8.1

	FOODHOME	FOODAWAY	ALCOHOL	HOUSING	FURNITUR	TEXTILES	DECORAT	CASCLOTH
FOODHOME	.078							
FOODAWAY	-.000	.048						
ALCOHOL	.003	.004	.287					
HOUSING	-.002	-.001	-.009	.126				
FURNITUR	.004	.006	-.002	-.003	.169			
TEXTILES	-.004	-.002	.006	-.006	.005	.093		
DECORAT	-.003	.003	.005	.005	.033	.006	.154	
CASCLOTH	-.003	.000	-.011	.004	-.013	.011	-.003	.055
DRSCLOTH	-.000	.001	.002	-.004	.008	-.004	-.002	.001
PERSCARE	.004	.001	-.004	.005	-.005	-.002	-.001	-.002
VACATION	-.002	-.000	-.007	-.007	-.001	.002	-.007	-.006
CLUBS	.014	-.004	.033	-.008	-.032	-.001	.019	-.013
TV	.002	.001	-.006	.000	.002	.013	-.006	-.006
MUSIC	-.009	-.006	.001	.049	.017	.007	-.007	.031
CAMP	.007	-.001	.002	.005	-.014	-.009	-.003	.003
READING	.002	.001	-.008	.007	-.005	-.004	-.012	-.006
GIFTS	-.010	-.010	.026	-.001	.015	.008	-.023	.009

EXHIBIT 8.2. *Continued*

	DRSCLOTH	PERSCARE	VACATION	CLUBS	TV	MUSIC	CAMP	READING	GIFTS
DRSCLOTH	.048								
PERSCARE	-.001	.062							
VACATION	-.004	-.001	.087						
CLUBS	.010	.001	-.004	.166					
TV	.002	-.006	.008	-.029	.553				
MUSIC	-.018	-.002	.017	-.034	.004	.542			
CAMP	.001	-.001	-.003	-.002	-.011	-.023	.178		
READING	.000	.003	.006	.010	.001	-.019	.011	.070	
GIFTS	.003	.001	.013	-.007	.037	-.021	-.008	-.007	.272

*R is the sample correlation matrix, $\hat{R}$ the matrix predicted under the model. The elements on the diagonal are uniquenesses, rather than residuals with value 0.

EXHIBIT 8.3*
Sorted Rotated Factor Loadings for the Four Factor Standardized Solution

	FACTOR 1	FACTOR 2	FACTOR 3	FACTOR 4
DECORAT	.972	.000	.000	.000
READING	.951	.000	.000	.000
CLUBS	.880	.000	.000	.000
HOUSING	.834	.000	.000	.000
VACATION	.777	.000	.000	.000
DRSCLOTH	.729	.261	.000	.000
FURNITUR	.686	.000	.000	.000
TEXTILES	.656	.291	.000	.000
GIFTS	.543	.297	.000	.000
CASCLOTH	.506	.400	.000	.000
PERSCARE	.315	.740	.000	.000
FOODHOME	.000	.696	.000	.458
ALCOHOL	.000	.000	.799	.000
TV	.000	.000	.000	.591
CAMP	.375	.000	.000	.491
FOODAWAY	.322	.312	.497	.000
MUSIC	.339	.000	.340	.000

*Loadings less than .250 are set to .000

expenditures (VACATION), and household furniture (FURNITUR) do not load on any other factor. For the second factor, the loadings are highest for FOODHOME and personal care expenditures (PERSCARE). The next highest loading is for the casual clothing variable (CASCLOTH). Smaller loadings are observed for food purchased away from home (FOODAWAY), gifts and contributions (GIFTS), household textiles (TEXTILES), and dress clothing (DRSCLOTH). From the regressions, recall that FOODHOME, PERSCARE, and CASCLOTH are either weakly superior or normal with respect to income at the levels of the socioeconomic hierarchy previously examined. In conjunction with the examination of the magnitudes of the other coefficients for the second factor, it appears that factor two is an "everyday, normal expenditures" factor. Factor three, on which the alcohol variable loads most highly, followed by FOODAWAY and MUSIC appears to represent an entertainment form that is rather different from the entertainment pattern represented by factor four, on which the variables FOODHOME, TV, and CAMP load.

Exhibit 8.4 presents the correlation matrix for the oblique factor solu-

EXHIBIT 8.4
Factor Correlations for the Rotated Factors in the Four Factor Solution

		FACTOR 1	FACTOR 2	FACTOR 3	FACTOR 4
FACTOR	1	1.000			
FACTOR	2	.545	1.000		
FACTOR	3	.847	.341	1.000	
FACTOR	4	.533	.436	.544	1.000

tion. Choosing $\gamma = 0$ allows for moderately correlated factors. Although it is perhaps more conventional in exploratory factor analysis to force the factors to be orthogonal, there is simply no reason to believe that such a constraint mirrors any existing state of affairs in the real world. Furthermore, if the factors are truly uncorrelated, Ω will be diagonal, so $\hat{\Omega}$ will be approximately diagonal. Not surprisingly, the factors are moderately to highly correlated, and factor 1, the general factor, is rather highly correlated with the other factors. The entertainment factors are also fairly highly correlated, and the normal expenditures factor is least highly correlated with the two entertainment factors. These results are consistent with the interpretation of the loading matrix and the consequent interpretation of the factors. Furthermore, the factor correlations provide additional evidence for the existence of stylistic unity by establishing some coherency among the stylistic unity variables.

Finally, we note that $v_1 = 6.373$, $v_2 = 1.600$, $v_3 = 1.165$, and $v_4 = .903$. While not amenable to the same interpretation as in the orthogonal case, large values of v_i may still indicate the relative salience of that factor. Thus, factor 1 appears most salient among the factors.

A Confirmatory Analysis

Having completed the task of determining the value of k and the task of specifying an initial pattern for the loading matrix, the full system of equations given by $\mathbf{y} = \Lambda(\mathbf{s.u.}) + \boldsymbol{\epsilon}$ and $\mathbf{s.u.} = \Gamma\mathbf{x} + \mathbf{v}$ can be considered. The notation is as previously defined. Assume that $\mathbf{v}$ and $\mathbf{x}$, and $\boldsymbol{\epsilon}$ and $\mathbf{s.u.}$ are uncorrelated, and also that $\boldsymbol{\epsilon}$ and $\mathbf{x}$ are uncorrelated. Now let Φ be the covariance matrix of $\mathbf{x}$, Ψ the covariance matrix of $\mathbf{v}$ and Θ the covariance matrix of $\boldsymbol{\epsilon}$. Then the covariance matrix of $(\mathbf{y}', \mathbf{x}')'$ is given as

$$\Sigma = \begin{bmatrix} \Sigma_{yy} & \Sigma_{yx} \\ \Sigma_{xy} & \Sigma_{xx} \end{bmatrix} = \begin{bmatrix} \Lambda \ (\Gamma\Phi\Gamma' + \Psi \ )\Lambda' + \Theta, & \Lambda\Gamma\Phi \\ \Phi\Gamma'\Lambda', & \Phi \end{bmatrix}$$

The equations specifying the model, in conjunction with the assumptions regarding the errors and disturbances, define a special case (a MIMIC model; see Jöreskog and Goldberger, 1975) of the general LISREL model (Jöreskog, 1970, 1973). Iterative minimization of the function $\log |\Sigma| + \mathrm{tr}(S\Sigma^{-1}) - \log |S| - (p + q)$ where S is the sample variance-covariance matrix, and p and q are as previously defined, with respect to the elements of Λ, Γ, Ψ, and Θ (Gruvaeus and Jöreskog, 1970) leads to maximum likelihood estimates of the parameters when the distribution of $(y', x')'$ is multivariate normal. Notice that f, the minimum value of the estimated function, is 0 when $\hat{\Sigma} = S$; that is, this function is small when $\hat{\Sigma}$ is close to S. There is no guarantee that the minimum is global rather than local. The minimization procedure is insensitive to the parameter boundaries and to the detection of alternative minima within the parameter bounds.

Let the null hypothesis correspond to the model estimated, and let the alternative specify that Σ is positive definite. As before, $nf = -2\log\lambda$, where n is the sample size, f is the minimum value of the fitting function, and λ is the likelihood ratio. Asymptotically, under the null, this statistic is distributed χ^2 with degrees of freedom $\frac{1}{2}(p + q)(p + q + 1) - A$, where A is the number of independent, free parameters estimated.

In Exhibit 8.5, a pattern matrix for the elements in Λ is specified. The entries are chosen in accordance with the results from the exploratory analysis and are of three types. The x's signify that the parameter in question is not a priori specified to take a given value, the 0's indicate that the parameter value in question is taken to be 0, and the 1's identify parameters set to 1. The parameters set to 1 establish a metric for the solution. This normalization is chosen in lieu of constraining the latent variables to have unit variances, as in the exploratory analysis, and the normalization is necessary to identify the model. The matrices Γ and Ψ are free, i.e., all the entries in a pattern matrix would be x's. Initially, Θ is chosen to be diagonal.

In Exhibit 8.6, the estimates, and in parentheses, the estimates divided by their standard errors for the initial model, are presented. No ratios are presented for the elements of Λ set to 1, since these are fixed. All elements of $\hat{\Lambda}$ are statistically significant at the .05 level. In the $\hat{\Gamma}$ matrix, the effects of the structural variables tend to be significant. This is true not only for the socioeconomic variables and the other structural variables that emerged from the regressions as important, but for marital status, and to some extent, location.

In the $\hat{\Psi}$ matrix, which is analogous to the covariance matrix of disturbances in a multivariate regression, there is evidence of significant

EXHIBIT 8.5
Pattern Matrix for Λ in the Initial LISREL Model (Model 1)

	FACTOR 1	FACTOR 2	FACTOR 3	FACTOR 4
FOODHOME	O	X	O	X
FOODAWAY	X	X	X	O
ALCOHOL	O	O	1	O
HOUSING	X	O	O	O
FURNITUR	X	O	O	O
TEXTILES	X	X	O	O
DECORAT	1	O	O	O
CASCLOTH	X	X	O	O
DRSCLOTH	X	X	O	O
PERSCARE	X	1	O	O
VACATION	X	O	O	O
CLUBS	X	O	O	O
TV	O	O	O	1
MUSIC	X	O	X	O
CAMP	X	O	O	X
READING	X	O	O	O
GIFTS	X	X	O	O

unexplained variance in factors two and three, but not in factors one and four. Additionally, the covariances between the disturbances may be taken to be 0, except for the covariance between the disturbances of factors two and three. Inspection of $\hat{\Theta}$ reveals that all the uniquenesses are significantly greater than 0. Finally, from the matrix of factor correlations, it appears that factors one, three, and four form a highly interrelated set, while factor two is only moderately correlated with the others.

As it stands, the model requires modification before any detailed substantive interpretation is warranted. With 298 degrees of freedom, minus twice the log likelihood ratio is 606.6138; to four digits the p value of the model is .0000, indicating that overall, the estimator of Σ under the model, $\hat{\Sigma}$, is not "close enough" to S. Inspection of the matrix $S - \hat{\Sigma}$ (Exhibit 8.7) reveals some irregularly large entries in the rows labeled HAGE and HSEON. In particular, the sample covariances between FURNITUR and HAGE, DECORAT and HAGE, VACATION and HAGE, CLUBS and HAGE, READING and HAGE, and GIFTS and HAGE are not adequately reproduced under the model. Similarly, the covariances between FURNITUR and HSEON, CASCLOTH and HSEON, DRSCLOTH and HSEON, CLUBS and HSEON, TV and HSEON, MUSIC and HSEON, CAMP and HSEON, and READING and

HSEON are inadequately reproduced. Recall that entries in Σ_{yx} are of the form $\Lambda\Gamma\Phi$, where Φ is fixed, and Γ is a free matrix. In order to more adequately reproduce this portion of the sample variance–covariance matrix, it might be appropriate to consider modifying the pattern matrix for Λ. Since the elements in the initial loading matrix are significantly different from 0 only the addition of x's to the initial pattern is considered. It

EXHIBIT 8.6

Parameter estimates and ratios of estimates to standard errors (in parentheses) for the initial model (Model I)

$\hat{\Lambda}$

	FACTOR 1	FACTOR 2	FACTOR 3	FACTOR 4
FOODHOME	0.000	.682	0.000	.595
		(11.399)		(6.181)
FOODAWAY	.335	.488	.308	0.000
	(7.714)	(9.794)	(4.866)	
ALCOHOL	0.000	0.000	1.000	0.000
HOUSING	.438	0.000	0.000	0.000
	(20.900)			
FURNITUR	.658	0.000	0.000	0.000
	(17.303)			
TEXTILES	.493	.663	0.000	0.000
	(11.580)	(10.636)		
DECORAT	1.000	0.000	0.000	0.000
CASCLOTH	.440	.704	0.000	0.000
	(10.545)	(15.096)		
DRSCLOTH	.731	.616	0.000	0.000
	(16.194)	(9.932)		
PERSCARE	.295	1.000	0.000	0.000
	(5.415)			
VACATION	.850	0.000	0.000	0.000
	(22.203			
CLUBS	1.184	0.000	0.000	0.000
	(19.014)			
TV	0.000	0.000	0.000	1.000
MUSIC	.409	0.000	.574	0.000
	(3.114)		(2.345)	
CAMP	.484	0.000	0.000	1.676
	(4.165)			(5.612)
READING	.625	0.000	0.000	0.000
	(22.969)			
GIFTS	.460	.531	0.000	0.000
	(10.935)	(5.782)		

continued on next page

EXHIBIT 8.6. *Continued*

$\hat{\Lambda}$ (standardized)	FACTOR 1	FACTOR 2	FACTOR 3	FACTOR 4
FOODHOME	0.000	.169	0.000	.188
FOODAWAY	.276	.121	.142	0.000
ALCOHOL	0.000	0.000	.461	0.000
HOUSING	.359	0.000	0.000	0.000
FURNITUR	.540	0.000	0.000	0.000
TEXTILES	.405	.165	0.000	0.000
DECORAT	.821	0.000	0.000	0.000
CASCLOTH	.361	.175	0.000	0.000
DRSCLOTH	.600	.153	0.000	0.000
PERSCARE	.243	.248	0.000	0.000
VACATION	.698	0.000	0.000	0.000
CLUBS	.972	0.000	0.000	0.000
TV	0.000	0.000	0.000	.316
MUSIC	.336	0.000	.265	0.000
CAMP	.398	0.000	0.000	.530
READING	.513	0.000	0.000	0.000
GIFTS	.378	.132	0.000	0.000

continued on next page

should be clear that it suffices to focus attention on the fifth, seventh, eighth, ninth, eleventh, twelfth, thirteenth, fourteenth, fifteenth, sixteenth, and seventeenth rows of the pattern matrix.

Exhibit 8.8 presents the matrix of first order partial derivatives for the minimizing function with respect to both the free and fixed elements in $\hat{\Lambda}$. Clearly, all the partials with respect to the free parameters are 0. Partials with respect to the parameters set to 0 are generally not 0, but should be near 0 when the parameter value is 0 (Sorbom, 1975). When this is not the case, it may indicate the need for freeing one or more elements in the pattern matrix. Inspection of the appropriate rows indicates that the partials with respect to the elements in the fifth row, second and fourth columns, are large. In the eighth row, entries in the third and fourth columns appear to be somewhat large, and in the eleventh row, the entry in the second column is large. Finally, in the sixteenth row, entries in the second and fourth columns are large. The other entries of interest are small. Before a new model which frees the parameters corresponding to the large entries is estimated, it pays to consider the fact that the value of the partials within a row of Λ depends upon the values of the other parameters within that row; therefore, it may not be necessary to free both elements within a row in order to achieve a more satisfactory solution.

EXHIBIT 8.6 *Continued*

$\hat{\Gamma}$

	FACTOR 1	FACTOR 2	FACTOR 3	FACTOR 4
R1	-.125	-.169	.643	.635
	(-.593)	(-.904)	(1.300)	(2.600)
R2	.100	-.151	.398	.193
	(.604)	(-1.033)	(1.030)	(1.092)
R3	.680	-.643	.774	.549
	(3.247)	(-3.415)	(1.599)	(2.362)
FAMSIZE	-.544	.802	-.889	.164
	(-3.727)	(6.089)	(-2.633)	(.985)
HMSTATUS	-.351	.585	-.029	-.748
	(-2.221)	(4.116)	(-.079)	(-3.788)
HAGE	-.006	.031	-.040	-.021
	(-.858)	(5.454)	(-2.703)	(-2.780)
L1	.053	.564	-.813	-.556
	(.250)	(2.990)	(-1.637)	(-2.283)
L2	-.359	.549	-.226	-.433
	(-2.196)	(3.754)	(-.597)	(-2.355)
L3	-.429	.658	.010	-.557
	(-1.719)	(2.960)	(.018)	(-2.020)
HINCOME	2.555	.719	1.710	-.681
	(5.974)	(2.139)	(2.073)	(-1.553)
HEDUC1	2.343	1.089	7.841	-4.615
	(1.598)	(.840)	(2.288)	(-2.674)
HSEI	-1.007	1.681	-5.066	-.183
	(-1.698)	(3.187)	(-3.614)	(-.287)
HEDSEI	.331	-.250	-.089	.084
	(4.020)	(-3.361)	(-.456)	(.950)
HEDON	-.308	-.040	-.862	.476
	(-1.855)	(-.270)	(-2.223)	(2.468)
HSEON	.040	-.115	.571	-.009
	(.616)	(-1.976)	(3.656)	(-.132)

continued on next page

Hence, as an initial strategy, in such rows the element in the pattern matrix that corresponds to the partial derivative of greatest magnitude is freed. Therefore, the entries in the fifth row and second column, eighth row and fourth column, and sixteenth row and second column of the pattern matrix are freed. In considering these elements for inclusion into a more refined model, it is also important to take into account the loadings estimated in the exploratory analysis. Respectively, the estimated rotated loadings for the large partials are .187, .147, .134, .119, .053, and − .033. With the exception of the elements in the eighth row, the loadings for the

EXHIBIT 8.6. *Continued*

$\hat{\Psi}$

	FACTOR 1	FACTOR 2	FACTOR 3	FACTOR 4
FACTOR 1	.003 (1.541)			
FACTOR 2	.001 (.921)	.003 (2.190)		
FACTOR 3	.001 (.233)	−.005 (−1.989)	.036 (2.877)	
FACTOR 4	−.002 (−1.395)	−.001 (−.742)	.002 (.680)	.001 (.391)

$\hat{\Theta}$

FOODHOME	.003 (3.682)	PERSCARE	.015 (7.340)
FOODAWAY	.012 (6.995)	VACATION	.047 (8.557)
ALCOHOL	.057 (4.369)	CLUBS	.201 (8.766)
HOUSING	.018 (8.580)	TV	.161 (8.811)
FURNITUR	.088 (8.808)	MUSIC	.376 (8.678)
TEXTILES	.027 (8.441)	CAMP	.199 (8.509)
DECORAT	.151 (8.773)	READING	.020 (8.425)
CASCLOTH	.011 (7.773)	GIFTS	.070 (8.765)
DRSCLOTH	.024 (8.182)		

$\hat{E}\left[(\underline{s.u.})(\underline{s.u.})' \right]$ (standardized)

	FACTOR 1	FACTOR 2	FACTOR 3	FACTOR 4
FACTOR 1	1.000			
FACTOR 2	.232	1.000		
FACTOR 3	.839	.084	1.000	
FACTOR 4	.724	.376	.683	1.000

parameters now freed, as well as the partials, have greater magnitude. The entry in the eleventh row, second column, has a loading of .053; since the loading in the exploratory solution is so close to 0, it does not seem worthwhile to allow the parameter to have nonzero value.

In short, our interpretation of the evidence indicates the desirability of relaxing the assumption that the parameters in the fifth row and second

EXHIBIT 8.7*

Residual Matrix S–$\hat{\Sigma}$ from Model 1

	FOODHOME	FOODAWAY	ALCOHOL	HOUSING	FURNITUR	TEXTILES	DECORAT	CASCLOTH	DRSCLOTH
FOODHOME	-0.000								
FOODAWAY	-0.001	0.000							
ALCOHOL	0.001	0.001	0.000						
HOUSING	-0.006	-0.002	0.000	0.000					
FURNITUR	0.033	0.015	-0.005	-0.004	0.000				
TEXTILES	0.004	-0.002	0.003	-0.005	0.028	0.000			
DECORAT	0.009	0.000	-0.010	0.001	0.033	0.017	-0.000		
CASCLOTH	0.002	0.001	0.004	-0.003	0.022	0.004	0.008	0.000	
DRSCLOTH	-0.002	0.000	-0.000	-0.006	0.025	-0.001	0.009	0.001	0.000
PERSCARE	-0.002	-0.000	-0.002	-0.006	0.030	-0.002	0.008	-0.001	0.003
VACATION	0.009	0.005	-0.001	-0.005	0.007	0.009	-0.000	0.010	0.004
CLUBS	0.007	-0.001	0.008	-0.005	-0.013	0.007	0.032	0.000	0.017
TV	-0.002	0.000	0.008	-0.002	0.022	0.015	0.008	0.005	-0.006
MUSIC	-0.005	-0.007	-0.009	0.014	0.002	-0.001	-0.016	0.010	-0.019
CAMP	0.001	0.003	0.016	-0.004	0.031	0.019	0.015	0.017	-0.005
READING	-0.012	-0.007	-0.002	0.001	-0.008	-0.010	-0.005	-0.011	-0.009
GIFTS	-0.005	-0.001	0.010	-0.003	0.022	0.001	-0.003	0.002	0.003
R1	0.000	-0.000	0.001	-0.001	-0.001	0.001	0.002	-0.001	0.001
R2	-0.000	0.000	-0.001	0.000	0.005	-0.000	0.002	0.002	-0.003
R3	-0.000	-0.001	0.001	0.001	-0.005	-0.000	-0.003	0.001	-0.001
FAMSIZE	-0.000	-0.001	0.001	-0.004	0.029	0.005	0.008	0.003	-0.001
HMSTATUS	0.000	0.000	-0.001	0.005	-0.024	-0.004	-0.000	-0.001	-0.000
HAGE	0.001	-0.022	0.033	-0.049	0.343	-0.017	0.153	-0.037	0.013
L1	-0.000	0.001	-0.001	0.001	-0.005	-0.001	-0.001	0.001	-0.000
L2	0.000	-0.000	0.000	-0.000	0.002	0.001	0.001	0.001	-0.001
L3	-0.000	-0.000	0.001	-0.000	0.001	0.001	0.002	0.000	0.000
HINCOME	-0.000	-0.000	-0.000	-0.003	0.019	0.002	0.004	0.001	-0.001

EXHIBIT 8.7. *Continued*

	FOODHOME	FOODAWAY	ALCOHOL	HOUSING	FURNITUR	TEXTILES	DECORAT	CASCLOTH	DRSCLOTH
HEDUC1	0.000	-0.001	0.002	0.007	-0.025	0.001	-0.000	0.000	-0.003
HSEI	0.002	0.005	-0.003	-0.006	-0.024	-0.014	-0.002	-0.017	0.018
HEDSEI	0.004	0.005	0.001	0.011	-0.153	-0.028	-0.001	-0.041	0.036
HEDON	0.001	-0.013	0.017	0.059	-0.189	0.013	0.011	0.005	-0.025
HSEON	0.015	0.037	-0.017	-0.059	-0.158	-0.115	-0.001	-0.152	0.159

EXHIBIT 8.7. *Continued*

	PERSCARE	VACATION	CLUBS	TV	MUSIC	CAMP	READING	GIFTS
PERSCARE	0.000							
VACATION	0.009	0.000						
CLUBS	0.012	-0.002	0.000					
TV	-0.012	0.009	-0.025	-0.000				
MUSIC	-0.011	0.005	-0.046	0.012	-0.000			
CAMP	-0.010	0.007	-0.017	0.018	-0.007	-0.000		
READING	-0.013	-0.003	0.003	-0.005	-0.012	-0.007	0.000	
GIFTS	0.001	0.011	0.005	0.004	-0.012	-0.008	-0.008	0.000
R1	-0.000	-0.000	0.003	0.001	-0.006	-0.004	0.001	0.000
R2	-0.000	0.002	-0.000	0.002	0.010	0.003	-0.003	-0.001
R3	0.000	-0.000	-0.003	-0.001	0.003	0.003	0.002	0.001
FAMSIZE	-0.003	0.005	-0.002	0.001	0.006	-0.001	-0.010	-0.009
HMSTATUS	0.002	-0.003	0.001	-0.000	0.003	0.000	0.005	0.003
HAGE	0.030	0.201	0.240	-0.009	-0.014	-0.008	-0.219	0.137
L1	0.000	-0.001	-0.002	0.002	0.001	0.002	0.001	-0.001
L2	-0.000	0.002	-0.002	-0.001	0.001	-0.000	-0.001	-0.000
L3	0.000	-0.002	0.001	-0.002	-0.001	0.002	0.000	-0.000
HINCOME	-0.001	0.006	0.001	0.000	0.003	0.001	-0.008	-0.001
HEDUC1	0.001	-0.010	-0.003	-0.003	0.001	0.000	0.010	-0.005
HSEI	0.005	-0.011	0.033	-0.016	-0.047	-0.025	0.018	0.007
HEDSEI	0.017	-0.064	0.071	-0.045	-0.099	-0.062	0.075	-0.002
HEDON	0.010	-0.080	-0.018	-0.037	0.021	0.007	0.069	-0.047
HSEON	0.043	-0.075	0.313	-0.148	-0.410	-0.234	0.130	0.061

*Entries in $S_{xx} - \hat{\Sigma}_{xx}$ are all 0.

137

EXHIBIT 8.8

First Order Partial Derivatives for the Minimizing Function with Respect to Free and Fixed Elements of $\hat{\Lambda}$ for Model 1

	FACTOR 1	FACTOR 2	FACTOR 3	FACTOR 4
FOODHOME	-0.000	0.000	0.122	-0.000
FOODAWAY	0.000	0.000	-0.000	0.142
ALCOHOL	-0.000	-0.005	-0.000	-0.034
HOUSING	0.000	0.308	-0.052	0.153
FURNITUR	-0.000	-0.359	0.016	-0.241
TEXTILES	-0.000	-0.000	-0.064	-0.259
DECORAT	-0.000	-0.075	0.060	-0.012
CASCLOTH	0.000	-0.000	-0.302	-0.356
DRSCLOTH	-0.000	0.000	0.112	0.071
PERSCARE	-0.000	-0.000	0.141	0.250
VACATION	0.000	-0.236	-0.053	-0.038
CLUBS	-0.000	-0.042	0.038	0.017
TV	0.000	0.009	-0.039	0.000
MUSIC	0.000	0.009	0.000	-0.018
CAMP	0.000	-0.005	-0.020	0.000
READING	-0.000	0.681	0.056	0.292
GIFTS	-0.000	-0.000	-0.071	0.112

column, sixteenth row and second column, and eighth row and fourth column are 0.

Let model 2 (not shown) be the new model that incorporates these three modifications. In this model each of the additional parameters is nonzero on the basis of a two tailed test at the .05 level of significance. The loading in the fifth row, second column, is given by .517, the loading for the sixteenth row and second column by .507, the loading for the eighth row and fourth column by .132. Respectively, the standardized loadings are .125, .123, and .042. Substantively, the parameter estimates for parameters included in both models are similar, as are the standard errors of the estimates. Admittedly, there are several instances in which certain estimates are statistically significant in one but not both models. However, the ratio of the estimated parameter to its standard error does not differ substantially in such instances.

The most remarkable feature of model 2 is the reduction in the value of the likelihood ratio test; with 295 degrees of freedom, $-2 \log \lambda$ is now 531.4075. That is, the reduction is 75.2063, or about one-eighth of the original value. Not only is the reduction statistically significant, it is also large, averaging more than 25 for each additional degree of freedom utilized. Clearly, model 2 is nontrivially superior to model 1. While the deviation matrix $S - \hat{\Sigma}$ for model 2 is not presented, it ought to be mentioned that the covariances between HAGE and the previously discussed items are now more adequately reproduced. This is also true of the covariances between HSEON and the items selected for closer examination. Nonetheless, some of the deviations are still considerable.

This does not necessarily mean that model 2 is adequate. While the reduction in χ^2 is substantial, the p value for the model itself is still .0000.

In considering how to modify model 2, the assumption that Θ is a diagonal matrix of uniquenesses is now examined. Exhibit 8.9 presents the first order partials of the minimizing function with respect to the free and fixed elements of $\hat{\Theta}$. Inspection of the exhibit indicates a potential gain in model adequacy from freeing elements in the pattern matrix for Θ. The question is which elements should be freed. Since items are not unique to a factor, i.e., some rows of $\hat{\Lambda}$ have more than one nonzero entry, and since the first column of $\hat{\Lambda}$ has 14 nonzero entries, it is not worthwhile to attempt to find a clear pattern of errors among the items comprising a factor, or for that matter, within items across factors. Therefore, an empirical criterion is justified. Whenever a first order partial derivative has magnitude greater than two, the corresponding entry in the pattern matrix for Θ is freed. This yields the pattern matrix in Exhibit 8.10. An additional 49 parameters are estimated in the revised version of model 2 (hereafter model 3). Comparison of parameter estimates and standard errors common to both models 2 and 3 (not shown) reveals no striking dissimilarities. Statistically, model 3 provides a more adequate fit to the data. With 49 additional free parameters minus twice the log likelihood ratio is reduced from 531.4075 to 413.2084, a reduction of 118.1991, or approximately 2.4 per degree of freedom. While not as dramatic as the difference between models 1 and 2, the reduction is clearly significant, despite the fact that many of the new estimates are not. Perhaps most importantly, with 246 degrees of freedom, the χ^2 value of 413.2084 has p value .0000, indicating a substantial lack of fit. The question now is whether further modifications are necessary, and if so, the specific modifications which ought to be incorporated.

In this vein, the following observations may be made. First, the likelihood ratio test statistic is a scalar multiple of the number of observations. Although 159 is by no means large, neither is it small, and the large χ^2 value is partially attributable to this fact. Second, the test statistic is asymptotically distributed χ^2 when the distribution of the observed variables is mutlivariate normal. Given the three location and three region variables, it should be obvious that the distribution of the observed variables is not multivariate normal. Third, if the deviation matrix $S - \hat{\Sigma}$ is

EXHIBIT 8.9

First Order Partial Derivatives for the Minimizing Function with Respect to Free and Fixed Elements of Θ for Model 2

	FOODHOME	FOODAWAY	ALCOHOL	HOUSING	FURNITUR	TEXTILES	DECORAT	CASCLOTH	DRSCLOTH
FOODHOME	-0.000								
FOODAWAY	4.413	0.000							
ALCOHOL	-1.103	-1.641	0.000						
HOUSING	14.939	0.400	0.539	-0.000					
FURNITUR	7.218	0.040	0.528	0.534	0.000				
TEXTILES	-0.626	6.367	-1.008	2.999	-3.348	0.000			
DECORAT	1.524	1.401	-.050	-0.628	-2.553	-2.218	0.000		
CASCLOTH	11.405	-3.196	0.420	-3.077	3.612	-9.724	-0.068	-0.000	
DRSCLOTH	7.769	-3.693	-2.131	5.175	-2.627	1.611	-0.223	-3.337	-0.000
PERSCARE	-15.190	-2.704	0.225	1.178	3.115	6.004	2.171	5.268	-6.601
VACATION	0.985	2.203	1.234	5.259	-0.339	-1.002	0.276	-4.737	2.951
CLUBS	-4.417	1.026	-1.366	1.278	1.291	-0.242	-1.006	2.078	-2.351
TV	2.549	-0.507	0.033	-0.201	-0.178	-2.070	-0.243	-0.950	0.776
MUSIC	6.021	1.172	.0439	-2.199	-0.245	-0.120	0.119	-2.209	1.545
CAMP	-0.543	-2.102	-0.765	-0.176	0.392	-1.248	-0.374	-4.102	0.514
READING	-7.047	-1.192	1.876	2.678	0.696	1.170	1.244	3.906	2.152
GIFTS	-0.624	3.012	-1.436	-0.204	-0.879	-0.415	0.979	-3.093	-1.612

EXHIBIT 8.9. *Continued*

	PERSCARE	VACATION	CLUBS	TV	MUSIC	CAMP	READING	GIFTS
PERSCARE	0.000							
VACATION	3.106	-0.000						
CLUBS	-1.202	0.443	-0.000					
TV	2.979	-0.995	0.658	-0.000				
MUSIC	1.193	-0.347	0.497	-0.012	-0.000			
CAMP	1.336	-0.346	0.279	-0.500	0.288	0.000		
READING	-5.275	0.907	-1.372	-0.065	1.855	-0.451	-0.000	
GIFTS	-0.504	-1.564	0.002	-1.166	0.478	-0.390	0.799	-0.000

EXHIBIT 8.10*
Pattern Matrix for Θ Derived from Exhibit 8.9

	FOODHOME	FOODAWAY	ALCOHOL	HOUSING	FURNITUR	TEXTILES	DECORAT	CASCLOTH	DRSCLOTH
FOODHOME	X								
FOODAWAY	X	X							
ALCOHOL	O	O	X						
HOUSING	X	O	O	X					
FURNITUE	X	O	O	O	X				
TEXTILES	O	X	O	X	X	X			
DECORAT	O	O	O	O	X	X	X		
CASCLOTH	X	X	X	X	X	X	O	X	
DRSCLOTH	X	X	O	O	X	O	X	X	X
PERSCARE	X	X	O	X	X	X	O	X	X
VACATION	O	X	O	O	O	O	O	X	X
CLUBS	X	O	O	X	O	X	O	X	X
TV	X	O	O	X	O	X	O	O	O
MUSIC	X	X	O	O	O	O	O	X	O
CAMP	O	O	O	X	O	O	O	X	O
READING	X	X	O	X	O	O	O	X	X
GIFTS	O	X	O	O	O	O	O	X	O

EXHIBIT 8.10. *Continued*

	PERSCARE	VACATION	CLUBS	TV	MUSIC	CAMP	READING	GIFTS
PERSCARE	X							
VACATION	X	X						
CLUBS	O	O	X					
TV	X	O	O	X				
MUSIC	O	O	O	O	X			
CAMP	O	O	O	O	O	X		
READING	X	O	O	O	O	O	X	
GIFTS	O	O	O	O	O	O	O	X

*X's correspond to diagonal elements of Θ and to off diagonal elements with entries greater than 2 in absolute value in Exhibit 8.9.

examined, or if a deviation matrix that has been proportionately adjusted is examined, almost all the covariances are closely reproduced under the model. This suggests that the fit is not so bad after all.

As it is not entirely clear that model 3 is unacceptable, neither is it clear how model 3 should be altered to achieve a better fit. There is no solid evidence to suggest including more factor loadings, and freeing more off-diagonal elements in the pattern matrix for Θ does not appear likely to decrease the likelihood ratio enough to substantially alter the p value of the model. Without straying drastically from the theoretical and empirical framework, there appears to be little that can be done to modify model 3. Furthermore, it is not at all clear that the need for modification is great. In this regard, it is important to note that the modifications of model 1 have so far done little to change the estimates of the parameters in model 1 or the standard errors of the estimates. That is, the substantive conclusions do not depend upon the set of estimates examined. This is probably the most important point of all.

There is, however, a need to fix some of the parameters to 0, in order to obtain more stable estimates of the remaining free parameters. Of particular importance are the coefficients for income, education, and occupational status, and the coefficients for the interactions. Thus, the coefficient for HEDON in the second row of $\hat{\Gamma}$, the coefficient for HEDSEI in the third row of $\hat{\Gamma}$, and the coefficient for HSEON in the fourth row of $\hat{\Gamma}$ are set to 0, as the ratio of the estimate to its standard error fails to exceed unity in model 3. The coefficients for HEDSEI and HSEI in the fourth row of $\hat{\Gamma}$ are not set to 0 at this time, because it is not unlikely that the removal of HSEON will cause the ratio of estimate to standard error for these coefficients to exceed unity. Continuing to use this criterion, $R1$ is removed from the first and second rows of $\hat{\Gamma}$, $R2$, $L2$ and FAMSIZE from the second row, HAGE and $L1$ from the first row, and HMSTATUS and $L3$ from the third row.

Turning to the symmetric matrices $\hat{\Psi}$ and $\hat{\Theta}$, and applying the same criterion, the factor 1 disturbance is assumed to be uncorrelated with the other factor disturbances. Additionally, the correlation between the factor 3 and factor 4 disturbances is assumed to be 0. However, the factor 4 residual variance is not set to 0, as the ratio of the estimate to its standard error merely indicates that the error variance in the fourth latent variable could be assumed to be 0. This possibility is not pursued here because a deterministic model for the fourth latent variable is arbitrarily rigid and not conceptually defensible. Furthermore, such a specification would require that the residual correlation between factors 2 and 4 be set to 0, in spite of the fact that the appropriate ratio for this parameter estimate exceeds one. Finally, in the matrix $\hat{\Theta}$ the 16 off-diagonal elements included in model 3 whose ratios do not exceed one are set to 0.

Exhibit 8.11 presents the final model (model 4) estimates and the estimates divided by their standard errors for the revised version of model 3. With 278 degrees of freedom, the χ^2 value is 425.5650 with p level .0000. Since model 4 is nested under model 3, comparison of χ^2 values is appropriate and indicates that model 3 is not an improvement over model 4. This is based on a difference in value of 12.3566 with 32 degrees of freedom.

EXHIBIT 8.11

Parameter estimates and ratios of estimates to standard errors (in parentheses) for the fourth model (Model 4)

$\hat{\Lambda}$

	FACTOR 1	FACTOR 2	FACTOR 3	FACTOR 4
FOODHOME	0.000	.690 (11.653)	0.000	.660 (6.010)
FOODAWAY	.357 (8.013)	.478 (9.603)	.295 (4.759)	0.000
ALCOHOL	0.000	0.000	1.000	0.000
HOUSING	.437 (20.853)	0.000	0.000	0.000
FURNITUR	.635 (14.741)	.524 (5.608)	0.000	0.000
TEXTILES	.516 (11.890)	.607 (9.377)	0.000	0.000
DECORAT	1.000	0.000	0.000	0.000
CASCLOTH	.426 (11.219)	.658 (14.037)	0.000	.126 (2.441)
DRSCLOTH	.752 (16.338)	.555 (8.961)	0.000	0.000
PERSCARE	.327 (5.511)	1.000	0.000	0.000
VACATION	.853 (22.451)	0.000	0.000	0.000
CLUBS	1.185 (19.076)	0.000	0.000	0.000
TV	0.000	0.000	0.000	1.000
MUSIC	.433 (3.482)	0.000	.509 (2.243)	0.000
CAMP	.413 (3.172)	0.000	0.000	1.896 (5.430)
READING	.638 (19.927)	-.301 (-5.261)	0.000	0.000
GIFTS	.479 (11.107)	.507 (5.427)	0.000	0.000

continued on next page

EXHIBIT 8.11. *Continued*

$\hat{\Lambda}$ (standardized)

	FACTOR 1	FACTOR 2	FACTOR 3	FACTOR 4
FOODHOME	0.000	.166	0.000	.202
FOODAWAY	.293	.115	.137	0.000
ALCOHOL	0.000	0.000	.465	0.000
HOUSING	.359	0.000	0.000	0.000
FURNITUR	.522	.126	0.000	0.000
TEXTILES	.424	.146	0.000	0.000
DECORAT	.821	0.000	0.000	0.000
CASCLOTH	.350	.158	0.000	.039
DRSCLOTH	.617	.134	0.000	0.000
PERSCARE	.268	.241	0.000	0.000
VACATION	.700	0.000	0.000	0.000
CLUBS	.973	0.000	0.000	0.000
TV	0.000	0.000	0.000	.306
MUSIC	.355	0.000	.236	0.000
CAMP	.339	0.000	0.000	.580
READING	.524	-.073	0.000	0.000
GIFTS	.393	.122	0.000	0.000

continued on next page

The preliminary factor analyses constitute the basis for the specification of free and fixed parameters in the loading matrix for the confirmatory analysis. Therefore, it should not be surprising if the previous interpretation of the factors is unaltered in the confirmatory models. For factors two, three, and four, this is the case. But factor one, which was previously interpreted as a general factor on the basis of the exploratory results, emerges as a conspicuous and specific luxury factor (see Exhibit 8.11), loading most highly on the by and large superior items CLUBS, VACATION, DECORAT, and DRSCLOTH. The qualifier "specific" appears to be necessary; for example, the loadings for the superior items GIFTS, FOODAWAY, and MUSIC are small. With this new interpretation in mind, the effects of the independent variables on the factors can be examined.

First, the region contrasts tend to to be insignificant, with the exception of the contrasts between Western and other regions. For the fourth factor, the contrast between the Northeastern region with the South and the North Central region is also significant. The location coefficients, on the other hand, tend to be significant. For the conspicuous luxury factor the effects of suburban residence in large metropolitan areas and residence in smaller cities are significant and negative, indicating lesser ex-

EXHIBIT 8.11. *Continued*

$\hat{\Gamma}$

	FACTOR 1	FACTOR 2	FACTOR 3	FACTOR 4
R1	0.000	-.219	.695	.468
		(-1.429)	(1.452)	(2.391)
R2	0.000	0.000	.279	0.000
			(.767)	
R3	.647	-.667	.744	.488
	(3.989)	(-4.210)	(1.571)	(2.646)
FAMSIZE	-.497	.742	-.839	.224
	(-3.672)	(5.947)	(-3.232)	(1.484)
HMSTATUS	-.277	.593	0.000	-.645
	(-2.200)	(4.723)		(-3.660)
HAGE	0.000	.029	-.041	-.020
		(6.850)	(-3.270)	(-3.207)
L1	0.000	.497	-.861	-.446
		(2.934)	(-2.048)	(-2.107)
L2	-.278	.431	0.000	-.312
	(-2.070)	(3.290)		(-2.003)
L3	-.449	.525	0.000	-.432
	(-2.125)	(2.583)		(-1.831)
HINCOME	2.613	.727	1.810	-.559
	(9.833)	(3.905)	(2.619)	(-1.798)
HEDUC1	3.187	.668	8.587	-3.948
	(3.174)	(3.005)	(2.703)	(-3.477)
HSEI	-1.028	1.867	-5.609	-.281
	(-1.911)	(5.405)	(-4.156)	(-1.546)
HEDSEI	.255	-.239	0.000	.095
	(3.527)	(-4.010)		(1.298)
HEDON	-.371	0.000	-.981	.400
	(-3.177)		(-2.900)	(3.216)
HSEON	.065	-.140	.608	0.000
	(1.092)	(-3.572)	(4.081)	

continued on next page

penditures on this factor. With respect to the second latent variable, the "everyday, normal expenditures" factor, the coefficients for these two variables are positive and significant. Turning to the entertainment factors, a curious result emerges. Given the opportunities in larger cities, the coefficients in the third equation (the "strongly superior entertainment" factor) are expected to increase with city size; conversely, in the fourth equation (for the "weakly superior entertainment" factor) the coefficients are expected to decrease with city size. In fact, in the third equation, residence inside cities of size 400,000 or more is negatively related to the third factor. In the fourth equation, the coefficients are negative, as ex-

EXHIBIT 8.11.   *Continued*

$\hat{\psi}$

	FACTOR 1	FACTOR 2	FACTOR 3	FACTOR 4
FACTOR 1	.003 (2.231)			
FACTOR 2	0.000	.004 (3.085)		
FACTOR 3	0.000	-.003 (-1.594)	.037 (2.915)	
FACTOR 4	0.000	-.002 (-1.459)	0.000	.001 (.541)

$\hat{E}\left((\underline{s.u.})(\underline{s.u.})'\right)$ (standardized)

	FACTOR 1	FACTOR 2	FACTOR 3	FACTOR 4
FACTOR 1	1.000			
FACTOR 2	.152	1.000		
FACTOR 3	.830	.025	1.000	
FACTOR 4	.762	.283	.690	1.000

continued on next page

pected, and significant by a one tailed criterion at the .05 level. However, the decline is not monotone, as initially expected.

The age coefficients are statistically significant in the second, third, and fourth equations, indicating that as head's age increases, expenditures shift away from both entertainment forms to those items constituting everyday normal expenditures. Of course, age has no effect on the conspicuous luxury factor. Recall that the coefficient was set to 0, on the basis of the evidence from model 3.

Examination of the family size and marital status coefficients reveals that increases in family size are negatively related to the first factor. But so is the percentage unmarried, indicating that the relationship between household size and "the specific luxury" factor is curvilinear. Similarly, both independent variables are positively related to the "normal, everyday expenditure" factor, again indicating a curvilinear relationship between household size and the factor. Marital status is not salient to differentiation in "strongly superior entertainment," but family size is and operates to diminish such expenditures, as expected. Thus, despite the

EXHIBIT 8.11. *Continued*

	FOODHOME	FOODAWAY	ALCOHOL	HOUSING	FURNITUR	TEXTILES	DECORAT	CASCLOTH	DRSCLOTH
FOODHOME	.004 (4.410)								
FOODAWAY	-.001 (-1.446)	.012 (6.833)							
ALCOHOL	0.000	0.000	.054 (4.044)						
HOUSING	-.001 (-2.202)	0.000	0.000	.018 (3.643)					
FURNITUR	-.002 (-1.852)	0.000	0.000	0.000	.071 (8.694)				
TEXTILES	0.000	-.003 (-2.032)	0.000	-.002 (-1.417)	.006 (1.738)	.028 (8.336)			
DECORAT	0.000	0.000	0.000	0.000	.029 (3.417)	.010 (1.845)	.150 (8.746)		
CASCLOTH	-.001 (-1.528)	0.000	0.000	0.000	-.003 (-1.414)	-.003 (2.030)	0.000	.012 (7.931)	
DRSCLOTH	-.002 (-1.982)	.001 (1.001)	0.000	-.002 (-1.020)	.007 (1.985)	0.000	0.000	.003 (2.116)	.027 (8.137)
PERSCARE	0.000	0.000	0.000	0.000	-.003 (-1.124)	-.002 (-.900)	0.000	0.000	.004 (2.120)
VACATION	0.000	0.000	0.000	-.006 (-2.484)	0.000	0.000	0.000	0.000	-.004 (-1.351)
CLUBS	0.000	0.000	0.000	0.000	0.000	0.000	0.000	0.000	.015 (2.677)
TV	0.000	0.000	0.000	0.000	0.000	.009 (1.653)	0.000	0.000	0.000

continued on next page

EXHIBIT 8.11. *Continued*

$\hat{\Theta}$ continued

	FOODHOME	FOODAWAY	ALCOHOL	HOUSING	FURNITUR	TEXTILES	DECORAT	CASCLOTH	DRSCLOTH
MUSIC	-.010 (-3.181)	0.000	0.000	.016 (2.393)	0.000	0.000	0.000	.012 (2.343)	0.000
CAMP	0.000	.008 (1.895)	0.000	0.000	0.000	0.000	0.000	-.010 (2.587)	0.000
READING	0.000	0.000	0.000	0.000	0.000	0.000	0.000	0.000	0.000
GIFTS	0.000	-.004 (-1.560)	0.000	0.000	0.000	0.000	0.000	.003 (1.139)	0.000

continued on next page

150

EXHIBIT 8.11. *Continued*

⊙

	PERSCARE	VACATION	CLUBS	TV	MUSIC	CAMP	READING	GIFTS
PERSCARE	.014 (7.004)							
VACATION	-.002 (-.873)	.044 (8.466)						
CLUBS	0.000	0.000	.199 (8.735)					
TV	-.007 (-1.681)	0.000	0.000	.161 (8.800)				
MUSIC	0.000	0.000	0.000	0.000	.384 (8.737)			
CAMP	0.000	0.000	0.000	0.000	0.000	.195 (8.371)		
READING	.002 (1.650)	0.000	0.000	0.000	0.000	0.000	.015 (7.918)	
GIFTS	0.000	0.000	0.000	0.000	0.000	0.000	0.000	.069 (8.757)

151

fact that marital status is unimportant, it is also true that single person families, who are presumably also single, do participate to a greater extent in "strongly superior entertainment," as expected. For "weakly superior entertainment," the family size coefficient is statistically insignificant, although the ratio of the estimate to its standard error does exceed unity, and the coefficient is positive, as expected. But the marital status coefficient is significant and negative, indicating that increases in the percentage unmarried lead to decreases in "weakly superior entertainment," which is not surprising. Thus, the evidence regarding the last two factors and the family size and marital status coefficients is consistent with expectation.

The Socioeconomic Effects

Net of the main effects of the socioeconomic variables, which tend to be significant, there are statistically significant interaction effects, two out of four times for HEDSEI and HSEON, and three out of four times for HEDON. Although it is technically incorrect, coefficients constrained to equal 0 on the basis of the model 3 evidence are treated as equivalent to statistically insignificant coefficients.

As in the previous chapter, the main effects of the socioeconomic variables cannot be discussed meaningfully. Therefore, as in that chapter, dependent variables are differentiated with respect to the socioeconomic variables income (HINCOME), education (HEDUC1) and occupational status (HSEI), and the partial derivatives are assessed for significance relative to an appropriate null hypothesis. Technically, it is no longer correct to refer to the partial derivatives as elasticities because the factors are (in the population) linear combinations of the items in logged form, and $\Sigma_{j=1}^{p} c_j \log y_{ij} \neq \log \Sigma_{j=1}^{p} c_j y_{ij}$. Nevertheless, the analogy to an elasticity is used.[1] For example, if the partial derivative with respect to HINCOME exceeds 1, the factor is interpreted as strongly superior.

The calculations in Exhibit 8.12 indicate that the partials with respect to income exceed unity at all levels of education and status examined for factors 1 and 3, indicating not just that these factors are strongly superior, but that they are so regardless of educational and occupational differentials. The income partials with respect to factor 1 shift monotonically downward as education and status are increased, at least at the levels examined. With respect to factor 3 the shift is monotone increasing. In both cases, the standard deviations are large, so that interpreting trends is risky. Therefore, the differences between partials at the middle and low

---

[1] In these data, use of the analogy does not appear to create undue distortion.

EXHIBIT 8.12*

Estimated First-Order Partial Derivatives, Standard Deviations (s.d.), and t ratios for Low, Middle, and High Levels of the Socioeconomic Hierarchy

	HINCOME,	s.d.,	t	HEDUC1,	s.d.,	t	HSEI,	s.d.,	t
LOW									
FACTOR 1	2.035,	.108,	9.612	.694,	.078,	8.897	.072,	.038,	1.873
FACTOR 2	.311,	.142,	-4.835	-.042,	.093,	-.446	.144,	.030,	4.859
FACTOR 3	1.576,	.207,	2.787	-.006,	.321,	-.020	-.283,	.074,	-3.806
FACTOR 4	.273,	.126,	-5.783	-.162,	.129,	-1.251	-.083,	.040,	-2.067
MIDDLE									
FACTOR 1	1.934,	.103,	9.060	.736,	.068,	10.864	.193,	.026,	7.336
FACTOR 2	.218,	.140,	-5.583	-.201,	.091,	-2.201	.003,	.022,	.118
FACTOR 3	1.601,	.222,	2.706	-.347,	.262,	-1.326	-.072,	.061,	-1.182
FACTOR 4	.428,	.124,	-4.608	.040,	.108,	.372	-.047,	.029,	-1.597
HIGH									
FACTOR 1	1.865,	.113,	7.654	.780,	.091,	8.510	.294,	.041,	7.142
FACTOR 2	.123,	.146,	-6.011	-.363,	.106,	-3.424	-.119,	.031,	-3.817
FACTOR 3	1.713,	.280,	2.544	-.687,	.247,	-2.777	.139,	.085,	1.634
FACTOR 4	.550,	.136,	-3.318	.243,	.111,	2.187	-.018,	.037,	-.487

*All calculations are rounded to 3 digits. For HINCOME, H_0 specifies that the partial has value 1; for the other two variables the value is 0. For the low level, HINCOME = 8.7598, HEDUC1 = 2.07944, and HSEI = 2.969388; for the middle level, HINCOME = 9.1069, HEDUC1 = 2.4663, and HSEI = 3.6362. For the high level, the values are 9.454, 2.7725887, and 4.31442, respectively. These correspond with the values chosen to define the levels in the previous chapter.

levels and at the middle and high levels have been computed, as well as the standard deviations of the differences and the ratios of the two. The calculations are presented in Exhibit 8.13. It is clear that the decline in factor 1 appears to represent a real trend, while the increase in factor 3 does not. For factors 2 and 4, the partial with respect to HINCOME is less than one. For factor 2, the partial declines monotonically from .311 to .123, and the decline is 60% of the original value. For factor 4, the partial increases monotonically and at the high level is over twice its value at the low level. Nonetheless, factors 2 and 4 are weakly superior regardless of levels of education and/or status.

The findings above are important for several reasons. First, they offer support for the substantive interpretation of the factors. Factor 1 has already been alluded to as a "specific luxury" factor; its partial should therefore be greater than one. Similarly, factor 2 has been interpreted as an "everyday, normal expenditures" factor; its partial should therefore be less than or equal to one. Second, the fact that the substantive interpretation of the partials is invariant over status and/or educational levels is important and indicates that, in some sense, income differentiates stylistic unity in a substantively similar fashion throughout the socioeconomic hierarchy. Nevertheless, the manner in which income operates on the factors is conditioned by levels of occupational status and/or education, as Exhibit 8.13 indicates. Factors 1 and 2 become less superior at higher levels of status and education, and higher levels of status, respectively. Simultaneously, factor four becomes markedly more income superior as levels of education are increased.

Inspection of the partials for HEDUC1 reveals that factor one is always education superior; the slight tendency for the partial to increase monotonically as status and income increase is not significant, as indicated by the ratios in Exhibit 8.13. With respect to factor 2, at the low level, the partial may be regarded as 0. Monotonic declines in the value of the partial are observed as the level of status increases, and the declines are real, as evidenced by the ratios in Exhibit 8.13. For factor 3, at both low and intermediate levels, the partial with respect to HEDUC1 may be taken to be 0. At the high level, the factor is education inferior. For factor 3 the differences are significant, indicating that the partials appear to decline monotonically as the level of income is increased. Inspection indicates the decline is sharp. For factor 4, only at the high level is the education partial significantly different from 0; here it is positive. Nevertheless, the trend toward increasing partials is real, indicating that the value of the partial increases with rising levels of status and income.

Putting together all the information, education has nontrivial effects

EXHIBIT 8.13*

Estimated Differences Between Partials, Standard Deviations (s.d.) and ratios of differences to standard deviations (r)

A. Differences between the Middle and Low levels

	HINCOME,	s.d.,	r	HEDUC1,	s.d.,	r	HSEI,	s.d.,	r
FACTOR 1	.100,	.042,	2.403	.041,	.051,	.805	.121,	.032,	3.780
FACTOR 2	-.093,	.026,	-3.572	-.159,	.040,	-4.010	-.141,	.023,	-6.029
FACTOR 3	.026,	.121,	.214	-.341,	.117,	-2.900	.211,	.052,	4.081
FACTOR 4	.155,	.048,	3.216	.202,	.055,	3.709	.037,	.028,	1.298

B. Differences between the High and Middle levels

	HINCOME,	s.d.,	r	HEDUC1,	s.d.,	r	HSEI,	s.d.,	r
FACTOR 1	-.070,	.037,	-1.867	.044,	.052,	.853	.101,	.028,	3.619
FACTOR 2	-.095,	.026,	-3.572	-.162,	.041,	-4.010	-.122,	.020,	-6.227
FACTOR 3	.011,	.105,	1.066	-.341,	.117,	-2.900	.211,	.052,	4.081
FACTOR 4	.123,	.038,	3.216	.202,	.055,	3.709	.029,	.022,	1.288

*All calculations are rounded to 3 digits. In panel A, the low partials are subtracted from the middle level partials; in panel B, the middle level partials are subtracted from the high partials. The null hypothesis is always that the difference is 0.

upon the differentiation of stylistic unity. Furthermore, the manner in which education operates is highly conditioned by the levels of the other explanatory variables, at least to a greater substantive extent than the effects of income are conditioned by levels of occupational status and education. The calculations reveal that as the level of occupational status increases, the "everyday, normal expenditures" factor becomes less desirable to marginal changes in education. For "strongly superior entertainment" a similar response can be observed as the level of income is increased. As levels of occupational status and income are increased, the desirability of "weakly superior entertainment" increases as education is marginally incremented. We shall return to this finding momentarily.

In the interim, consider the partials with respect to occupational status. As was true of the partial of factor 1 with respect to education, its partial with respect to occupational status is positive at all three levels. Unlike the education partial, the increase across levels of education and income is real and dramatic; over the range of interest it quadruples. The partials for the second factor are significant at both low and high levels and change sign. At the low level, factor 2 is status superior, but at the high level of education and income, the decrement that results from increases in status is similar to the increment at the low level. The partial for factor 3 is significant at the low level and almost significant at the high level. The trend toward increasing partials at the different levels is real, however. Taken together, the results indicate that at low levels of income, "strongly superior entertainment" is status inferior. But as the level of income rises, the relationship changes, and "strongly superior entertainment" is almost status superior. For factor 4, it appears that the monotonic rise toward 0 is artificial. However, at the low level, the partial is less than 0, that is, "weakly superior entertainment" is status inferior.

Like education, occupational status has nontrivial effects upon the differentiation of stylistic unity. As with education, the relations between status and the factors are conditioned to a large extent by the levels of the other explanatory variables, particularly income.

From the account above, it should be clear that education and occupational status do not always operate in the same fashion. With respect to "strongly superior entertainment," the education partials decline while the status partials rise. With respect to "weakly superior entertainment," the education partials rise until they are positive, while the status partials are negative or not statistically different from 0. With respect to factor 2, both sets of elasticities decline, but at low levels of education and income, status has a positive effect, while at high levels, the effect is negative. Apart from indicating the differential operation of these characteristics, which shows the value of not combining them into an index, there is an interesting story buried in these calculations.

With respect to "strongly superior entertainment," the education partial declines from low to high levels, but the partials with respect to occupational status increase and become descriptively positive. The differential operation of education and status, in conjunction with status inferiority at the low level, may illustrate either the responsiveness of status to forces engendering "conspicuous consumption," or the relatively conscious unresponsiveness of education (snobbishness) to this phenomenon, or both at the high level. Corroborating evidence is the unresponsiveness of education and responsiveness of status to shifts across levels of the socioeconomic hierarchy for factor one, which is also strongly superior with respect to income. For factor four, which is weakly superior with respect to income, the partials with respect to education become positive at the high levels, while the partial with respect to status is not different from 0 at that point. Thus, particularly at the high level, status consciousness may well dictate increments to strongly superior factors. But education, if anything, shows either no change or changes in the other direction with respect to strongly superior factors as levels of the socioeconomic hierarchy are varied. However, factor one is education superior at the levels of the stratification system examined. Furthermore, the fact that the evidence is strongest at the high level serves to corroborate the argument. After all, it is at this level that conspicuous consumption and/or snobbishness should be most evident.

One other piece of information must be discussed. In exhibit 8.11 the correlation matrix between the latent variables is presented. As in the exploratory analysis, factor two is moderately correlated with the others, at least by comparison with the larger correlations between factors one and three, one and four, and three and four. The implication is that the "everyday normal expenditures" factor stands apart from the other three, which might be said to form a set. In terms of stylistic unity, information on factor two (factors one, three, and four) yields little information on factors one, three, and four (factor two). That is, there is little consistency across the two sets of variables.

Descriptive form, Spatio-Temporal Invariance, and Social Structure: A Speculative and Nontechnical Exegesis

Up to this point, the descriptive form of stylistic unity has received only marginal attention. In part, this is attributable to the primary focus on the sociological processes underlying what is regarded as an otherwise arbitrary form. Since process is of utmost importance, the focus itself is quite reasonable.

But there is also an abstract sense in which descriptive form is not entirely arbitrary, and this point demands attention as well. To be sure, the specific items that indicate a lifestyle are culturally arbitrary. So is the specific and concrete manner in which lifestyle forms are differentiated, as previously discussed. But the manner in which the lifestyle items hang together (as revealed by the factor analyses) is another story. For it is quite possible that the items themselves are patterned in a manner that is not entirely spatio-temporally specific. And, to the extent that this is true, it is possible to reach conclusions about the abstract organization of a lifestyle that cut across time and space.

For example, it is almost impossible to imagine concrete lifestyle forms in America 100 years from now. But unless there is some great disaster, man will undoubtedly still travel, vacation, love, play, entertain, sleep, eat, drink, cope, attempt to enrich his life, and try to outdo his peers. At the abstract level, what matters is the way in which a lifestyle reflects and is organized about these concerns; it is precisely this form of organization that we might expect to transcend a specific spatio-temporal context. In other words, the abstract patterns that the factor analysis reveals may reflect an abstract stylistic unity that is not at all idiographic.

In this vein, the most important conclusion is that factor one appears prestige oriented and taps a component of lifestyle that is a priori universal. While the factor is specific and strongly superior, as noted, the luxury items on which the loadings are low (Exhibit 8.11) are food purchased away from home (FOODAWAY), expenditures on musical equipment (MUSIC), gifts and contributions (GIFTS), and expenditures on camping, health, and sports equipment (CAMP), which is strongly superior at the middle and high levels of the socioeconomic hierarchy. In this vein, the basically normal items reading materials (READING) and furniture (FURNITUR) have larger loadings. But the largest loadings are for the strongly superior items household decorations (DECORAT), dress clothing (DRSCLOTH), membership fees for clubs and organizations (CLUBS) and vacation expenditures (VACATION), which is strongly superior except at the high level, where it is normal.

While it is difficult to pin a coherent label on this factor, it appears that the primary dimension of a lifestyle is a priori conspicuous, traditional, materially oriented, and prestige related, a dimension on which individuals indicate to others their place or desired place within the stratification system. That is, the elements on which the loadings are highest are of the type that have been singled out as prestige-indicative (Chapin, 1935; Laumann and House, 1970; Shils, 1970; Veblen, 1966; Warner, Meeker, and Eells, 1960; Warner and Lunt, 1941, 1942). Others have adversely associated such elements with conformity, ambition, status drive, self-aggrandizement, pretentiousness, respectability, family life, suburban and small town living, and the American dream.[2] In future reference, we shall often call this factor "visible success" or "prestige acquisition."

Factor two loads most highly (Exhibit 8.11) on the generally weakly superior items personal care expenditures (PERSCARE) and food at home (FOODHOME). Next is the loading for the basically normal item casual clothing (CASCLOTH), followed, respectively, by the loadings for household textiles (TEXTILES), DRSCLOTH, FURNITUR, GIFTS, FOODAWAY, and READING. In the context of the larger loadings, it appears that factor two captures an aspect of lifestyle that is mundane and maintenance oriented, i.e., oriented to sustaining everyday life. Thus, we shall often refer to this factor as "maintenance."

Factor three was originally labeled "strongly superior entertainment" because it loaded on items that were predominantly strongly superior. But it also appears to represent an entertainment form that is youthful, active, other oriented, evening oriented, and nonfamilial, and the structural effects are consistent with this interpretation. With some hesitancy, we might even label this latent variable a "high life" factor.

The fourth factor has already been interpreted as weakly superior. But it also appears to be a priori traditional, familial, and home centered, and it appears to represent a "home life" entertainment form that is qualitatively different from that which factor three taps.

We have no data per se with which to support an argument that stylistic unity is always organized about the lifestyle components that have been identified. But there is every reason to believe that the structure that has been uncovered is in its broad outline typical of advanced Western societies, and there is also reason to believe that this characterization will apply in the future. For several centuries, novelists have written about the relationship between prestige and "visible success" among selected parts of the population, drawing out the often undesirable consequences of excessive personal concern with such phenomena. Since that time, larger segments of the population have been freed from the overwhelming concern with subsistence, thereby incorporated into a position in which this relation is of import. Barring a long-term economic disaster,

[2] These themes are developed in the following novels: *Le Père Goriot* and *Eugénie Grandet* (Honoré de Balzac), *The Red and the Black* (Stendhal), *The Great Gatsby* (F. Scott Fitzgerald), *Madame Bovary* (Gustave Flaubert), *The Rise of Silas Lapham* (William Dean Howells), *The Bostonians* (Henry James), *Babbitt* (Sinclair Lewis), *Point of No Return* (John P. Marquand), *The Razor's Edge* (William Somerset Maugham), *The House of Mirth* and *The Age of Innocence* (Edith Wharton).

or the rise of the "1984 society," there is no a priori reason to expect the relationship itself to deteriorate.

Man also needs to maintain his everyday existence. The manner in which this is accomplished is culturally differentiated in a complex fashion, but the need itself is spatio-temporally invariant. In the society of the future, robots and computers may provide the basic services, but the specific form itself is not the issue.

Similarly, man needs to relax and to enjoy the company and fellowship of others to fulfill his own existence. The entertainment factors point to two different fashions in which man satisfies these needs. Again, there is no inherent reason to expect that the specific manner in which these needs are fulfilled is invariant. But it would be surprising if either of these abstract modes disappeared entirely. Several centuries ago, when most people did not live in large cities, everyday entertainment was centered about the home, or perhaps an occasional fair.[3] Thus, the home life was the predominant mode, and by comparison, the high life was less important. This is clearly no longer the case: recreational forms are differentiated along a variety of new dimensions. But there is no reason to expect the home life to lose its significance: it is a traditional activity and a major form of psychic and economic investment.

While there is every reason to believe that the abstract organization of stylistic unity, and hence lifestyle, is spatio-temporally invariant, there is less reason to have confidence in the assertion that the relationship between social structure and stylistic unity is spatio-temporally invariant. Therefore, in reconsidering the broad outlines of this relation, the notion of spatio-temporal invariance is not stressed, with a few exceptions. The results apply to the particular context, although it is expected that similar findings could be generated in other advanced Western societies, both at this particular point in time, and at points in time not too far removed. Because the regional effects are relevant only in the American context, they are not considered here.

The data show that "visible success" is related to location, but unrelated to age; the latter indicates the invariance of the level of participation

---

[3] In previous historical periods, the high life appears to have been a predominantly urban phenomenon. In several instances (the age of Pericles in ancient Athens), the existing evidence indicates a fairly egalitarian distribution of high life activities among a large proportion of the population (Robinson, 1933; Van Hook, 1937). Similarly, in Renaissance Florence, there is evidence for a high life which is not confined solely to the upper classes (Cellini, 1979; Vasari, 1971). In other periods, for example, Tokugawa Japan, high life activities were structured more rigidly by economic or political status, and participation was characteristic of the nobility and/or merchant class, depending upon the particular historical circumstances (Kirkwood, 1970).

across the levels of the age distribution examined. Participation in the process of "prestige acquisition" is, however, related positively to marriage, though the effect itself is counterbalanced by the presence of additional household members. That is, all other things equal, increasing family size, typically through the siring of children, moderates participation by chaneling resources away from prestige acquisition; this occurs despite the fact that marriage itself is positively associated with visible success. As expected, and as previously discussed, the complex of socioeconomic variables differentiates participation in the dominant mode. Increments to income, occupational status, and education increase participation, and the proportion of marginal income allotted to prestige acquisition decreases as one moves to the top of the income hierarchy.

Not surprisingly, sustaining everyday existence requires a larger fraction of income (and we suspect more attention) on the part of older persons with well established multiple person households. But this relationship is differentiated by location, presumably because it is easier and more acceptable to generate maintenance from within the home in a smaller rather than a larger area. The socioeconomic cluster does not operate uniformly on maintenance, and the effects depend upon location in the socioeconomic hierarchy. Increases in the level of income generate increasing expenditures on maintenance, but a decline in the relative proportion of income allocated to maintenance. At the high end of the hierarchy, the effect of occupational status is negative, so that an increment to status decrements total expenditures on maintenance, and at the low end, the effect is positive. This is consistent with the interpretation that high status individuals (with higher levels of education and income) channel their greater resources differentially into other forms, such as prestige acquisition and high life, while lower status individuals, who are unable to compete as effectively in prestige acquisition thereby place more value on maintaining everyday existence at a higher level and attach importance to this activity. In fact, the popular stereotype that upper-middle-class children go to school in the morning with long hair and tattered jeans, while working-class children go to school neatly groomed is the prime example of this phenomenon.

Our interpretation of the high life factor as youthful and nonfamilial is borne out by the data. First, the effects of the age variable are negative. Similarly, the effect of the family size variable is negative. While the effect of the marital status variable is itself 0, unmarried individuals tend to have single person households, and married individuals tend to have larger households. Thus, for an unmarried individual in a one person household, the effect of marital status is 0, while the effect of the family size variable (FAMSIZE) does not matter, since its value is 0 for that observation. But for larger households, the family size variable has value greater than 0, so the overall effect is negative. Thus the assertion that the factor appears nonfamilial, while not strictly true, is not contradicted by the data. But it does not appear to be the case that high life is predominantly an urban phenomenon, as was initially expected.

The income effects are greater than 1 at all the levels of the socioeconomic hierarchy that have been examined. Thus, not only is an increment to income accompanied by an increase in "high life" expenditures, but as the level of income is raised, the relative proportion of marginal income devoted to high life is increased. Unlike the "visible success" factor, the high life factor is unrelated to education, except at the upper end of the socioeconomic hierarchy, and here its effect is negative. Similarly, the effect of occupational status on high life expenditures is essentially 0, except at the low end of the socioeconomic hierarchy, where the effect is negative; at the high level, the effect is almost positive. Nevertheless, expenditures on "high life" are related primarily to money. With respect to the home life factor, the independent variables operate more or less as expected. Both marriage and large household size augment home life expenditures. Furthermore, the home life is most prevalent outside SMSAs, as might be expected on the basis of the hypothesis of differential opportunity. As income is increased, home life expenditures are increased, but the relative proportion of income allotted to home life expenditures declines. At the high level of the socioeconomic hierarchy, home life expenditures are positively related to education and unrelated to occupational status. Other than this, only the status effect at the low level is significantly different from 0, and here it is negative.

Suppose that we add the income elasticities in Exhibit 8.12 together at each level of the socioeconomic hierarchy; within each level, the sum of the elasticities is approximately 4, the average approximately 1. This indicates that the relative proportion of income spent on the aggregate of the four factors is constant.[4] But the manner in which this constant proportion

---

[4] The fact that the elasticities sum to approximately four is not a mathematical necessity in the strict sense, but an empirical regularity that is true for these data, and, I suspect, for similar data as well.

Intuitively, this empirical regularity reflects the fact that a 1% increment to income is of necessity accompanied by a 1% increment to total expenditures, so long as total expenditures is defined to equal income.

To demonstrate mathematically why the result is even approximately true is exceedingly difficult because there are interactions between income and other variables present, and because the estimation procedure is nonlinear, among other things.

Heuristically, however, we can see that the result is approximately true as follows: let $f_{ik}^* = \exp(f_{ik})$, where f_{ik} is the kth factor score for the ith observation. Suppose, contrary to

is distributed across the factors is not constant. If the income effects for high life and home life are added and halved, values near 1 are obtained at all levels of the socioeconomic hierarchy. That is, the proportion of income spent on entertainment is approximately constant, although its distribution among forms is not. For the present, consider this average as the effect of income on entertainment. Also note that by implication, the proportion of income allotted jointly to maintenance and visible success is approximately constant.

The deviations from constancy, while small, are nonetheless of considerable interest. At the low level of the socioeconomic hierarchy, the effect of income on entertainment is closer to .9 than to 1, at the middle the effect is close to 1, and at the high level, the effect is close to 1.15. Therefore, the effect of income on the first two factors (defined analogously as an average) must be greater than 1, 1, and less than 1, respectively, at the low, medium, and high levels of the socioeconomic hierarchy. Casual inspection of Exhibit 8.12 bears out this assertion and reveals that the separate income effects decline monotonically as successively higher levels of the hierarchy are examined. Thus, the share of additional income allotted to maintenance and visible success is greatest at the low-

---

fact, that $\Sigma_{k=1}^4 f_{ik}^* = y_i$ for all i, where y_i is the income variable (in unlogged form) for the ith observation. Then we know that $\Sigma_{k=1}^4 f_{ik} = \log \Pi_{k=1}^4 f_{ik}^* \le 4\log(y_i/4)$. Suppose that for all i, and all k, the model is given by $f_{ik} = \alpha_k + B_k \log y_i + \delta_k' w_i + \epsilon_{ik}$, where δ_k' and w_i are row and column vectors of parameters and explanatory variables, respectively, that do not include the aforementioned interactions with income, and ϵ_{ik} is a stochastic term with 0 expectation.

$$f_k = [1, \log y, W] \begin{bmatrix} \alpha_k \\ B_k \\ \delta_k \end{bmatrix} + \epsilon_k = [x_1, x_2, W] \begin{bmatrix} \alpha_k \\ B_k \\ \delta_k \end{bmatrix} + \epsilon_k$$

$$= X \begin{bmatrix} \alpha_k \\ B_k \\ \delta_k \end{bmatrix} + \epsilon_k, k = 1, \dots, 4.$$

Suppose that the matrix of explanatory variables has full column rank, and that the model is estimated by ordinary least squares. Suppose also that

$$\sum_{k=1}^4 f_{ik} = 4 \log(y_i/4) = 4 \log y_i - 4 \log 4 \qquad \text{for all } i.$$

Then

$$(X'X)^{-1}X' \left[\sum_{k=1}^4 f_k \right] = \left[\sum_{k=1}^4 \hat{\alpha}_k, \sum_{k=1}^4 \hat{B}_k, \sum_{k=1}^4 \hat{\delta}_k' \right]' = (X'X)^{-1}X' \left[4 \log y - 4 \log 4 \right]$$

$$= 4 (X'X)^{-1}X'x_2 - 4 \log 4 ((X'X)^{-1}X'x_1) = [-4 \log 4, 4, 0']'$$

and note that the result $\Sigma_{k=1}^4 B_k = 4$ is also true when the variables are deviated about their means.

est end of the socioeconomic hierarchy. In other words, the relative proportion of income spent on maintenance declines as income increases, but the decline is least sharp at the lower end of the hierarchy. The share of additional income allotted to prestige acquisition is also greatest at the lower level, and here the increase in the relative proportion of income spent on prestige acquisition is most sharp.

Individuals at the lower end of the hierarchy are only able to increase the relative proportion of income allotted to maintenance and visible success by decreasing the relative proportion allocated to entertainment. Conversely, at the high end of the hierarchy, entertainment becomes marginally more important, and the fraction of additional income devoted to prestige acquisition and maintenance is smaller than at the low end. In other words, those who have already achieved a modicum of success (objective success) appear to be less concerned, at the margin, with its display (visible success) and channel additional resources disproportionately to entertainment. But those who have been less successful are clearly more concerned with the accumulation of visible success. The idea that one must keep up with the Joneses, at least in its traditional form, appears to be rooted most strongly at the lower end of the hierarchy, in contradistinction to a large body of literary and popular writing. Does this mean that individuals at the top of the socioeconomic hierarchy are less concerned with the accumulation of honor? On the face of it, the argument would appear to indicate this. But the data is also consistent with the interpretation that at the top of the hierarchy, entertainment is prestige related. And it is already known that interaction outside the kinship network during nonwork hours is more likely at the top of the hierarchy than at the bottom. If the interpretation itself is correct, it may indicate that persons at the low end of the hierarchy think of symbolic success more conventionally than persons at the high end.

CHAPTER 9

Lifestyle, Stratification, and Alienation: Conclusions and Speculations

In the first part of this study the concept of lifestyle was examined and an analytical theory of lifestyle differentiation presented. In order to formulate the theory it was necessary to decide what a lifestyle is, as previous authors have not used the word systematically or analytically. Thus, it is not clear whether a lifestyle is a property of some loosely defined aggregate or a property of an individual. Not unrelatedly, it is also not clear how to differentiate the causes and consequences of lifestyle from the phenomenon itself; that is, the domain of content is not well specified.

The process of specifying a suitable domain of content was initiated in the third chapter, which delves into the ordinary use of the word *style* and contains an explication of usage among art historians, for whom the concept of style is central. After defining style as "any distinctive, and therefore recognizable, way in which an act is performed or an artifact made or ought to be performed and made [Gombrich, 1968, p. 352]," implications of the definition were considered. Next, a lifestyle was defined by analogy. Then, the derived implications were used as a set of primary criteria to exclude various phenomena from the domain of content. Application of the criteria lead to the conclusion that a lifestyle consists of behaviors that are physically observable or deducible from observation over which an individual has considerable discretionary power.

The application of these criteria lead to a considerable reduction in the domain of content as conceptualized by others. But while the criteria help to pare down the problem, they cannot logically be used to differentiate among the phenomena that satisfy the conditions. In order to "index" lifestyles in some fashion, further reduction of the domain of content is warranted.

To achieve this reduction, the secondary criterion of spatio-temporal salience was applied to those phenomena that satisfy previous criteria. An important implication, not necessarily disadvantageous, is that the particular phenomena may vary over time and/or space. It was argued that in post–World War II America, consumption best indexes lifestyle. The link between psychological gratification and consumption in contemporary American society was historically sketched, and other obvious candidates, e.g., work and leisure, were excluded on the basis of primary and/or secondary criteria.

Logically, this completed that part of the work not subject to empirical disconfirmation. The value of the conceptual work stands apart from any and all analytical theories of lifestyle differentiation, although not from any test of such a theory. This is the case because any such test will utilize data on consumption. If consumption is an inappropriate phenomenon to single out conceptually, then no model that utilizes such data can test any theory about lifestyle differentiation. If, however, consumption is an appropriate phenomenon to focus attention on, no implementation of the theory bears any relationship to the value of the conceptual work.

The theory of lifestyle differentiation that is postulated is twofold. First, lifestyle differentiation was hypothesized to stem from the variety of "referents" and orientations that compose an individual's experience. Second, the variation in these social psychological phenomena was viewed as a function of the variation in the positions individuals occupy within society and the demands that stem from the occupation of these positions, that is, the variation stems from differentiation within the social structure. Thus, lifestyle variation stems from structural differentiation.

The remainder of this work is concerned with implementing and testing the hypothesized theory of lifestyle differentiation.

Data limitations force an exclusive focus on expenditures, as discussed in Chapter 6. These, in conjunction with limitations imposed by the substantive theoretical structure, force us to confine the analysis to white heads of household aged 25–64 in the appropriate survey year.

For this sample, the individual observations were grouped, as described in Chapters 6 and 7, and 17 logged expenditure items regressed, using weighted least squares, upon the structural variables. Effect parameters were estimated for region, location, family size, marital status, head's age, and various combinations of income, education, occupational status, and the interactions among the socioeconomic characteristics. Effects of age and region were found, but these do not conform to a substantively meaningful pattern. The effects of family size, which are significant in many of the equations, appear to be orderly. When the effects are significant, the elasticity of family size is positive for weakly superior items and negative for strongly superior items, indicating that increasing family size is tantamount to placing a constraint upon the disposition of family income. However, marital status in and of itself does not appear to have significant effects upon the production of lifestyle variation. It is believed this occurs because family size, which is strongly associated with marital status, produces that variation which might otherwise be attributed to marital status differentials. Before considering the effects of the socioeconomic variables, the lack of location effects must be explained. Although a variety of interpretations are consistent with the evidence, the preferred explanation asserts the existence of differences in opportunity by location; since there are no effects, it must be the case that these are not capitalized upon.

Finally, the effects of the socioeconomic variables were considered. Education is much less important to lifestyle differentiation than either status or income, and there is little support for Michael's theory that education operates as an efficiency variable. Across levels of the socioeconomic hierarchy, substantively and statistically significant differences in the education elasticities were found. This is even more true of the status and income elasticities. The calculations indicate that the socioeconomic effects are intertwined; that is, the effect of a variable depends upon levels of one or both of the others. Furthermore, it is demonstrated that the effects of education are unrelated to the effects of occupational status and income. But the effects of status and income are positively related, indicating some substitutability with respect to the process of lifestyle differentiation.

In Chapter 8 the preliminary analysis was brought a step further. Relying heavily upon the distinction between *stylistic unity* and *style,* a statistical model in which stylistic unity intervenes between social structure and lifestyle, and in which the effects of social structure on lifestyle are indirect, was postulated and estimated. Substantively, the effects of the structural variables on the stylistic unity variables are of great importance.

After some exploratory analysis, a "MIMIC" model with four latent variables was estimated by means of maximum likelihood. The effects of region are often 0, but there are location effects. There are also effects of head's age on the second, third, and fourth factors, which have been called, respectively, "everyday, normal maintenance," "high life entertainment," and "home life entertainment"; the first factor is a "prestige" factor. The pattern indicates that as head's age increases, expenditures are shifted from factors three and four to factor two. Effects of family size and marital status were also found.

The conclusion that education is not salient to the differentiation of lifestyle, based on the regressions, is somewhat premature. Education appears to have indirect effects, if not total effects, by operating on stylistic unity. Furthermore, the manner in which education differentiates stylistic unity is conditioned by place in the socioeconomic hierarchy.

As before, both income and occupational status are salient. Status operates differentially throughout the socioeconomic hierarchy, and it appears that status is superior (inferior) for strongly superior (weakly superior) factors, while education sometimes displays an inverse pattern. This is particularly true at the high level of the stratification system and suggests both the existence of status-related conspicuous consumption and the partial unresponsiveness of education to this behavior. Income also operates differentially throughout the socioeconomic hierarchy, but substantively the income effects tend toward invariance across levels. This is not true of the effects of the other socioeconomic variables.

Descriptive reexamination of the factors leads to the conclusion that the first factor taps visible success, the second maintenance, the third a form of entertainment we call high life, and the fourth a form of entertainment we call home life. It is argued that this pattern, in its abstract form, represents an underlying organization that is common, at least among advanced Western societies, an organization that is likely to continue into the future.

Conclusions and Speculations

The primary focus of the empirical work is on the effects of the socioeconomic variables. The results minimally indicate that income, status, and education are salient, either directly or indirectly, to lifestyle differentiation, irrespective of level. Thus, both economic and noneconomic aspects of stratification are germane to lifestyle. By implication, the findings provide no support for the simplified Weberian hypothesis (Chapter 2) that class differentiates production while status differentiates consumption. The effects of the three variables are intertwined, so that the effects of the economic variables tend to depend upon levels of the noneconomic variables and vice-versa. Hence, the economic aspects of stratification condition the fashion in which the noneconomic aspects differentiate lifestyle; similarly, the noneconomic aspects condition the relationship between lifestyle and economic dimensions of stratification. However, the extent to which the noneconomic aspects of stratification condition the economic aspects is less than the converse.

In Chapter 2 it is argued that the study of lifestyle is a legitimate sociological enterprise, in part because the notion itself is related to phenomena that sociologists already consider important. Thus, it is important to construct the concept independently, in a general fashion that facilitates the study of these relations. While the empirical work has focused on the relationship between lifestyle, stylistic unity, and social structure, we have yet to indicate those other phenomena that are related to lifestyle and/or stylistic unity. Nor have we indicated why lifestyle (stylistic unity) is an important sociological concept. An exploration of these issues appears to be warranted, indeed, necessary. In the process of this inquiry, it becomes clear that the concept of lifestyle should command a more important place in stratification research and in general sociological thought.

At a fixed point in time, an individual's lifestyle stems from both his relationship to the social system (structured choice) and choices that are viewed as idiosyncratic. Embedded in this set of choices are implications regarding other phenomena; for example, certain lifestyle choices imply a low rate of saving. Furthermore, lifestyle choices are antecedents (perhaps causal) to both future lifestyle choices and to those social roles that are not ascribed. Individual lifestyle choices may by means of aggregation effect energy utilization, household formation and dissolution, migration patterns, crime rates, health and the distribution of health care services, to cite a few examples. Hence, the concept of lifestyle should be of direct interest to a broad variety of social researchers, at both micro and macro analytic levels.

While the preceeding is sufficient to establish the potential utility of the concept, it dodges the ill-defined question of meaning. This is indeed a difficult question, and as we shall see, even a partial answer is multi-faceted.

Social stratification, however defined, is at the center of sociological theory and research. Recent American research on the question of who gets what and why has focused on three characteristics, education, income, and occupational status (occupational prestige), these being perceived as the major reward axes in American society. Together, these characteristics form a moderately correlated set of elements that are causally related. Separately each component of this triptych serves as a basis for general social standing (prestige, honor, deference-position).

The theory of lifestyle differentiation, per se, merely places lifestyle at the end of this set of relations. But lifestyle is also a basis for social standing because, at least in part it reflects "a voluntary participation in an order of values [Shils, 1970; p. 425]." In addition, while financial position is an initial condition for a lifestyle, lifestyle should not be treated as a mirror image of wealth and income. For example, old wealth begets more deference than new wealth precisely because of lifestyle differences between the old and new rich. Lifestyle, because it is a nondeterministic transformation of financial position, is thus a conceptually independent and empirically distinct source of standing.[1] Furthermore, along with occupation, lifestyle constitutes "the most substantial and continuous of the various deference-entitlements [Shils, 1970, p. 430]," and it is the most visible basis of standing. Finally, of the four characteristics under consideration, lifestyle, at the individual level, stands furthest away from those relations that govern production and closest to the realm of culture (Shils, 1970, p. 426).

In addition to the theoretical argument, two other points should be noted. First, the historical record provides descriptive and suggestive evidence for the notion that lifestyle is a source of standing.[2] Second, the empirical results in the previous chapter appear to support the theoretical argument.

To predict the future import of lifestyle as a status generating characteristic is a perilous activity, dependent upon a vision of the future itself. Nevertheless, I shall argue that the import of lifestyle may well increase. But as the conclusion derives most naturally from the next level of meaning I wish to consider, the discussion of this point is deferred.

In Chapter 3, it is argued that Americans create individual lifestyles that are profoundly shaped by consumption. Furthermore, it is argued that in American society a lifestyle is an important property of an individual, and that a fair amount of self-esteem (or lack of it) derives from distinctive lifestyle choices. From the individual's standpoint, a lifestyle choice is not important because it contributes to the maintenance and creation of social relationships in the abstract, nor does the importance lie

[1] In fact, Shils (1970, p. 424) argues that financial position serves as a deference-entitlement only when conjoined with a certain style of life.

[2] This observation indicates that lifestyle is not merely a modern but also a conventional basis of esteem. It also highlights the potentiality of the concept in historical research.

in the fact that lifestyle choices are partially structured by position in the social system. Neither does the importance reside in the baseline provision of food and shelter; in contemporary America, this is taken for granted, and by itself, subsistence merely provides a partial context around which a broad range of possibilities are organized. Rather, lifestyle is important because it manifests both social and individual identity, because lifestyle has become an increasingly important center of meaning, in short, because the creation of lifestyle itself is a time-intensive activity with a heavy investment of ego. In this context, the modern significance of a lifestyle may arise as a solution to the existential problems of boredom, meaninglessness, and lack of control, problems created by the confluence of affluence and the destruction of the traditional centers of meaning, religion, work, family, and community.

No doubt this view, as posed, is somewhat naive. Alienation, in any of these three forms, is hardly unique to modern man. Nor can it be said that any of the aforementioned institutions have withered away. On the other hand, majority affluence is a historically unprecedented form of existence that provides the initial conditons for the de-emphasis of the subsistence problem, thereby allowing for secondary motivations to enter the forefront of everyday consideration. Furthermore, while religion, work, family, and community are still prevalent institutional forms, each of these has undergone a dramatic transformation in twentieth century America. Religion lost "salience" as "scientific explanation" entered the foreground. Urbanization transformed traditional community structure, and social relations became increasingly rationalized. The nuclear family remains intact, despite theorizing to the contrary, yet the broader kinship networks lost ground as the separate nuclear units scattered across the country. And work, as previously discussed, appears to be increasingly losing much of its intrinsic importance among a large fraction of the population. Thus, the existential view is at least partially grounded in empirical reality, and the notion that lifestyle increasingly fills a partial void must be taken seriously.

In fact, it is precisely this notion, albeit stated somewhat differently, that has formed the starting point for a variety of modern thinkers. There are those who see a nascent form of community arising out of the modern city, just as there are others who espouse the return to occupational salience as a basis of meaning. Similarly, others blame the decline of family and/or religion for the "insidious" nature of contemporary life and advocate the restoration of these institutions to their proper place in the social system. On the psychological side there are the futurist–humanist–individualists, advocating nonmaterial potentiality and self-actualization as truly meaningful sources of truly meaningful satisfaction. And finally there are those who have abandoned all hope, who believe that "1984" is just around the corner.[3]

However, our concern is with the probable course of the future and the place of lifestyle in future society, not with the merit of these particular points of view. In this vein, it seems likely that, barring any gross disaster (e.g., nuclear war), a scenario of the future based on some extrapolation of the present constitutes a more likely vision, particularly in the short run.

Ceteris paribus, extrapolation of a decline in the intrinsic significance of work leads to the conclusion that the salience of lifestyle will increase. In the limit, if work is perceived as an activity that generates only extrinsic rewards, then occupational role no longer qualifies as a status generating characteristic. In addition, since there is no intrinsic meaning to the activity itself, a transfer of meaning from work to some other center of meaning is required. The contention here is that lifestyle is not an unlikely recipient of the transfer.[4]

We could easily muster additional evidence for the conclusion that lifestyle is likely to increase in importance. But by now, the implications of the discussion should be clear: The concept of lifestyle is a valuable analytic tool, and its potentiality in sociological research is likely to increase. Thus, it is time for researchers to focus attention on the concept, its implications, and its measurement.

There is a great amount of work to be done, and as a first step it is of value to more accurately pin down the relationship of lifestyle to social structure. In this study, for example, the interpretation of the socioeconomic effects depends upon the levels of the hierarchy chosen for examination, not the joint probability density function of education, occupation, and income.

Beyond this, the research reported upon here is predominantly exploratory. While this is reasonable, given the approach to the problem, the work inevitably suffers from both the usual problems of statistical inference in exploratory research and the lack of a basis from which to extend findings and rethink issues. It is hoped that this research will provide a basis for these activities.

[3] In actuality, modern critical thought cannot be divided so clearly into well-defined camps, nor is it as superficial as portrayed. Nevertheless, it is useful to establish boundaries by drawing out the stereotypes in this fashion.

[4] An alternative view of the future that leads to similar conclusions postulates the automatization of work and a consequent shrinkage of the working population (see Shils, 1970, pp. 429–430). In this vein, it might also be noted that the disappearance of educational and/or income differentials could also increase the importance of lifestyle.

There are several directions in which future work should go. First, attention should be paid to other dimensions of consumption, as indicated in the data and methods chapter. To the extent that it is difficult to measure activity through consumption, some data on activities may need to be generated and utilized. The expenditures data itself could be better, and perhaps a longer time frame is needed to more accurately measure expenditures on certain items, in particular, major durables. Additionally, some thought as to other methods of data analysis might be fruitful. Stylistic unity need not be conceptualized as it is in this work. More importantly, given the data and methods of analysis employed here, there are an insufficient number of blacks in the sample to merit a black–white comparison. Additionally, there are an insufficient number of household heads aged 65 and above.

Cross-sectional and cross-cultural comparisons also need to be made, at least in those instances where such comparisons would be temporally and spatially appropriate. Among other things, such comparisons would shed light on the validity of the hypothesis that abstract descriptive form is spatio-temporally invariant (with appropriate qualifications, of course). In addition, it would be desirable to study lifestyles longitudinally in order to assess both the stability of the phenomenon and the nature of change.

Besides this, there is also a need for more conceptual and theoretical work. I have argued that the concept of lifestyle is important and have attempted to back up this assertion with a variety of examples and reasons. The argument itself is suggestive, but at best it scratches the surface of social reality. More penetrating analyses are called for.

In short, only after new data has been collected, and after more intensive and extensive inquiries have been conducted will researchers better understand the concept of lifestyle and its place in sociological thought.

Creation of the Education Codes

The Bureau of Labor Statistics used the following scheme to code respondents' education, using the highest level completed:

1   Some grade school
2   Some high school
3   High school graduate
4   Some college
5   College graduate, graduate work
6   None, no response, invalid code

In order to transform this scheme into regular years of schooling completed, we first treated all respondents coded 6 as missing data. For the others, transformed values were computed by taking weighted averages over the appropriate grades, within the B.L.S. levels, by sex, age, and race. That is, within these groups, we computed the conditional probability, for a given grouping of grades, that respondent had a particular level of education, as defined in single years of completed schooling. Then the frequencies, by single year, within a sex, age, and race level, are weighted by the probabilities to compute the specific average.

The data utilized are the 1970 Census cross-classification of education by sex by race by age. Although the study utilizes only the data pertaining to nonblack females aged 25 to 64 and to nonblack males 25 to 64, the transformed values are presented for three age groups, and for blacks as well as nonblacks.

NON-BLACK MALES

Age:	20-24	25-64	65+
1.	6.76	6.80	6.47
2.	10.11	10.00	9.83
3.	12.00	12.00	12.00
4.	13.88	13.83	13.86
5.	16.53	16.95	16.88

BLACK MALES

Age:	20-24	25-64	65+
1.	6.32	5.57	4.80
2.	10.17	10.01	9.81
3.	12.00	12.00	12.00
4.	13.72	13.79	13.88
5.	16.48	17.01	16.94

NON-BLACK FEMALES

Age:	20-24	25-64	65+
1.	6.82	6.92	6.62
2.	10.11	10.04	9.89
3.	12.00	12.00	12.00
4.	13.87	13.80	13.84
5.	16.29	16.66	16.63

BLACK FEMALES

Age:	20-24	25-64	65+
1.	6.43	5.96	5.22
2.	10.13	10.01	9.80
3.	12.00	12.00	12.00
4.	13.74	13.75	13.87
5.	16.30	16.82	16.63

Creation of the SEI Scores

The BLS used the following occupation codes:

1   self employed, including farm operators
2   salaried professional, technical and kindred workers
3   salaried managers and administrators, and kindred workers
Wage and other salaried:
4   clerical workers
5   sales workers
6   craftsmen
7   operatives
8   unskilled laborers, including household workers
9   service workers
10   not working, not retired
11   retired
12   other (Armed forces living off post, working without pay, invalid codes, not reported)

The BLS industry codes are

1   agriculture, forestry, fishing, mining
2   construction
3   manufacturing
4   transportation, communications, utilities, finance, insurance, real estate
5   trade
6   nonprofessional service
7   professional service
8   public administration
9   not reported
0   other (retired, invalid codes, not applicable)

First, the BLS occupational codes must be made into a set of categories that more closely correspond with Census definitions. Using BLS occupation as the row variable and BLS industry as the column variable, we create a matrix whose entries are the transformed codes. The matrix is as follows:

	1	2	3	4	5	6	7	8	9	0
1	8	2	2	2	2	2	2	2	2	2
2	1	1	1	1	1	1	1	1	1	1
3	2	2	2	2	2	2	2	2	2	2
4	4	4	4	4	4	4	4	4	4	4
5	3	3	3	3	3	3	3	3	3	3
6	5	5	5	5	5	5	5	5	5	5
7	6	6	6	6	6	6	6	6	6	6
8	9	7	7	7	7	7	7	7	7	7
9	10	10	10	10	10	10	10	10	10	10
10	13	13	13	13	13	13	13	13	13	13
11	13	13	13	13	13	13	13	13	13	13
12	13	13	13	13	13	13	13	13	13	13

Entry codes are

1   professional, technical and kindred workers
2   managers, officials and proprietors
3   sales workers
4   clerical workers
5   craftsmen
6   operatives, including transportation
7   unskilled laborers, including private household workers
8   farmers

9   farm workers
10   service workers, excluding private household
13   missing or inappropriate

Conditional probabilities, race and sex specific, are computed by detailed occupational categories within each entry code, using frequencies from the 1970 Census of Population. These are multiplied into the detailed SEI scores (Featherman, Sobel and Dickens, 1975) and summed within entry codes, so that the SEI score attached to an entry category is a weighted average of the detailed occupational scores within the category.
The scores are as follows:

	NON-BLACK MEN	BLACK MEN	NON-BLACK WOMEN	BLACK WOMEN
1.	74.77	68.61	63.11	64.19
2.	63.30	61.51	58.34	59.76
3.	52.80	48.29	41.13	41.82
4.	45.24	43.13	52.13	50.35
5.	33.10	28.87	36.99	34.10
6.	19.48	18.81	17.98	17.57
7.	9.23	8.86	9.79	8.21
8.	15.00	15.08	14.92	14.97
9.	7.96	6.72	10.17	6.92
10.	19.20	14.84	17.16	14.36 .

APPENDIX C

Creation of the Dependent Variables

FOODHOME - Food at home (excluding vacation or nonpleasure trips) is defined as the sum of the following:

    Food purchases at grocery store
    Food purchases at specialty store
    Bulk food purchases for canning and freezing
    Board

FOODAWAY - Food away from home (excluding vacation or nonpleasure trips) is defined as the sum of the following:

    Meals in restaurant, cafeteria, etc.
    School meals purchased
    Other meals purchased
    Weddings catered
    Confirmations or Bar Mitzvahs catered
    Other affairs catered

ALCOHOL - Alcohol (excluding vacation or nonpleasure trips) is defined as the sum of the following:

    Alcoholic beverages purchased at grocery stores
    Wine and beer purchased at other stores
    Other alcoholic beverages purchased at other stores
    Alcohol purchased at restaurants, taverns, etc.

HOUSING - Housing (excluding vacation homes, vacation and non-pleasure trips) is defined as the sum of the following:

    Rent (current home)
    Rent (previous home in survey year, part year CU)
    Rent (previous home in survey year, full year CU)
    Rent (previously rented home in survey year, excluding
      vacation home)
    Rent as pay
    Repairs and redecorating fees charged to renters
    Special fees and commissions charged to renters
    Garage and parking fees charged to renters

HOUSING continued

Interest paid on first mortgage (present home)
Interest paid on first mortgage (previous home in survey
   year)
Interest paid on second mortgage (present home)
Interest paid on second mortgage (previous home in survey
   year)
Refinancing charges (present home)
Refinancing charges (previous home in survey year)
Prepayment penalty on mortgage (present home)
Prepayment penalty on mortgage (previous home in survey
   year)
Property taxes (present home)
Property taxes (previous home in survey year)
Real property insurance (present home)
Real property insurance (previous home in survey year)
Comprehensive (homeowners) insurance (present home)
Comprehensive (homeowners) insurance (previous home in
   survey year)
Other property insurance (present home)
Other property insurance (previous home in survey year)
Ground rent (present home)
Ground rent (previous home in survey year)
Land rent for mobile home (present home)
Land rent for mobile home in survey year (previous home in
   survey year)
Interior painting and papering, contracted out (present
   home)
Interior painting and papering, contracted out (previous
   home in survey year)
Interior painting and papering, materials only (present
   home)
Interior painting and papering, materials only (previous
   home in survey year)
Exterior painting, contracted out (present home)
Exterior painting, contracted out (previous home in survey
   year)
Exterior painting, materials only (present home)
Exterior painting, materials only (previous home in survey
   year)
Water heater and plumbing, contracted out (present home)
Water heater and plumbing, contracted out (previous home in
   survey year)
Water heater and plumbing, materials only (present home)

HOUSING continued

Water heater and plumbing, materials only (previous home in survey year)
Heating or air conditioning, contracted out (present home)
Heating or air conditioning, contracted out (previous home in survey year)
Heating or air conditioning, materials only (present home)
Heating or air conditioning, materials only (previous home in survey year)
Electrical work, contracted out (present home)
Electrical work, contracted out (previous home in survey year)
Electrical work, materials only (present home)
Electrical work, materials only (previous home in survey year)
Roofing or gutters, contracted out (present home)
Roofing or gutters, contracted out (previous home in survey year)
Roofing or gutters, materials only (present home)
Roofing or gutters, materials only (previous home in survey year)
Pest control service contracts
Lawn maintenance service contracts
Pool maintenance service contracts
Furnace or air conditioning service contracts
Other service contracts
Maintenance charges included in mortgage payments (present home)
Maintenance charge included in mortgage payments (previous home in survey year)
Periodic maintenance charges (present home)
Periodic maintenance charges (previous home in survey year)
Plastering and paneling, contracted out (present home)
Plastering and paneling, contracted out (previous home in survey year)
Plastering and paneling, materials only (present home)
Plastering and paneling, materials only (previous home in survey year)
Siding, contracted out (present home)
Siding, contracted out (previous home in survey year)
Siding, materials only (present home)
Siding, materials only (previous home in survey year)
Flooring, linoleum or vinyl tile, contracted out (present home)
Flooring, linoleum or vinyl tile, contracted out (previous home in survey year)

HOUSING continued

Flooring, linoleum or vinyl tile, materials only (present home)
Flooring, linoleum or vinyl tile, materials only (previous home in survey year)
Other hard surface floor coverings, contracted out
Windows, screens, awnings, etc., contracted out (present home)
Windows, screens awnings, etc., contracted out (previous home in survey year)
Windows, screens, awnings, etc., materials only (present home)
Windows, screens, awnings, etc., materials only (previous home in survey year)
Pest control not covered by contracts, contracted out (present home)
Pest control not covered by contracts, contracted out (previous home in survey year)
Pest control not covered by contracts, materials only (present home)
Pest control not covered by contracts, materials only (previous home in survey year)
Small repair jobs around the house, contracted out, (present home)
Small repair jobs around the house, contracted out, (previous home in survey year)
Small repair jobs around the house, materials only (present home)
Small repair jobs around the house, materials only (previous home in survey year)
Materials not for specific repairs (present home)
Materials not for specific repairs (previous home in survey year)
Lodging at school or college
Other lodging, excluding vacations
Reduction of principal (present home) negative
Reduction of principal (previous home) negative
Mortgage interest due in survey year but not paid
Rent due in survey year but not paid

TEXTILES - Household textiles (including vacation homes) is defined as the sum of the following:

Sheets
Pillowcases
Pillows excluding decorator pillows and cushions
Decorative pillows and cushions

TEXTILES   continued

    Bedspreads
    Electric blankets
    Other blankets and quilts
    Table linens, woven or plastic
    Towels and washcloths
    Bathmats and toilet seat covers
    Shower curtains
    Kitchen towels
    Custom-made curtains
    Ready-made curtains
    Custom-made draperies
    Custom-made slipcovers
    Other furniture protectors
    Other bedroom linens
    Other bathroom linens
    Other kitchen or dining room linens
    Materials for draperies, etc.
    Crochet thread, yarn, etc.

FURNITUR - Household furniture and floor coverings (including
    vacation homes) is defined as the sum of the following:

    Nonconvertible sofa or couch
    Convertible sofa or couch
    Nonreclining chairs
    Recliner chairs
    Living room suites
    Desks
    Tables
    Bookcases or record cabinets
    Other living room furniture
    Bar or portable bar
    Other recreation and house furnishings
    Dining room tables
    Dining room chairs
    China cabinets or buffet
    Dining room suites
    Dinette sets
    Serving table or cart
    Other dining room furniture
    Kitchen tables
    Uninstalled kitchen cabinets
    Other kitchen furniture
    Headboards and bedframes

FURNITUR continued

    Mattresses, springs, rollaway beds
    Bedroom dressers, chests and vanities
    Nightstands
    Bedroom chairs
    Bedroom suites
    Other bedroom furniture
    Cribs and mattresses
    Playpens
    Other infants furniture
    Nursery chests or dressers
    Baby carriage or stroller
    Wooden outdoor furniture
    Metal outdoor furniture
    Plastic and vinyl outdoor furniture
    Other outdoor furniture
    Installed wall to wall carpet other than kitchen or bath
    Uninstalled wall to wal carpet other than kitchen or bath
    Installed wall to wall carpet for kitchen or bathroom
    Uninstalled wall to wall carpet for kitchen or bathroom
    Room size rugs
    Other soft floor covering

DECORAT - Household Decorations (including vacation homes) is
    defined as the sum of the following:

    Lamps
    Chandeliers and other light fixtures
    Custom-made window shades, blinds and rods
    Ready-made window shades, blinds and rods
    Paintings and pictures (greater than $10)
    Clocks
    Other decorative items (greater than $15)
    Mirrors

CASCLOTH - Casual clothing is defined as the sum of the following:

    Casual slacks and dress jeans for men
    Other slacks for men
    Dungarees, jeans and work pants for men
    Other dungarees or jeans for men
    Short pants for men
    Other shorts and short sets for men
    Other trousers and slacks for men
    Swim suits for men

CASCLOTH   continued

Beach robes and other swim wear for men
Special sport clothing for men
Uniforms not reimbursed for men
Other special clothing for men
Sport shirts for men
Work shirts for men
Blouses for men
Other shirts for men
Casual slacks and dress jeans for boys
Other slacks for boys
Dungarees, jeans, and work pants for boys
Other dungarees or jeans for boys
Short pants for boys
Other shorts and short sets for boys
Other trousers and slacks for boys
Uniforms not reimbursed for boys
Other special clothing for boys
Swim suits for boys
Beach robes and other swim wear for boys
Special sport clothing for boys
Sport shirts for boys
Work shirts for boys
Blouses for boys
Other shirts for boys
Street dresses including two-piece pant-dresses for women
Jumpers for women
Sport shirts for women
Work shirts for women
Blouses or tops for women
Other shirts for women
Skirts or culottes for women
Items similar to dresses for women
Other casual slacks and dress jeans for women
Other dungarees, jeans and work pants for women
Other shorts for women
Slacks for women
Dungarees or jeans for women
Shorts and short sets for women
Other trousers and slacks for women
Uniforms not reimbursed for women
Other special clothing for women
Swim suits for women
Beach robes and other swim wear for women
Special sport clothing for women

CASCLOTH continued

```
T-shirts for women
Street dresses for girls
Jumpers for girls
Sport shirts for girls
Work shirts for girls
Blouses or tops for girls
Other shirts for girls
Skirts or culottes for girls
Items similar to dresses for girls
Other casual slacks and dress jeans for girls
Other dungarees, jeans and work pants for girls
Other shorts for girls
Slacks for girls
Dungarees or jeans for girls
Shorts and short sets for girls
Other trouser and slacks for girls
Uniforms not reimbursed for girls
Other special clothing for girls
Swim suits for girls
Beach robes and other swim wear for girls
Special sport clothing for girls
Undershirts or t-shirts for girls
Sweaters and sweater sets for infants
Street dresses for infants
Jumpers for infants
Skirts or culottes for infants
Items similar to dresses for infants
Other outerwear for infants
Casual slacks and dress jeans (male) for infants
Dungarees and jeans (male) for infants
Short pants (male) for infants
Slacks (female) for infants
Dungarees or jeans (female) for infants
Shorts or short sets (female) for infants
Other trousers or slacks for infants
Sport shirts for infants
Unclassified shirts for infants
Blouses or tops for infants
Other shirts for infants
Swim suits for infants
Beach robes and other swim wear for infants
Special sport clothing for infants
Other special clothing for infants
```

DRSCLOTH - Dress clothing is defined as the sum of the following:

2 or 3 piece suits for men
Other 2 or 3 piece suits for men
Sports coats and tailored jackets for men
Vests for men
Unclassified suits for men
Items similar to suits for men
Unclassified suits for men
Unclassified suits for men
Unclassified suits for men
Unclassified suits for men
Unclassified suits for men
Unclassified suits for men
Dress trousers or slacks for men
Dress shirts for men
2 or 3 piece suits for boys
Other 2 or 3 piece suits for boys
Sports coats and tailored jackets for boys
Vests for boys
Unclassified suits for boys
Items similar to suits for boys
Unclassified suits for boys
Unclassified suits for boys
Unclassified suits for boys
Unclassified suits for boys
Unclassified suits for boys
Unclassified suits for boys
Dress trousers or slacks for boys
Dress shirts for boys
Sport coats and tailored jackets for women
One-piece pant-dresses for women
Formal or semiformal dresses for women
Other 2 or 3 piece suits for women
2 or 3 piece suits for women
Pantsuits for women
Dress shirts for women
Vests for women
Items similar to suits for women
Other dress slacks for women
Sports coats and tailored jackets for girls
One-piece pant dresses for girls
Formal or semiformal dresses for girls
Other 2 or 3 piece suits for girls
2 or 3 piece suits for girls
Pantsuits for girls

DRSCLOTH   continued

Dress shirts for girls
Vests for girls
Items similar to suits for girls
Other dress slacks for girls
2 or 3 piece suits (male) for infants
2 or 3 piece suits (female) for infants
Pantsuits for infants
Sports coats and tailored jackets for infants
Vests for infants
Items similar to suits for infants
Formal or semiformal dresses for infants
One-piece pant-dresses for infants
Dress trousers or slacks (male) for infants
Dress shirts for infants

PERSCARE - Personal Care (selected items) is defined as the sum
    of the following:

Haircuts and other barber shop services for males
Shampoos and sets for females
Haircuts for females
Other beauty parlor services for females including wig
    care
Males hairpieces or toupees
Females hairpieces or wigs

VACATION - Recreation, Vacation Trips is defined as the sum of
    the following:

Car or camper (gas, oil en route), domestic trips partly
    for business
Car or camper (gas, oil en route), domestic trips to summer
    camp
Car or camper (gas, oil en route), domestic trips for
    vacation or pleasure
Car or camper (gas, oil en route), foreign trips partly for
    business
Car or camper (gas, oil en route), foreign trips to summer
    camp
Car or camper (gas, oil en route), foreign trips for
    vacation or pleasure
Other vehicle expense, domestic trips partly for business
Other vehicle expenses, domestic trips to summer camp
Other vehicle expenses, domestic trips for vacation or
    pleasure

VACATION continued

Other vehicle expenses, foreign trips partly for business
Other vehicle expenses, foreign trips to summer camp
Other vehicle expenses, foreign trips for vacation or
   pleasure
Toll charges, domestic trips partly for business
Toll charges, domestic trips to summer camp
Toll charges, domestic trips for vacation or pleasure
Toll charges, foreign trips partly for business
Toll charges, foreign trips to summer camp
Toll charges, foreign trips for vacation or pleasure
Own car at destination, domestic trips partly for business
Own car at destination, domestic trips to summer camp
Own car at destination, domestic trips for vacation or
   pleasure
Other own transportation at destination, domestic trips
   partly for business
Other own transportation at destination, domestic trips to
   summer camp
Other own transportation at destination, domestic trips for
   vacation or pleasure
Vehicle owned by other outside CU at destination, domestic
   trips partly for business
Vehicle owned by other outside CU at destination, domestic
   trips to summer camp
Vehicle owned by other outside CU at destination, domestic
   trips for vacation or pleasure
Own car at destination, foreign trips partly for business
Own car at destination, foreign trips to summer camp
Own car at destination, foreign trips for vacation or
   pleasure
Other own transportation at destination, foreign trips partly
   for business
Other own transportation at destination, foreign trips to
   summer camp
Other own transportation at destination, foreign trips for
   vacation or pleasure
Vehicle owned by other outside CU at destination, foreign
   trips partly for business
Vehicle owned by other outside CU at destination, foreign
   trips to summer camp
Vehicle owned by other outside CU at destination, foreign
   trips for vacation or pleasure
Plane fares to and from domestic trips partly for business

VACATION continued

Plane fares to and from domestic trips to summer camp
Plane fares to and from domestic trips for vacation or
   pleasure
Plane fares at destination on domestic trips partly for
   business
Plane fares at destination on domestic trips to summer camp
Plane fares at destination on domestic trips for vacation
   or pleasure
Plane fares to and from foreign trips partly for business
Plane fares to and from foreign trips to summer camp
Plane fares to and from foreign trips for vacation or
   pleasure
Plane fares at destination on foreign trips partly for
   business
Plane fares at destination on foreign trips to summer camp
Plane fares at destination on foreign trips for vacation or
   pleasure
Train or bus fares to and from domestic trips partly for
   business
Train or bus fares to and from domestic trips to summer camp
Train or bus fares to and from domestic trips for vacation
   or pleasure
Train or bus fares at destination on domestic trips partly
   for business
Train or bus fares at destination on domestic trips to
   summer camp
Train or bus fares at destination on domestic trips for
   vacation or pleasure
Train or bus fares to and from foreign trips partly for
   business
Train or bus fares to and from foreign trips to summer camp
Train or bus fares to and from foreign trips for vacation
   or pleasure
Train or bus fares at destination on foreign trips partly
   for business
Train or bus fares at destination on foreign trips to
   summer camp
Train or bus fares at destination on foreign trips for
   vacation or pleasure
Boat fares to and from domestic trips partly for business
Boat fares to and from domestic trips to summer camp
Boat fares to and from domestic trips for vacation or
   pleasure
Boat fares at destination on domestic trips partly for
   business

VACATION   continued

Boat fares at destination on domestic trips to summer camp
Boat fares at destination on domestic trips for vacation
or pleasure
Boat fares to and from foreign trips partly for business
Boat fares to and from foreign trips to summer camp
Boat fares to and from foreign trips for vacation or
pleasure
Boat fares at destination on foreign trips partly for
business
Boat fares at destination on foreign trips to summer camp
Boat fares at destination on foreign trips for vacation or
pleasure
Rented vehicle to and from domestic trips partly for
business
Rented vehicle to and from domestic trips to summer camp
Rented vehicle to and from domestic trips for vacation or
pleasure
Rented vehicle at destination on domestic trips partly for
business
Rented vehicle at destination on domestic trips to summer
camp
Rented vehicle at destination on domestic trips for vacation
or pleasure
Rented vehicle to and from foreign trips partly for business
Rented vehicle to and from foreign trips to summer camp
Rented vehicle to and from foreign trips for vacation or
pleasure
Rented vehicle at destination on foreign trips partly for
business
Rented vehicle at destination on foreign trips to summer
camp
Rented vehicle at destination on foreign trips for vacation
or pleasure
Limousine or taxi to and from domestic trips partly for
business
Limousine or taxi to and from domestic trips to summer camp
Limousine or taxi to and from domestic trips for vacation
or pleasure
Limousine or taxi at destination on domestic trips partly
for business
Limousine or taxi at destination on domestic trips to
summer camp
Limousine or taxi at destination on domestic trips for
vacation or pleasure

VACATION   continued

Limousine or taxi to and from foreign trips partly for
   business
Limousine or taxi to and from foreign trips to summer camp
Limousine or taxi to and from foreign trips for vacation or
   pleasure
Limousine or taxi at destination on foreign trips partly for
   business
Limousine or taxi at destination on foreign trips to summer
   camp
Limousine or taxi at destination on foreign trips for
   vacation or pleasure
Combined travel expenses on domestic trips partly for
   business
Combined travel expenses on domestic trips to summer camp
Combined travel expenses on domestic trips for vacation or
   pleasure
Combined travel expenses on foreign trips partly for business
Combined travel expenses on foreign trips to summer camp
Combined travel expenses on foreign trips for vacation or
   pleasure
Food to be prepared on domestic trips partly for business
Food to be prepared on domestic trips to summer camp
Food to be prepared on domestic trips for vacation or
   pleasure
Food to be prepared on foreign trips partly for business
Food to be prepared on foreign trips to summer camp
Food to be prepared on foreign trips for vacation or
   pleasure
Meals purchased on domestic trips partly for business
Meals purchased on domestic trips to summer camp
Meals purchased on domestic trips for vacation or pleasure
Meals purchased on foreign trips partly for business
Meals purchased on foreign trips to summer camp
Meals purchased on foreign trips for vacation or pleasure
Alcoholic beverages by the drink on domestic trips partly
   for business
Alcoholic beverages by the drink on domestic trips to
   summer camp
Alcoholic beverages by the drink on domestic trips for
   vacation or pleasure
Alcoholic beverages by the drink on foreign trips partly for
   business
Alcoholic beverages by the drink on foreign trips to summer
   camp

VACATION   continued

Boat fares at destination on domestic trips to summer camp
Boat fares at destination on domestic trips for vacation
  or pleasure
Boat fares to and from foreign trips partly for business
Boat fares to and from foreign trips to summer camp
Boat fares to and from foreign trips for vacation or
  pleasure
Boat fares at destination on foreign trips partly for
  business
Boat fares at destination on foreign trips to summer camp
Boat fares at destination on foreign trips for vacation or
  pleasure
Rented vehicle to and from domestic trips partly for
  business
Rented vehicle to and from domestic trips to summer camp
Rented vehicle to and from domestic trips for vacation or
  pleasure
Rented vehicle at destination on domestic trips partly for
  business
Rented vehicle at destination on domestic trips to summer
  camp
Rented vehicle at destination on domestic trips for vacation
  or pleasure
Rented vehicle to and from foreign trips partly for business
Rented vehicle to and from foreign trips to summer camp
Rented vehicle to and from foreign trips for vacation or
  pleasure
Rented vehicle at destination on foreign trips partly for
  business
Rented vehicle at destination on foreign trips to summer
  camp
Rented vehicle at destination on foreign trips for vacation
  or pleasure
Limousine or taxi to and from domestic trips partly for
  business
Limousine or taxi to and from domestic trips to summer camp
Limousine or taxi to and from domestic trips for vacation
  or pleasure
Limousine or taxi at destination on domestic trips partly
  for business
Limousine or taxi at destination on domestic trips to
  summer camp
Limousine or taxi at destination on domestic trips for
  vacation or pleasure

VACATION continued

Limousine or taxi to and from foreign trips partly for
   business
Limousine or taxi to and from foreign trips to summer camp
Limousine or taxi to and from foreign trips for vacation or
   pleasure
Limousine or taxi at destination on foreign trips partly for
   business
Limousine or taxi at destination on foreign trips to summer
   camp
Limousine or taxi at destination on foreign trips for
   vacation or pleasure
Combined travel expenses on domestic trips partly for
   business
Combined travel expenses on domestic trips to summer camp
Combined travel expenses on domestic trips for vacation or
   pleasure
Combined travel expenses on foreign trips partly for business
Combined travel expenses on foreign trips to summer camp
Combined travel expenses on foreign trips for vacation or
   pleasure
Food to be prepared on domestic trips partly for business
Food to be prepared on domestic trips to summer camp
Food to be prepared on domestic trips for vacation or
   pleasure
Food to be prepared on foreign trips partly for business
Food to be prepared on foreign trips to summer camp
Food to be prepared on foreign trips for vacation or
   pleasure
Meals purchased on domestic trips partly for business
Meals purchased on domestic trips to summer camp
Meals purchased on domestic trips for vacation or pleasure
Meals purchased on foreign trips partly for business
Meals purchased on foreign trips to summer camp
Meals purchased on foreign trips for vacation or pleasure
Alcoholic beverages by the drink on domestic trips partly
   for business
Alcoholic beverages by the drink on domestic trips to
   summer camp
Alcoholic beverages by the drink on domestic trips for
   vacation or pleasure
Alcoholic beverages by the drink on foreign trips partly for
   business
Alcoholic beverages by the drink on foreign trips to summer
   camp

VACATION   continued

Alcoholic beverages by the drink on foreign trips for
   vacation or pleasure
Alcoholic beverage package sale on domestic trips partly
   for business
Alcoholic beverage package sale on domestic trips to
   summer camp
Alcoholic beverage package sale on domestic trips for
   vacation or pleasure
Alcoholic beverage package sale on foreign trips partly for
   business
Alcoholic beverage package sale on foreign trips to summer
   camp
Alcoholic beverage package sale on foreign trips for
   vacation or pleasure
Lodging on domestic trips partly for business
Lodging on domestic trips to summer camp
Lodging on domestic trips for vacation or pleasure
Lodging on foreign trips partly for business
Lodging on foreign trips to summer camp
Lodging on foreign trips for vacation or pleasure
All expense trips on domestic trips partly for business
All expense trips on domestic trips for vacation or
   pleasure
All expense trips on foreign trips partly for business
All expense trips on foreign trips for vacation or pleasure
All expense trips on domestic trips to summer camp
All expense trips on foreign trips to summer camp
Entertainment, admissions to events, etc. on domestic trips
   partly for business
Entertainment, admissions to events, etc. on domestic trips
   to summer camp
Entertainment, admissions to events, etc. on domestic trips
   for vacation or pleasure
Entertainment, admissions to events, etc. on foreign trips
   partly for business
Entertainment, admissions to events, etc. on foreign trips
   to summer camp
Entertainment, admissions to events, etc. on foreign trips
   for vacation or pleasure
Sport fees for bowling, golfing, etc. on domestic trips
   partly for business
Sport fees for bowling, golfing, etc. on domestic trips to
   summer camp

VACATION   continued

    Sport fees for bowling, golfing, etc. on domestic trips for
      vacation or pleasure
    Sport fees for bowling, golfing, etc. on foreign trips
      partly for business
    Sport fees for bowling, golfing, etc. on foreign trips to
      summer camp
    Sport fees for bowling, golfing, etc. on foreign trips for
      vacation or pleasure
    Rental of sports equipment on domestic trips partly for
      business
    Rental of sports equipment on domestic trips to summer camp
    Rental of sports equipment on domestic trips for vacation
      or pleasure
    Rental of sports equipment on foreign trips partly for
      business
    Rental of sports equipment on foreign trips to summer camp
    Rental of sports equipment on foreign trips for vacation or
      pleasure
    Other expenses for souvenirs, passports, etc. on domestic
      trips partly for business
    Other expenses for souvenirs, passports, etc. on domestic
      trips to summer camp
    Other expenses for souvenirs, passports, etc. on domestic
      trips for vacation or pleasure
    Other expenses for souvenirs, passports, etc. on foreign
      trips partly for business
    Other expenses for souvenirs, passports, etc. on foreign
      trips to summer camp
    Other expenses for souvenirs, passports, etc. on foreign
      trips for vacation or pleasure

CLUBS - Membership fees for clubs, organizations is defined as
    the sum of the following:

    Membership fees for country clubs of swimming pools
    Membership fees for other social, recreational or fraternal
      organizations
    Membership fees for civic or charitable organizations

THEATRE - Subscription for cultural events - is defined as the
    sum of the following:

    Subscriptions for theatre series
    Subscriptions for concert, opera or other musical series

SPORTS - Subscription to sporting events

    Subscriptions for seasons tickets to sporting events

TV - TV is defined as the sum of the following:

    Black and white portable TV
    Black and white console TV
    Color portable TV
    Color console TV
    Black and white TV combined with other items
    Color TV combined with other items

MUSIC - Music type equipment is defined as the sum of the
    following:

    Tape recorder
    Separate stereo components
    Other sound equipment

CAMP - Major camping, health and sports equipment is defined as
    the sum of the following:

    Major camping equipment
    Health and exercise equipment
    Major sports equipment including golf clubs, skis, etc.
    Other major sports and recreation equipment

READING - Reading materials is defined as the sum of the following:

    Newspaper subscriptions
    Magazine or periodical subscriptions
    Book or record club subscriptions
    Encyclopedias and other sets of books
    Nonsubscription books, paperbacks, newspapers and magazines

GIFTS - Gifts and contributions (to persons outside Consumer Unit)
    is defined as the sum of the following:

    Other gifts of cash, bonds, stocks
    Living room suite gifts
    Couch or sofa gifts
    Convertible couch or sofa gifts
    Upholstered lounge chair gifts
    Recliner gifts
    Living room table gifts
    Other living room furniture gifts

GIFTS continued

        Dining room suite gifts
        Dinette set gifts
        Dining room table gifts
        Dining room chair gifts
        Serving table or cart gifts
        China closet or buffet gifts
        Other dining room furniture gifts
        Kitchen table gifts
        Kitchen cabinet (not built-in) gifts
        Other kitchen furniture gifts
        Bedroom suite gifts
        Headboard and/or frame gifts
        Springs and mattress (including rollaways) gifts
        Chest-dresser and vanity gifts
        Night table gifts
        Bedroom chair gifts
        Other bedroom furniture gifts
        Crib and/or mattress gifts
        Playpen gifts
        Infants chest or dresser gifts
        Other infants furniture and equipment gifts
        Wooden outdoor furniture gifts
        Metal outdoor furniture gifts
        Plastic or vinyl outdoor furniture gifts
        Other outdoor furniture gifts
        Bar or porta-bar gifts
        Bookcases or record cabinet gifts
        Electric Stove gifts
        Gas stove gifts
        Other stove gifts
        Refrigerator gifts
        Refrigerator-freezer gifts
        Home freezer gifts
        Built-in dishwasher gifts
        Portable dishwasher gifts
        Garbage disposal gifts
        Range hood gifts
        Automatic clothes washer gifts
        Semiautomatic clothes washer gifts
        Combination washer-dryer gifts
        Other clothes washer gifts
        Electric clothes dryer gifts
        Gas clothes dryer gifts
        Vacuum cleaner gifts

GIFTS   continued

Electric broom gifts
Rug shampooer and floor polisher gifts
Other electric floor cleaning equipment gifts
Sewing machine with cabinet gifts
Sewing machine without cabinet gifts
Reverse cycle air conditioner gifts
Nonreverse cycle air conditioner gifts
Toaster gifts
Portable mixer gifts
Mixer with stand gifts
Blender gifts
Electric can opener gifts
Coffeemaker gifts
Indoor broiler or rotisserie gifts
Electric pot or pan gifts
Electric knife gifts
Electric food warmer gifts
Electric iron gifts
Other electrical kitchen appliance gifts
Portable heater or stove gifts
Dehumidifier gifts
Humidifier or vaporizer gifts
Window or portable fan gifts
Other cooling or heating equipment gifts
Dinnerware gifts
Silver flatware gifts
Stainless flatware gifts
Glassware gifts
Cooking ware (excluding electric) gifts
Other dish or dinnerware gifts
Pillow case gifts
Sheet gifts
Bathroom towels and wash cloths gifts
Kitchen towel gifts
Tablecloths, place mats and napkin gifts
Other kitchen or dining room linen gifts
Bedspread gifts
Electric blanket gifts
Other blankets or quilt gifts
Pillows, excluding decorative gifts
Other bedroom linen gifts
Bathmats and toilet seat cover gifts
Shower curtain gifts
Other bathroom linen gifts

GIFTS continued

    Material for slipcovers and curtains gifts
    Material for handwork gifts
    Manual typewriter gifts
    Electric typewriter gifts
    Power mower gifts
    Riding mower or garden tractor gifts
    Manual mower gifts
    Other power lawn equipment gifts
    Electric drill gifts
    Electric saw gifts
    Electric sander gifts
    Other power tool gifts
    Baby carriage or stroller gifts
    Barbeque grill gifts
    Installed wall-to-wall carpet (other than kitchen and bathroom) gifts
    Noninstalled wall-to-wall carpet (other than kitchen and bathroom) gifts
    Installed wall-to-wall carpet for kitchen and bathroom gifts
    Noninstalled wall-to-wall carpet for kitchen and bathroom gifts
    Room-size rugs gifts
    Other soft floor covering gifts
    Other hard surface floor covering gifts
    Custom-made curtains gifts
    Ready-made curtains gifts
    Custom-made drapes gifts
    Ready-made drapes gifts
    Custom-made venetian blinds and window shades gifts
    Ready-made venetian blinds and window shades gifts
    Custom-made slipcover gifts
    Ready-made slipcover gifts
    Decorative pillows and cushions gifts
    Other household item gifts
    Pingpong table gifts
    Pool table gifts
    Other recreational or house furnishing gifts
    Original paintings and other pictures (greater than $10) gifts
    Clock gifts
    Lamp gifts
    Mirror gifts
    Chandeliers and other lighting fixture gifts
    Other decorative items (greater than $15) gifts

GIFTS   continued

Hair dryer gifts
Electric shaver gifts
Electric hair setter gifts
Electric toothbrush gifts
Other electric personal care item gifts
Shoes, casual or dress, gifts
Sandals gifts
Sneakers or gym shoes gifts
Sport shoes gifts
Boots, leather and leather type, gifts
Rubbers, rubber boots and galoshes gifts
House slippers gifts
Other footwear gifts
Alterations or repair to women's and girl's clothing gifts
Alterations or repair to men's and boy's clothing gifts
Alterations or repair to women's and girl's shoes gifts
Alterations or repair to men's and boy's shoes gifts
Other alteration or repair gifts
Material for making clothes gifts
Sewing notion gifts
Heavy weight coats for men gifts
Light weight coats for men gifts
Snow-ski suits for men gifts
All-weather coats for men gifts
Plastic raincoats for men gifts
Other coats for men gifts
Heavy jackets for men gifts
Light jackets for men gifts
Sweaters and sweater sets for men gifts
Fur jackets for men gifts
Other jackets for men gifts
2 or 3 piece suits for men gifts
Other 2 or 3 piece suits for men gifts
Unclassified suits for men gifts
Sports coats and tailored jackets for men gifts
Vests for men gifts
Items similar to suits for men gifts
Dress trousers or slacks for men gifts
Causal slacks and dress jeans for men gifts
Dungarees, jeans and work pants for men gifts
Short pants for men gifts
Other slacks for men gifts
Other dungarees or jeans for men gifts
Other shorts and short sets for men gifts

GIFTS continued

    Other trousers and slacks for men gifts
    Unclassified suits for men gifts
    Unclassified suits for men gifts
    Unclassified suits for men gifts
    Unclassified suits for men gifts
    Unclassified suits for men gifts
    Unclassified suits for men gifts
    Dress shirts for men gifts
    Work shirts for men gifts
    Sport shirts for men gifts
    Blouses for men gifts
    Other shirts for men gifts
    Undershorts for men gifts
    Undershirts or t-shirts for men gifts
    Other undershirts for men gifts
    Girdles for men gifts
    Body stockings for men gifts
    Unclassified underwear for men gifts
    Other undershorts for men gifts
    Thermal underwear for men gifts
    Other undergarments for men gifts
    Pajamas for men gifts
    Robes for men gifts
    Nightgowns for men gifts
    Other robes for men gifts
   ·Other nightwear or lounge wear for men gifts
    Socks for men gifts
    Stockings for men gifts
    Unclassified hosiery for men gifts
    Tights for men gifts
    Other hosiery for men gifts
    Hats, caps and helmets for men gifts
    Dress gloves for men gifts
    Work gloves for men gifts
    Mittens for men gifts
    Handbags for men gifts
    Wallets for men gifts
    Other accessories for men gifts
    Ties for men gifts
    Swim suits for men gifts
    Beach robes and swim wear for men gifts
    Uniforms, not reimbursed for men gifts
    Special sport clothing for men gifts
    Other special clothing for men gifts

GIFTS   continued

Heavy weight coats for boys gifts
Light weight coats for boys gifts
Snow-ski suits for boys gifts
All-weather coats for boys gifts
Plastic raincoats for boys gifts
Other coats for boys gifts
Heavy jackets for boys gifts
Light jackets for boys gifts
Sweaters and sweater sets for boys gifts
Fur jackets for boys gifts
Other jackets for boys gifts
2 or 3 piece suits for boys gifts
Other 2 or 3 piece suits for boys gifts
Unclassified suits for boys gifts
Sports coats for boys gifts
Vests for boys gifts
Items similar to suits for boys gifts
Dress trousers or slacks for boys gifts
Casual slacks and dress jeans for boys gifts
Dungarees, jeans and work pants for boys gifts
Other slacks for boys gifts
Short pants for boys gifts
Other dungarees or jeans for boys gifts
Other shorts and short sets for boys gifts
Other trousers and slacks for boys gifts
Unclassified suits for boys gifts
Unclassified suits for boys gifts
Unclassified suits for boys gifts
Unclassified suits for boys gifts
Unclassified suits for boys gifts
Unclassified suits for boys gifts
Dress shirts for boys gifts
Sport shirts for boys gifts
Work shirts for boys gifts
Blouses for boys gifts
Other shirts for boys gifts
Undershorts for boys gifts
Undershirts or t-shirts for boys gifts
Other undershirts for boys gifts
Girdles for boys gifts
Body stockings for boys gifts
Unclassified underwear for boys gifts
Other undershorts for boys gifts
Thermal underwear for boys gifts

GIFTS   continued

    Other undergarments for boys gifts
    Pajamas for boys gifts
    Robes for boys gifts
    Nightgowns for boys gifts
    Other robes for boys gifts
    Other nightwear or loungewear for boys gifts
    Socks for boys gifts
    Stockings for boys gifts
    Unclassified hosiery for boys gifts
    Tights for boys gifts
    Other hosiery for boys gifts
    Hats, caps and helmets for boys gifts
    Dress gloves for boys gifts
    Work gloves for boys gifts
    Mittens for boys gifts
    Handbags for boys gifts
    Wallets for boys gifts
    Other accessories for boys gifts
    Ties for boys gifts
    Swim suits for boys gifts
    Beach robes and other swim wear for boys gifts
    Uniforms, not reimbursed for boys gifts
    Special sport clothing for boys gifts
    Other special clothing for boys gifts
    Heavy weight coats for women gifts
    Light weight coats for women gifts
    Snow-ski suits for women gifts
    All-weather coats for women gifts
    Plastic raincoats for women gifts
    Other coats for women gifts
    Heavy jackets for women gifts
    Light jackets for women gifts
    Sweaters and sweater sets for women gifts
    Fur jackets and stoles for women gifts
    Other jackets for women gifts
    Other 2 or 3 piece suits for women gifts
    2 or 3 piece suits for women gifts
    Pantsuits for women gifts
    Sports coats and tailored jackets for women gifts
    Vests for women gifts
    Items similar to suits for women gifts
    Other dress slacks for women gifts
    Other casual slacks and dress jeans for women gifts
    Other dungarees, jeans and work pants for women gifts

GIFTS   continued

Other shorts for women gifts
Slacks for women gifts
Dungarees or jeans for women gifts
Shorts and short sets for women gifts
Other trousers and slacks for women gifts
Street dresses for women gifts
Formal or semiformal dresses for women gifts
Skirts or culottes for women gifts
Jumpers for women gifts
One-piece pant-dresses for women gifts
Items similar to dresses for women gifts
Dress shirts for women gifts
Sport shirts for women gifts
Work shirts for women gifts
Blouses or tops for women gifts
Other shirts for women gifts
Other panties for women gifts
T-shirts for women gifts
Slips for women gifts
Girdles or foundations for women gifts
Body stockings for women gifts
Bras for women gifts
Panties for women gifts
Thermal underwear for women gifts
Other undergarments for women gifts
Pajamas for women gifts
Robes for women gifts
Nightgowns for women gifts
Housecoats and brunch coats for women gifts
Other nightwear or lounge wear for women gifts
Socks for women gifts
Stockings for women gifts
Pantyhose for women gifts
Tights for women gifts
Other hosiery for women gifts
Hats, caps and helmets for women gifts
Dress gloves for women gifts
Work gloves for women gifts
Mittens for women gifts
Handbags or purses for women gifts
Wallets for women gifts
Other accessories for women gifts
Ties for women gifts
Swim suits for women gifts

GIFTS   continued

Beach robes and other swim wear for women gifts
Uniforms, not reimbursed for women gifts
Special sport clothing for women gifts
Other special clothing for women gifts
Heavy weight coats for girls gifts
Light weight coats for girls gifts
Snow-ski suits for girls gifts
All-weather coats for girls gifts
Plastic raincoats for girls gifts
Other coats for girls gifts
Heavy jackets for girls gifts
Light jackets for girls gifts
Sweaters and sweater sets for girls gifts
Fur jackets and stoles for girls gifts
Other jackets for girls gifts
Other 2 or 3 piece suits for girls gifts
2 or 3 piece suits for girls gifts
Pantsuits for girls gifts
Sports coats and tailored jackets for girls gifts
Vests for girls gifts
Items similar to suits for girls gifts
Other dress slacks for girls gifts
Other casual slacks and dress jeans for girls gifts
Other dungarees, jeans and work pants for girls gifts
Other shorts for girls gifts
Slacks for girls gifts
Dungarees or jeans for girls gifts
Shorts and short sets for girls gifts
Other trousers and slacks for girls gifts
Street dresses for girls gifts
Formal or semiformal dresses for girls gifts
Skirts or culottes for girls gifts
Jumpers for girls gifts
One-piece pant-dresses for girls gifts
Items similar to dresses for girls gifts
Dress shirts for girls gifts
Sport shirts for girls gifts
Work shirts for girls gifts
Blouses or tops for girls gifts
Other shirts for girls gifts
Other panties for girls gifts
Undershirts or t-shirts for girls gifts
Slips for girls gifts
Girdles or foundations for girls gifts

GIFTS   continued

Body stockings for girls gifts
Bras for girls gifts
Panties for girls gifts
Thermal underwear for girls gifts
Other undergarments for girls gifts
Pajamas for girls gifts
Robes for girls gifts
Nightgowns for girls gifts
Housecoats and brunch coats for girls gifts
Other nightwear or lounge wear for girls gifts
Socks for girls gifts
Stockings for girls gifts
Pantyhose for girls gifts
Tights for girls gifts
Other hosiery for girls gifts
Hats, caps and helmets for girls gifts
Dress gloves for girls gifts
Work gloves for girls gifts
Mittens for girls gifts
Handbags or purses for girls gifts
Wallets for girls gifts
Other accessories for girls gifts
Ties for girls gifts
Swim suits for girls gifts
Beach robes and other swim wear for girls gifts
Uniforms, not reimbursed for girls gifts
Special sport clothing for girls gifts
Other special clothing for girls gifts
Heavy weight coats for infants gifts
Light weight coats for infants gifts
Snow-ski suits for infants gifts
All-weather coats for infants gifts
Plastic raincoats for infants gifts
Other coats for infants gifts
Heavy jackets for infants gifts
Light jackets for infants gifts
Sweaters and sweater sets for infants gifts
Fur jackets and stoles for infants gifts
Other jackets for infants gifts
2 or 3 piece suits (male) for infants gifts
2 or 3 piece suits (female) for infants gifts
Pantsuits for women and girls for infants gifts
Sport coats and tailored jackets for infants gifts

GIFTS   continued

Vests for infants gifts
Items similar to suits for infants gifts
Dress trousers or slacks (male) for infants gifts
Casual slacks and dress jeans (male) for infants gifts
Dungarees and jeans (male) for infants gifts
Short pants (male) for infants gifts
Slacks (female) for infants gifts
Dungarees or jeans (female) for infants gifts
Shorts and short sets (female) for infants gifts
Other trousers and slacks for infants gifts
Street dresses for infants gifts
Formal or semiformal dresses for infants gifts
Skirts or culottes for infants gifts
Jumpers for infants gifts
One-piece pant-dresses for infants gifts
Items similar to dresses for infants gifts
Dress shirts for infants gifts
Sport shirts for infants gifts
Unclassified shirts for infants gifts
Blouses or tops for infants gifts
Other shirts for infants gifts
Under shorts for infants gifts
Undershirts or t-shirts for infants gifts
Slips for infants gifts
Unclassified outerwear for infants gifts
Body stockings for infants gifts
Unclassified underwear for infants gifts
Panties for infants gifts
Thermal underwear for infants gifts
Other undergarments for infants gifts
Pajamas for infants gifts
Robes for infants gifts
Nightgowns for infants gifts
Unclassified sleepwear for infants gifts
Other nightwear or lounge wear for infants gifts
Socks for infants gifts
Stockings for infants gifts
Other hosiery for infants gifts
Tights for infants gifts
Other hosiery for infants gifts
Hats, caps and helmets for infants gifts
Dress gloves for infants gifts
Other gloves for infants gifts
Mittens for infants gifts

GIFTS   continued

    Handbags or purses for infants gifts
    Wallets for infants gifts
    Other accessories for infants gifts
    Ties for infants gifts
    Swim suits for infants gifts
    Beach robes and other swim wear for infants gifts
    Unclassified outerwear for infants gifts
    Special sport clothing for infants gifts
    Other special clothing for infants gifts
    Coats, snow suits, 2 or 3 piece sets for infants gifts
    Caps and hoods for infants gifts
    Other outerwear for infants gifts
    Undershirts and slips for infants gifts
    Washable diapers for infants gifts
    Disposable diapers for infants gifts
    Sleeping garments for infants gifts
    Socks and booties for infants gifts
    Layettes for infants gifts
    Other infants clothing for infants gifts
    Combined clothing expenses for infants gifts
    Watch gifts (all sex-age groups)
    Costume jewelry gifts (all sex-age groups)
    Jewelry other than costume (all sex-age groups)
    Infants jewelry gifts
    Suitcase or luggage gifts
    Trunk gifts
    Garment bag and closet storage item gifts
    Other suitcase or storage bag type item gifts
    Portable black and white TV gifts
    Console black and white TV gifts
    Black and white TV combined with other items gifts
    Portable color TV gifts
    Console color TV gifts
    Color TV combined with other items gifts
    Piano gifts
    Organ gifts
    Radio gifts
    Phonograph gifts
    Tape recorder gifts
    Separate stereo component gifts
    Other sound equipment gifts
    Musical instruments other than piano or organ gifts
    Musical accessories
    Subscriptions and membership gifts
    Still camera gifts

GIFTS continued

    Slide projector gifts
    Movie camera gifts
    Movie projector gifts
    Other photographic equipment gifts
    Bicycles gifts
    Tricycles and battery power cart gifts
    Playground equipment gifts
    Swimming pool gifts
    Unpowered sports vehicle gifts
    Major sports equipment gifts
    Health and exercise equipment gifts
    Major camping equipment gifts
    Other major sports and recreation equipment gifts
    Minor sports equipment (less than $10) gifts
    New subcompacts and compacts excluding AMC compacts post
       1967 gifts
    New intermediates and AMC compacts post 1967 gifts
    New standard and medium excluding Chrysler medium post
       1967 gifts
    New luxury, Chrysler medium, Chevrolet, Pontiac, Buick,
       Oldsmobile, Cadillac and foreign sports post 1967 gifts
    New Lincoln/Mercury, Plymouth, Dodge, AMC sports; AMC,
       other domestic miscellaneous purchase of post 1967; all
       Chevrolet, Pontiac, Buick and Oldsmobile pre 1968 car
       gifts
    New Cadillac, Ford, Lincoln/Mercury, Plymouth, Dodge,
       Chrysler, AMC pre 1968 gifts
    New post 1967 from Japan, Germany, England and other
       countries gifts
    New trucks domestic and foreign gifts
    New other automobile gifts
    New other truck gifts
    New unclassified domestic post 1967 subcompact gifts
    New unclassified domestic post 1967 compact gifts
    New unclassified domestic post 1967 intermediate gifts
    New unclassified domestic post 1967 standard gifts
    New unclassified domestic post 1967 medium gifts
    New unclassified domestic post 1967 luxury gifts
    New unclassified domestic post 1967 sports gifts
    New Unclassified domestic post 1967 miscellaneous gifts
    Other new unclassified vehicle gifts
    Used subcompacts and compacts excluding AMC compacts post
       1967 gifts
    Used intermediates and AMC compacts post 1967 gifts

GIFTS   continued

  Used standard and medium excluding Chrysler medium post
    1967 gifts
  Used luxury, Chrysler medium, Chevrolet, Pontiac, Buick,
    Oldsmobile, Cadillac and Ford sports post 1967 gifts
  Used Lincoln/Mercury, Plymouth, Dodge, AMC sports; AMC
    and other domestic miscellaneous purchases of post 1967;
    all Chevrolet, Pontiac, Buick, and Oldsmobile pre 1968
    car gifts
  Used Cadillac, Ford, Lincoln/Mercury, Plymouth, Dodge,
    Chrysler, AMC pre 1968 gifts
  Used post 1967 from Japan, Germany, England and other
    countries gifts
  Used trucks, domestic and foreign gifts
  Used automobile gifts
  Used truck gifts
  Used invalid or not reported domestic post 1967 subcompact
    gifts
  Used invalid or not reported domestic post 1967 compact
    gifts
  Used invalid or not reported domestic post 1967 inter-
    mediate gifts
  Used invalid or not reported domestic post 1967 standard
    gifts
  Used invalid or not reported domestic post 1967 medium gifts
  Used invalid or not reported domestic post 1967 luxury gifts
  Used invalid or not reported domestic post 1967 sports gifts
  Used invalid or not reported domestic post 1967 miscellaneous
    gifts
  Used invalid or not reported vehicles
  New self-propelled camper gifts
  New trailer type camper gifts
  New other attachable camper gifts
  New motorcycles gifts
  New noncamper type trailer gifts
  New plane gifts
  New other type of vehicles gifts
  Used self-propelled camper gifts
  Used trailer type camper gifts
  Used other attachable camper gifts
  Used motorcycles gifts
  Used noncamper type trailer gifts
  Used plane gifts
  Used other type of vehicles gifts

GIFTS   continued

       Finance charges for gift vehicles
       New boat gifts
       Used boat gifts
       Toy gifts
       Pets gifts
       Encyclopedia and other sets of books gifts
       Other gifts costing more than $15
       Miscellaneous nonpowered hand tool gifts
       Vacation or trip expenses for persons outside the CU
       Expenses for persons outside of the CU during trips
       Other contributions or gifts

References

Ackerman, James S.
  1963 "Style." Pp. 164–186 in James S. Ackerman and Rhys Carpenter, *Art and Ar-
        chaeology.* Englewood Cliffs, N.J.:Prentice-Hall.
Allen, R. G. D., and A. L. Bowley
  1935 *Family Expenditures.* London:Staples Press.
Ando, A., and F. Modigliani
  1963 "The 'life cycle' hypothesis of saving: Aggregate implications and tests." *Amer-
        ican Economic Review* 53:55–84.
Aronowitz, Stanley
  1973 *False Promises.* New York:McGraw-Hill.
Barber, Bernard
  1957 *Social Stratification.* New York:Harcourt, Brace and World.
Bell, Clive
  1958 *Art.* New York:Capricorn.
Bell, Wendell
  1958 "Social choice, life styles, and suburban residence." Pp. 225–247 in William M.
        Dobriner (ed.), *The Suburban Community.* New York:Putnam.
Bendix, R., and S. M. Lipset
  1966 "Karl Marx's theory of social classes." Pp. 6–11 in R. Bendix and S. M. Lipset
        (eds.), *Class, Status, and Power.* New York:The Free Press.
Berger, Bernard
  1960 *Working Class Suburb.* Berkeley:University of California Press.

Blau, Peter M., and Otis Dudley Duncan
1967 *The American Occupational Structure*. New York:Wiley.
Bloch, Marc L. B.
1961 *Feudal Society*. Translated by L.A. Manyon. Chicago:University of Chicago Press.
Blum, Alan F., and Peter McHugh
1971 "The social ascription of motives." *American Sociological Review* 36(February): 98–109.
Blumer, Herbert
1969 *Symbolic Interactionism: Perspective and Method*. Englewood Cliffs, N.J.: Prentice-Hall.
Bowles, Samuel, and Herbert Gintis
1976 *Schooling in Capitalist America: Educational Reform and the Contradictions of Economic Life*. New York:Basic Books.
Branson, William H.
1972 *Macroeconomic Theory and Policy*. New York:Harper and Row.
Bronfenbrenner, Urie
1958 "Socialization and social class through time and space." Pp. 400–425 in E. E. Macoby, T. M. Newcombe, and E. L. Hartley (eds.), *Readings in Social Psychology*. New York:Holt, Rinehart and Winston.
Brown, J. A. C., and A. S. Deaton
1972 "Surveys in applied economics: Models of consumer behavior." *Economic Journal* 82:1145–1236.
Burdge, Rabel
1969 "Levels of occupational prestige and leisure activity." *Journal of Leisure Research* 1: 262–274.
Carlson, Michael D.
1974 "The 1972–73 consumer expenditure survey." *Monthly Labor Review* 97:16–23.
Cellini, B.
1979 *The Autobiography of Benvenuto Cellini*. Translated by George Bull. New York:Penguin.
Chapin, Francis S.
1935 *Contemporary American Institutions: A Sociological Analysis*. New York:Harper and Row.
Christensen, Laurits R., Dale W. Jorgenson and Lawrence J. Lau
1975 "Transcendental logarithmic utility functions." *American Economic Review* 65:367–382.
Clarke, Alfred C.
1956 "Leisure and occupational prestige." *American Sociological Review* 21:205–214.
Coleman, J.
1974 *Youth: Transition to Adulthood*. Chicago:University of Chicago Press.
Coser, Lewis A.
1977 *Masters of Sociological Thought*. New York:Harcourt, Brace, Jovanovich.
Davis, Kingsley
1949 *Human Society*. New York:Macmillan.
DeGrazia, Sebastian
1962 *Of Time, Work, and Leisure*. New York:The Twentieth Century Fund.
Demerath, N. J.
1965 *Social Class in American Protestantism*. Chicago:Rand-McNally.
Dowd, Douglas F.
1974 *The Twisted Dream*. Cambridge, Mass:Winthrop.

Duncan, Otis Dudley
1961 "A socioeconomic index for all occupations." Pp. 109–138 in A. J. Reiss, Jr., *Occupations and Social Status*. New York:The Free Press.

Ewen, Stuart
1976 *Captains of Consciousness*. New York:McGraw-Hill.

Featherman, David L., Michael E. Sobel, and David Dickens
1975 "Manual for coding occupations into detailed 1970 categories and a listing of 1970-basis Duncan socio-economic and NORC prestige scores." Center for Demography and Ecology Working Paper 75-1. University of Wisconsin-Madison.

Feldman, Saul D., and Gerald W. Thielbar
1972 *Life Styles: Diversity in American Society*. Boston:Little, Brown.

Focillon, Henri
1948 *The Life of Forms in Art*. Translated by Charles B. Hogan and George Kubler. New Haven:Yale University Press.

Friedman, M.
1957 *A Theory of the Consumption Function*. Princeton:Princeton University Press.

Galbraith, John Kenneth
1958 *The Affluent Society*. Boston:Houghton Mifflin.

Gans, Herbert J.
1951 "Park Forest: Birth of a Jewish community." *Commentary* 2:16–30.
1962 *The Urban Villagers: Group and Class in the Life of Italian Americans*. New York:The Free Press.

Glaab, Charles N., and A. Theodore Brown
1967 *A History of Urban America*. New York:Macmillan.

Goldthorpe, John D., and David Lockwood
1962 "Not so bourgeois after all." *New Society* 3(October 18):18–19.

Gombrich, E. H.
1968 "Style." Pp. 352–361 in the *International Encyclopedia of the Social Sciences* (Vol. 15). New York:The Free Press.

Gordon, M.
1964 *Assimilation in American Life*. New York:Oxford University Press.

Gruvaeus, G. T., and K. G. Jöreskog
1970 "A computer program for minimizing a function of several variables." Research Bulletin 70-14. Princeton, N.J.:Educational Testing Service.

Hamilton, Richard F.
1964 "The behavior and values of skilled workers." Pp. 42–57 in Arthur B. Shostak and William Gomberg (eds.), *Blue Collar World:Studies of the American Worker*. Englewood Cliffs, N.J.:Prentice-Hall.

Handel, G., and Lee Rainwater
1964 "Persistence and change in working-class life." Pp. 36–41 in Arthur B. Shostak and William Gomberg (eds.), *Blue Collar World:Studies of the American Worker*. Englewood Cliffs, N.J.:Prentice-Hall.

Harman, H. H.
1967 *Modern Factor Analysis*. Chicago:University of Chicago Press.

Hauser, Arnold
1958 *The Philosophy of Art History*. New York:Knopf.

Havighurst, Robert J., and Kenneth Feigenbaum
1959 "Leisure and life style." *American Journal of Sociology* 64(January):396–404.

Heckman, James
1974 "Shadow prices, market wages, and labor supply." *Econometrica* 42:679–694.

1976 "The common structure of statistical models of truncation, sample selection and limited dependent variables and a simple estimator for such models." *The Annals of Economic and Social Measurement* 5:475–492.

Hoffman, Martin
1972 "The public places of gay life." Pp. 351–362 in Saul D. Feldman and Gerald W. Thielbar (eds.), *Life Styles:Diversity in American Society.* Boston:Little, Brown.

Inkeles, Alex
1960 "Industrial man: The relation of status to experience, perception, and values." *American Journal of Sociology* 66(July):13–18.

Jennrich, R. I., and P. F. Sampson
1966 "Rotation for simple loadings." *Psychometrika* 31:313–323.

Jöreskog, K. G.
1970 "A general method for analysis of covariance structures." *Biometrika,* 57:239–251.
1973 "A general method for estimating a linear structural equation system." Pp. 85–112 in A. S. Goldberger and O. D. Duncan (eds.), *Structural Equation Models in the Social Sciences.* New York:Seminar Press.

Jöreskog, K. G., and A. S. Goldberger
1975 "Estimation of a model with multiple indicators and multiple causes of a single latent variable." *Journal of the American Statistical Association,* 70:631–639.

Kakwani, N. C.
1967 "The unbiasedness of Zellner's seemingly unrelated regression equations estimators." *Journal of the American Statistical Association,* 62:141–142.

Katona, George
1964 *The Mass Consumption Society.* New York:McGraw-Hill.
1971 *Aspirations and Affluence.* New York:McGraw-Hill.

Kinsey, Alfred C., Wardell B. Pomeroy, and Clyde E. Martin
1948 *Sexual Behavior in the Human Male.* Philadelphia:Saunders.

Kirkpatrick, E. L.
1923 The Standard of Life in a Typical Section of Diversified Farming. New York Agricultural Experiment Station Bulletin 423. Ithaca, New York.

Kirkwood, K. P.
1970 *Renaissance in Japan.* Rutland, Vermont:Charles E. Tuttle.

Klein, Philip A.
1971 "The cyclical timing of consumer credit, 1920–1967." Occasional Paper 113, National Bureau of Economic Research. New York:Columbia University Press.

Kroeber, A. L.
1957 *Style and Civilizations.* Ithaca, N.Y.:Cornell University Press.
1963 *An Anthropologist Looks at History.* Berkeley:University of California Press.

Laumann, Edward O., and James S. House
1970 "Living room styles and social attributes: The patterning of material artifacts in a modern urban community." Pp. 189–203 in Edward O. Laumann, Paul M. Siegel and Robert W. Hodge (eds.), *The Logic of Social Hierarchies.* Chicago: Markham.

Lawley, D. N., and A. E. Maxwell
1971 *Factor Analysis as a Statistical Method.* London:Butterworth.

Lefebvre, Henri
1971 *Everyday Life in the Modern World.* Translated by Sacha Rabinovitch. London:A. Lane.

Liebow, Elliot
1967 *Tally's Corner.* Boston:Little, Brown.

Liviatan, Nissan
 1961 "Errors in variables and Engel curve analysis." *Econometrica* 29:336–362.
Lofland, John
 1970 "The youth ghetto." Pp. 756–778 in Edward O. Laumann, Paul Siegel, and Robert W. Hodge (eds.), *The Logic of Social Hierarchies*. Chicago:Markham.
Loomis, C. P.
 1934 The Growth of the Farm Family in Relation to its Activities. North Carolina Agricultural Experiment Station Bulletin 298.
Mandell, Lewis
 1972 *Credit Card Use in the United States*. Ann Arbor:University of Michigan Press.
Martineau, Pierre
 1958 "Social classes and spending behavior." *Journal of Marketing* 23:121–131.
Maslow, Abraham Harold
 1954 *Motivation and Personality*. New York:Harper.
Matras, Judah
 1975 *Social Inequality, Stratification, and Mobility*. Englewood Cliffs, N.J.:Prentice-Hall.
Matza, David
 1967 *Delinquency and Draft*. New York:Wiley.
Mayer, Kurt B.
 1955 *Class and Society*. New York:Random House.
McCord, W., Howard J. Friedberg, and E. Harwood
 1969 *Life Styles in the Black Ghetto*. New York:Norton.
Mead, George Herbert
 1934 *Mind, Self and Society*. Chicago:University of Chicago Press.
Merton, Robert K.
 1968 *Social Theory and Social Structure*. New York:The Free Press.
Merton, T.
 1969 *Mystics and Zen Masters*. New York:Delta.
Meyersohn, Rolf
 1968 "Television and the rest of leisure." *The Public Opinion Quarterly* 32(Spring):102–112.
Michael, Robert T.
 1972 "The effect of education on efficiency in consumption." Occasional Paper 116, National Bureau of Economic Research. New York:University of Columbia Press.
Mowry, George E.
 1965 *The Urban Nation, 1920–1960*. New York:Hill and Wang.
Murry, F. Middleton
 1965 *The Problem of Style*. London:Oxford University Press.
Myers, James H., and Jonathan Gutman
 1974 "Life style: The essence of social class." Pp. 235–256 in William D. Wells (ed.), *Life Style and Psychographics*. American Marketing Association.
Noe, Frank P.
 1974 "Leisure life styles and social class: A trend analysis 1900–1960." *Sociology and Social Research* 58:286–294.
Packard, Vance Oakley
 1959 *The Status Seekers*. New York:David Mckay.
Parks, Richard W.
 1969 "Systems of demand equations: An empirical comparison of alternative functional forms." *Econometrica* 37:629–650.

Phlips, Louis
1974 *Applied Consumption Analysis.* Amsterdam:North Holland.
Prais, S. J. and H. S. Houthakker
1955 *The Analysis of Family Budgets.* Cambridge:Cambridge University Press.
Reed, J. S.
1972 *The Enduring South: Subcultural Persistence in Mass Society.* Lexington, Mass.: Heath.
Reynolds, Fred D., and R. Darden
1974 "Construing life style and psychographics." Pp. 71–96 in William D. Wells (ed.), *Life Style and Psychographics.* American Marketing Association.
Rich, Stuart U. and S. C. Jain
1970 "Social class and life cycle as predictors of shopping behavior." Pp. 170–185 in Stuart Henderson Britt (ed.), *Psychological Experiments in Consumer Behavior.* New York:Wiley.
Robinson, C. P.
1933 *Everyday Life in Ancient Greece.* Oxford:Oxford University Press.
Rodman, H.
1964 "Middle-class misconceptions about lower-class behavior." Pp. 59–69 in Arthur B. Shostak and William Gomberg (eds.), *Blue Collar World: Studies of the American Worker.* Englewood Cliffs, N.J.:Prentice-Hall.
Ryder, N. B., and C. Westoff
1971 *Reproduction in the United States, 1965.* Princeton:Princeton University Press.
Schapiro, Meyer
1961 "Style." Pp. 81–113 in Morris Philipson (ed.), *Aesthetics Today.* Cleveland, Ohio:World.
Schatzman, Leonard, and Anselm Strauss
1955 "Social class and modes of communication." *American Journal of Sociology* 60:329–338.
Sewell, William H.
1940 The Construction and Standardization of a Scale for the Measurement of Oklahoma Farm Families Socioeconomic Status. Agricultural Experiment Station, Technical Bulletin No. 9. Stillwater:Oklahoma Agricultural and Mechanical College.
Shils, Edward A.
1970 "Deference." Pp. 420–448 in Edward O. Laumann, Paul M. Siegel and Robert W. Hodge (eds.), *The Logic of Social Hierarchies.* Chicago:Markham.
Sorbom, D.
1975 "Detection of correlated errors in longitudinal data." *British Journal of Mathematical and Statistical Psychology* 28:138–151.
Soule, George H.
1947 *Prosperity Decade; from War to Depression: 1917–1929.* New York:Rinehart.
Summers, R.
1959 "A note on least squares bias in household expenditure analysis." *Econometrica* 27:121–126.
Taeuber, Conrad, and Irene B. Taeuber
1975 *The Changing Population of the United States.* New York:Russell and Russell.
Tallman, Irving, and Ramona Morgner
1970 "Life-style differences among urban and suburban blue-collar families. *Social Forces* 48:334–348.
Theil, Henri
1971 *Principles of Econometrics.* New York:Wiley.

Thurstone, L. L.
  1947 *Multiple-Factor Analysis.* Chicago: University of Chicago Press.
Timm, Neil H.
  1975 *Multivariate Analysis with Applications in Education and Psychology.* Monterey, California:Brooks/Cole.
Tobin, James
  1958 "Estimation of relationships for limited dependent variables." *Econometrica* 26:24–36.
Tomeh, Aida K.
  1964 "Informal group participation and residential patterns." *American Journal of Sociology* 29(October):718–729.
Tumin, Melvin M.
  1970 *Readings on Social Stratification.* Englewood Cliffs, N.J.:Prentice-Hall.
U.S. Bureau of the Census
  1949 *Historical Statistics of the United States, 1789–1945.* Washington, D.C.:U.S. Government Printing Office.
Vanek, Joan
  1974 "Time spent in housework." *Scientific American* 231(5):116–120.
Van Hook, L. R.
  1937 *Greek Life and Thought.* New York:Columbia University Press.
Vasari, G.
  1971 *Lives of the Artists.* Translated by George Bull. New York:Penguin.
Veblen, Thorsten
  1966 Exerpts from "The Theory of the Leisure Class." Pp. 36–42 in R. Bendix and S. M. Lipset (eds.), *Class, Status, and Power.* New York:The Free Press.
Warner, William Lloyd, and Paul S. Lunt
  1941 *The Social Life of a Modern Community.* New Haven:Yale University Press.
  1942 *The Status System of a Modern Community.* New Haven:Yale University Press.
Warner, William Lloyd, Marchia Meeker, and Kenneth Eells
  1960 *Social Class in America.* New York:Harper and Row.
Weber, Max
  1966 "Class, status and party." Pp. 21–28 in R. Bendix and S. M. Lipset (eds.), *Class, Status, and Power.* New York:The Free Press.
White, Clyde
  1955 "Social class differences in the use of leisure." *American Journal of Sociology* 61:145–150.
Willmott, Peter, and Michael Young
  1960 *Family and Class in a London Suburb.* London:Routledge and Kegan Paul.
Wirth, Louis
  1938 "Urbanism as a way of life." *American Journal of Sociology* 44:1–24.
Wölfflin, Heinrich
  1932 *Principles of Art History.* Translated by M. D. Hottinger. New York:Henry Holt.
Zablocki, B.
  1971 *The Joyful Community.* Baltimore:Penguin.
Zablocki, B. and R. M. Kanter
  1976 "The differentiation of life-styles." *Annual Review of Sociology* 2:269–298.
Zellner, Arnold
  1962 "An efficient method of estimating seemingly unrelated regressions and tests for aggregation bias." *Journal of the American Statistical Association* 57:348–368.

Zimmerman, C. C.
  1929 Income and Expenditures of Minnesota Farm and City Families, 1927–28. Minnesota Agricultural Experiment Station Bulletin 255. St. Paul, Minnesota.
  1936 *Consumption and Standards of Living.* New York: D. Van Nostrand.
Zimmerman, C. C., and J. D. Black
  1924 Factors Affecting Expenditures of Farm Family Incomes in Minnesota. Minnesota Agricultural Experiment Station Bulletin 246. St. Paul, Minnesota.
  1927 How Minnesota Farm Family Incomes are Spent: An Interpretation of a One Year Study. Minnesota Agricultural Experiment Station Bulletin 239. St. Paul, Minnesota.

Subject Index

A

Age
  effects of in MIMIC models, 148, 160–162
  effects of in preliminary regressions, 77–78
  effects of in regressions, 95, 100, 115, 167
  in theory of lifestyle differentiation, 59, 62
  measurement, 69–70
  sample restrictions 69

B

Bureau of the Census, U.S., 33, 44–45, 67, 175
Bureau of Labor Statistics, 67, 69, 175, 177

C

Coherency, *see* Stylistic unity
Collectivity, 51, 54

Commodity set, 56
Consistency, *see* Stylistic unity
Consumer unit, defined, 68
Consumption, *see also* Lifestyle
  advertising and, 36–38
  as a basic need, 41–42, 50, 171
  conspicuous, 5, 9, 157
  credit use and, 37–39
  dimensions of, 5, 64–65
  expressiveness and, 32, 40–42, 170
  free time and, 43–47
  gratification and, 32, 35–37, 166
  hypothesis of induced demand, 32–33
  in Soviet Union, 41
  leisure and, 2, 43–47, 166
  lifestyle and, 2–3, 61, 63–65, 166
  motion picture and, 37
  product differentiation and, 32–33, 40, 65
  rise of consumption society, 32–40
  self-esteem and, 41–42, 170
  utility theory and, 56–59
Consumption items, *see* Expenditure variables
Correlation matrix
  of expenditure variables, 123–124

Position, *see* Role
Prestige acquisition, *see also* General factor
    effects of independent variables, 160–161, 168
    form of, 158–159
    levels of socioeconomic hierarchy and, 161, 163–164
    spatio-temporal invariance and, 159–160
Prices, *see also* Engel curve
    possible effects of, 62, 100, 115

R

Race
    in theory of lifestyle differentiation, 59, 62
    sample restrictions and, 69
Reduced form equations, *see* Expenditure system
Reference group, 51, 53
Referents, 52–55, 166
Region
    effects of in MIMIC models, 146, 148
    effects of in preliminary regressions, 79
    effects of in regressions, 100, 115, 167
    in theory of lifestyle differentiation, 62
    measurement, 69–70
    prices and, 62, 100, 115
Regression analysis
    analysis of residuals, 86–89
    efficiency of OLS vs. GLS, 93
    final regressions, 96–99
    iterative generalized least squares (GLS), 92–94
    ordinary least squares (OLS), 92–94
    model building strategies, 70–72, 79, 82–92
    multicollinearity, 82–83
    preliminary regression models, 80–81
    specification error and, 94
    weighted least squares (WLS), 67, 69
    weights, defined, 76, 88
Role, 3, 52–55, 62
Role set, 52–55

S

Sample, 67–68
    age restrictions, 68, 166

race restrictions, 68, 166
    subpopulations, 68
Social category, defined, 51
Social control, of work-force, 34–35
Socioeconomic hierarchy, *see also* specific socioeconomic variables
    effects of differences between levels in MIMIC models, 154–157, 162–164
    effects of differences between levels in regressions, 4, 111–114
    effects of socioeconomic variables in MIMIC models, 5, 152–157, 160–164
    effects of socioeconomic variables in regressions, 4, 102–106, 111–114, 116, 167–168
    levels, defined, 102
Spatio-temporal invariance, *see* Stylistic unity
Spatio-temporal salience, criterion of, *see* Lifestyle
Specific luxury factor, 146, 148, 154–157, *see also* Prestige acquisition
Status, *see* Role
Status set, 54
Stratification system-see Socioeconomic hierarchy
Style, *see also* Stylistic unity
    as activity vs. product, 21, 26–27
    as a descriptive concept in art history, 24
    as an esthetic concept, 22–23
    as a theoretical framework for art history, 2
    Baroque, 24
    defined, 2, 26, 165
    descriptive labels and, 25
    descriptive use in ordinary language, 20–21, 23
    expressiveness and, 20–21, 26, 27
    idiosyncratic use in ordinary language, 20–21, 23
    normative use in ordinary language, 20
    period, 24
    relationship between period style and theoretical style in art history, 24
    stylistic unity in art history and, 4–5, 23, 25, 26–27, 118–119
    uniformity and, 20–21, 26

QUANTITATIVE STUDIES IN SOCIAL RELATIONS

Consulting Editor: Peter H. Rossi

UNIVERSITY OF MASSACHUSETTS
AMHERST, MASSACHUSETTS